THE

RACEHORSE IN TRAINING

WITH

Hints on Racing and Racing Reforms

By WILLIAM DAY

London

CHAPMAN AND HALL, LIMITED, 193, PICCADILLY

1880

PREFACE.

In bringing before the public a work that has for its specific subject the training of the racehorse, and incidentally offers some observations on turf matters generally, the author feels the need of its indulgence.

The experience gathered as the result of thirty years unwearied labour in the management of a large racing-stud, is, he feels, the best apology he can put forward for the attempt to write comprehensively on matters never before so treated by a trainer. In order to inform, to please, and to encourage the student, a thorough knowledge of the subject must be supplemented by facts clearly stated, and by arguments based on experiences that have stood the test of time. It is perhaps too common to represent technical or professional matters as full of mystery to the unlearned. Such a pretence would be out of place here. Our subject is one easy of comprehension, and it is the intention and desire of the writer to apply to it the simple treatment of which it is susceptible; to set forth practical knowledge and important and ascertained truths deduced from daily observation in a manner intelligible to the ordinary reader.

This is the work that the author has undertaken to do. He feels there is something of presumption in the attempt to write on a topic of so wide an interest and of so national an importance, whilst so many of his professional contemporaries, pre-eminently fitted for the task, are silent. It is a task which only a trainer can hope to complete with any degree of satisfaction to himself or benefit to others. No one seeking information would read a book on Pathology written by any one but a fully qualified physician, or on Political Economy, unless its author were thoroughly versed through experience and study in the features and necessities of his country. It is, therefore, not assuming too much to conclude that the fittest person to write on training, and on matters more immediately connected with the turf, must be a trainer. He has knowledge and practical experience which are denied others moving in a different sphere, however exalted, except at second-hand. Information, however good, if transmitted by a process of delegation, cannot fail to lose in its course something of its value. For these reasons the author has ventured to record his own experiences of the training of the racehorse and of other matters connected with the turf; and has supplemented the opinions deduced therefrom with those of able and practical men.

The design of the book is to treat, in the first place, as exhaustively as the writer's ability and experience will permit, the process of perfecting the horse for the course; then briefly to review and compare racing as it was and as it is, and to draw such inferences as the study of the subject suggests; and, lastly, to offer a few suggestions for reform of turf proceedings, which, in his humble opinion, would be of considerable benefit to this chief of our national sports. To treat the subject comprehensively is his desire. It will be found, therefore, that his suggestions are not confined to the technical and ordinary affairs of the every-day routine of a training-stable. He has endeavoured to the best of his ability to examine other matters which are certainly not inferior in interest. Thus, he attempts to show under what circumstances some horses vanquish or are vanquished in their public engagements. He has added, so far as memory serves him, many memorable sayings, and the accounts of notable doings of the most successful men and conspicuous characters on the turf; as well as of others who have left it for their long home, who, whilst here, were known for their parsimony or their extravagance, as makers or as spenders of fortunes, with other anecdotes which have occurred to him as having some public interest.

This then, being the scope of the work, the author ventures to launch it before the world, leaving it as it stands with all its shortcomings and inadvertencies to the lenient consideration which may be asked for a book that has no other pretence than to advance the results of practical knowledge, and to supply what may be a possible need. That all should have been said that may be said on the various matters discussed, is impossible. The writer must be content in the knowledge of having done the best in his power to lay before the public the results of the experience of many years in a concise and intelligible form.   He should perhaps add, in conclusion, that in the rare instances in which recent events show his facts or suggestions in a new or altered light, it has been thought better not to attempt to remodel that which has been already written, but to draw attention to any apparent discrepancies by the use of footnotes.

WOODYATES, *February,* 1880.

CONTENTS.

x CONTENTS.

THE RACEHORSE IN TRAINING.

CHAPTER I.

THE TRAINING STABLES.

Introduction--Scope and design of the work—The training stables—The buildings described—Tile roof recommended—The loose-boxes, stalls, and partitions—Corn and hay stores ; screening the corn—Windows and airholes—Boxes and stalls both necessary, and why—Disposal of the manure—Supply of water—The pavement ; its material and slope—Drains condemned—The yard.

BEFORE proceeding to give the results of my experience for the last thirty years as a trainer and for many years previously as a jockey, it will possibly be some convenience to the reader to sketch shortly the plan followed in the different chapters.

First, in precedence, and deservedly so—as on the hygienic principles upon which they are built and conducted so much of success or failure depends—will be treated the Stables, and their interior economy, with a glance at some of the casualties arising from neglect of salutary rules in this important department.

Next will come remarks upon that very interesting subject, Condition. It is one that deserves a separate notice, for on none is there more divergence of opinion and, it may be added, general misconception.

In their proper order will follow observations on the Training-ground, and on the vital and arduous work of

B

preparation, matters which cannot be dismissed without an attempt, at least, to handle them exhaustively. As horses have to be bought as well as trained, a few hints on purchasing will here fitly find a place.

Trials will appropriately come next, and will occupy a good deal of our attention. The subject is a technical one little understood, and will warrant, it is hoped, the space devoted to it. Then with some notice of the jockeys of to-day, old and young, heavy and light, and the anxious moments they frequently occasion to the trainer, we shall come to the duties imposed upon owner and trainer alike when the racehorse is brought to the post fit to run. In connection with this portion of the subject some observations will be offered on the weights for old and young horses and the different courses.

The difficulties, it may be almost said hardships, which at every step beset the trainer cannot be omitted, however personal the matter may appear, from a work that attempts to be comprehensive. Few can imagine how great and varied these difficulties are, or the important bearing they have upon racing results.

A short review of the turf of to-day and of past times, and a few suggestions obviously arising in the treatment of our subject, will, as has been said, form what it is hoped may be found an appropriate conclusion.

This design will, it is believed, give scope for the introduction of many matters of genuine interest to the lover of the racehorse. Under their respective headings, the following subjects will find a place : Casualties and sickness chiefly traceable to deficient stable arrangements ; their causes, symptoms, and remedies. The breaking of the yearling ; its training and trials. The treatment of older horses whilst in training. A minute comparison between horses of the present day and those of past years, with the object of ascertaining their relative merits. Suggestions to clerks of courses, lessees, and other functionaries ; and hints for a different manner and time of entries for many of the large stakes and other matters relating to them. The formation of an outer ring, on all race-courses, for the convenience and protection of the small bettor, as well as his more opulent opponent. The interest owners have in their horses, and how far they may be called private or public property. Commission agents and their emissaries. Notes on trainers and jockeys. The purchase of yearlings, showing the fallibility of the best judges in giving high prices for useless animals; and how the high and low priced horses, ranging from 10 to 1,000 guineas, have turned out ; with hints which to reject and which to choose. The consideration of engagements ; a serious item for the economist and needy sportsman. Low and high standards of weights and long and short courses. Our foreign competitors and their studs. The subversion of the old and the introduction of the new system of training. The abolition of sweating, and the circumstances under which it was brought about. The superabundant clothing once in use, and the paucity that succeeded it. All these, and many other interesting matters which cannot well be enumerated here, will be found embodied in the work ; exhibited as fully and intelligibly as the author's best efforts and anxious desire to do justice to his subject will permit.

IN PURSUANCE of the plan sketched out, the training stables take precedence of the description of other matters. They demand our first attention, for unless they are properly built, and their internal arrangements perfect, their inmates will fall into a state of chronic disease, rather than enjoy robust health, and will be more in need of the veterinary surgeon than the trainer.

The stables I intend describing (which though not a model of perfection, have probably fewer faults than most others) are those I built here some twenty-eight years ago. They have met the approbation of competent judges, and in a sanitary point of view have stood the test of time.

They are built of brick and faced flint in the proportion of two of the former to four of the latter without the least attempt at ornamentation, square shaped with lofts above ; the roof being composed of tile, which is better than slate, being cooler in summer and warmer in winter—both desirable objects of attainment. The nineteen boxes and thirty-one stalls are intermixed for the more equal diffusion of heat ; for a uniform temperature throughout is very desirable. Each set of four stalls is divided from the others by sliding partitions of deal, fastened with iron latches. The boxes are opened and shut by a screen running on rollers at the top. This plan is safer than to have the rollers at the bottom, for in the latter case, horses may, by kicking or other violence, force the partitions open and get together. With the rollers at the top, this is simply impossible, unless something should break, a thing I never knew to occur.

In size they are eleven-and-a-half feet by twelve, which leaves a clear space of six feet behind the horses, giving sufficient room to pass from stable to stable, and to keep the animals from the draught of the windows and air-holes ; for without this safeguard a sudden fall in the temperature during the night may be the cause of colds, if of nothing worse.

The stalls are of the following dimensions; width, six feet two inches in the clear; height at head, seven feet six inches tapering to five feet one inch at the tail—both ends being unusually high for the safety and well-being of the horses; two paramount objects. This height may appear extreme, and has the effect of dwarfing the occupants in appearance. But for racing purposes there is no object in adding to their stature, and the advantages of the plan are obvious. For one thing, the additional height prevents horses from seeing each other and so becoming restless and kicking over the lower end, and injuring themselves, which in ordinary stalls they may do. Behind the stalls there is a space of nine feet; ample room for removing the dung every morning and for traversing the stable with pleasure and safety. The length of the stall from manger to lower stall-post is ten feet five inches. This prevents the inmates kicking each other, which in shorter stalls may very easily be done. The height from floor to ceiling is ten feet. The partitions consist of a two inch planking of beech or oak, joined in three places to prevent the possibility of separation through kicking or other violence.

Over three sides of the square are spacious lofts for the storage of hay, corn, and straw in separate compartments. The ends are partitioned off and ceiled, forming sleeping-rooms for the boys; the head lad having a room to himself, or sleeping at home if married. In one angle are two saddle-rooms; the one for keeping the saddlery when clean, the other for cleaning it. In an adjoining room the clothes are dried, and a copper in a small room next to it supplies hot water.

The corn is conducted from the stores to the feeding bins by means of a tube, before entering which it has to pass over a broad wire screen, which mechanically separates the dust and small seeds from the corn. Thus a saving of labour is effected ; for, though all the corn is again thoroughly sifted, or should be, it is less trouble to do so after than before, and it is done more effectually. The hay is kept in lofts, and sufficient only for each day's consumption is removed to the closed bins below; by this means it is kept from the tainted smell of the stables and when given is fresh and sweet.

The lofts are approached by a side entrance so that no fodder passes through the yard in transit to them.

The stables are lighted through thirty-nine windows in iron frames, each four feet square. This is most desirable, as giving the needful amount of light in which most stables are deficient. The ventilation is effected through air-holes at the top and bottom about a foot square each, behind and over the heads of the horses in proportion of about two to each horse; which is ample. For entering and leaving the stables there are thirteen doors, eight feet nine inches high, opening inside flush with the wall, and four feet broad.

Something may be said about the relative merits of boxes and stalls, which respectively have their advocates. The fact is, both are necessary in every stable. If a horse is a weaver put him into a box, for in it he is more contented and often forgets his tricks. On the other hand, some horses, that in a box would walk themselves to a standstill (being as restless as a caged hyena) in a stall will rest comfortably and consequently do better.

The manure is carted away to a distance every morning. In town, where space cannot be had for money, it is necessarily economised, a dung pit being made in the centre of the yard, where the manure is deposited and left, too often only to generate deleterious gases by fermentation ; the cause of much sickness. To lessen this, the pit should be cleared of all manure twice a week and rinsed with a solution of disinfecting fluid or sprinkled with chloride of lime; offensive drains too should be treated in the same way if there be any in or out of the stable.

The whole of the water from the roofs is conveyed from the shooting by iron pipes to two large tanks, placed at opposite sides of the yard, capable of holding about 400 hogsheads. This supply is sufficient for all purposes, as I have never known them to be dry longer than a few days together, barely sufficient for occasionally cleaning them out.

The pavement of the stalls is flint, which offers an uneven, yet not an uncomfortable surface. It is preferable to bricks, which are liable to become slippery and may cause injury to the horse on rising. It has a fall of about four inches from head to tail. A greater fall would be bad, for it would cause the back sinews to be always in a state of tension. In dealers' stables you may see the animals standing across the stalls to avoid this. The great rise in such places is obviously to make the horses look of more importance, to engage the attention of the purchasers. But this would be an evil in the racing stable ; nor do I think any horses would remain comfortable long in so unnatural a position. The flooring behind the stalls is of brick, but I think ground clinkers are better, for they are not so slippery, and certainly are more durable, and look nicer.

Drains are bad. They cause dampness, and often produce the unpleasant smells they are designed to prevent. When undrained stables are kept scrupulously clean by frequently removing the dung, no such smells will be generated, and less dampness will be found than in those that have drains.

Having described all the necessary internal parts and arrangements with, it is hoped, sufficient accuracy, I need only say that a turret clock on the north side of the building, with the cardinal points, is surmounted by a horse (*Joe Miller*) as a weather vane. In the centre of the yard is a grass plot encircled by an evergreen hedge. A gravel path runs between it and the doors, before which a space of a few yards is pitched with pebbles. The whole is shaded in summer by a choice specimen of the horse-chestnut

CHAPTER II.

VENTILATION AND LIGHT.

Light and air essentials—Cool stables the best—Stifling condition of certain stables; its effects and attractiveness to those preferring looks to health—Mr. Burns and Dr. Southwood on the value of pure air and principles of ventilation—Another excellent authority and his arguments—Simple experiments in proof of my theory—Temptations to an opposite course and direful results—Extra clothing preferred to exclusion of air—Light equally necessary—A worn-out theory, "the tinsel of glossy coats."

LIGHT and fresh air are essentials to the health of all domestic animals. Nevertheless, in olden times, when knowledge was limited, owners of horses used to, and in some instances, even in the present day (be it said to their folly) do, shut up the animals in ill-built stables, low and narrow, in fact, insufficient in every dimension; air-holes too small, too few and improperly placed, with small windows, made as though never meant to be opened. I have seen trainers in their zeal for the welfare of the animal, or his appearance, have the very keyhole stopped with a small wisp of hay or straw, and the outside of the doors barricaded, as if to resist an onslaught of some terrible enemy—half embedded in dung suffered to remain till it has become in a high state of fermentation, disengaging deleterious gases—for the sole purpose of producing excessive heat, poisoning the circumambient air that beneficent nature has provided.

From the exterior of such premises you may judge of the state of the interior, which on entering will be found to be filled with unpleasant odours, the thermometer standing at seventy in the depth of winter, whilst - on all sides not only the olfactory nerves but the eyes are assailed by the effects of ammoniacal gas produced by the imprisoned ordure and urine.

The sensation is one to make the visitor only anxious to escape into the open air once more. If we are to judge, then, by the result produced upon the human being by contact for a few minutes only with the contaminated air that pervades the whole place; what must be the feeling of the wretched horse that has to live in it, or rather to die by inches, or become blind from such pernicious treatment?

To a superficial observer, and even at times to owners, this state of things has a fascinating attraction. The horses appear with coats like satin, full of flabby fat (engendered by heat) often mistaken for muscle. Such people never think of the weakness, the languor, the loss of appetite, from which the poor horses are suffering, as the result of continually inhaling and re-breathing the same poisoned atmosphere; every day, and day by day intensifying its more deadly effects on animal existence. Pearl-like drops are seen in countless numbers standing on most projections, even on the hairs of the rugs, on the side walls, the ceiling; in fact, every particle of the furniture of the stables is wet and clammy with the same impurely heated air.

My own views on the question of ventilation are embodied in a book on this subject, which I remember to have read some twenty years ago. It is entitled *Practical Ventilation*, by R. S. Burns, and I cannot do better than here submit an extract from it :—

"The proper supply," the author says, "of fresh air is as necessary to the health of the inferior animals as it undoubtedly is to man.   Baneful as is the influence of impure air on the constitution of human beings exposed to its influence, it is no less so to the valuable animals, the horse and the cow. Many are the diseases which affect our domestic animals that are brought on by exposure to foul air, and many a valuable animal is sacrificed to a close and ill-ventilated stable."

In the same work Dr. Southwood Smith is quoted :—

"Nor is there one," says the Doctor, "among the many questions thus forced upon the attention of every civilised community, which is itself so important, or the correct solution of which is so indispensable to the preservation of health, as the investigation and subject-means for providing in every space occupied by human beings a gradual but constant change of air."

These quotations testify to the absolute necessity for both man and the lower animals of air in sufficient quantities, and to the evils of withholding it.   The suggestions they contain cannot be too highly commended to the study of all who have anything to do with the care and management of horses.

Nor are these my sole authorities.   I can refer for confirmation of my conclusions—for I can hardly call that theory, which has been demonstrated by practice—to a work on stable management and ventilation which I think one of great merit :—

"The principle of ventilation," says the writer, "has been till lately but ill understood.   If we thoroughly ventilate, we run the risk of increasing the cold atmosphere of the stable below the requisite heat.   Not that heat should

be so great as to starve the animal when he is turned
out, for though it is said to economise corn and lay on flesh
to have the animals kept warm, still it may be carried to an
improper excess.   There is not generally sufficient discrimination exercised in the distinction between hot air and pure
air.   Hot air is not always impure, nor is cold innocuous.
The fact is, other things being equal, a cubic yard of hot air
is certainly less nourishing than an equal quantity of cold air ;
because being more rarefied the former will of necessity
have less of the vivifying principle—the oxygen.   Pure
atmospheric air ought to contain in one hundred measures,
seventy-three of nitrogen and twenty-seven of oxygen, nearly.
There is usually more or less carbonic acid gas mixed with
it, seldom, however, as much as one per cent.   Now the
warmer the air in any confined place, the thinner it becomes
—it will be rarefied.   Hence a stable filled with hot air, will
contain less oxygen than one maintained in cold, though
neither the one nor the other may be absolutely impure.
The operation of breathing destroys the oxygen and leaves
in its place a poisonous atmosphere, carbonic acid gas.
Now this is a heavy gas.   It will remain at the bottom of
the stable unless forced upwards ; whereas the vapour and
hot air will always tend upwards whether there is an aperture
or not.   So long therefore as the air in the stable and that
of the atmosphere are the same warmth, there will be little
ventilation.   It is this interchange from hot to cold, which
causes the principle to be set in motion to its fullest extent ;
and the most perfect ventilation of air is when the cold and
pure air is admitted at the bottom of the building and the
hot air allowed to escape at the top.   It is a mistake also to
imagine that the foul air from a stable can possibly escape
unless fresh and pure air is allowed free access."

On such excellent and clearly defined principles comment
is needless.   Having in a measure traced the cause, I will
pass to discuss the effect of inattention to these essential
rules.   The effect, indeed, may be readily discovered in a

very simple fashion. Remove a horse from a cold place to one much warmer, and, invariably, the result will be he will cough ; a sufficient proof of the injury he receives. Reverse the process ; take him from a warm to a cool stable and it is not so.

The result of this easy experiment may seem paradoxical ; at variance with reason, if you will. Nevertheless it is true ; and, it may be admitted, is well worthy the consideration of every owner or manager of a stable. Yet for one object—looks—the simple lesson it teaches is wholly disregarded. Servants will willingly stake their own reputation, and their employer's interest, on what is here shown to be a fallacy.

The temptation to do so, is comprehensible enough. The beautiful effect produced by a hot stable on the coats of its inmates, ensures unbounded admiration and lavish praise. But few, very few, know the many diseases of which it is the lamentable cause. In such a state, it may fairly be said, the horse is constantly shedding his coat, and as a necessary result becomes weak and enervated ; in fact in a state of disease rather than of health.

There is reason in all things. No one should, to escape one extreme, blindly rush into another, and in order to avoid a stable too hot, have one too cold. But when the temperature is chilly, and your horses uncomfortably cold, supply additional clothing rather than close windows and air-holes. The latter expedient may improve their looks, but it is a poor object gained at the cost of appetite, condition, nay, more, not unoften the very animals themselves.

What must men of science, our veterinary surgeons, for example, and other reasonable persons, think on entering the stables of those adhering with such pertinacity to an exploded theory, the effete doctrine of a worn-out age? Yet whatever they may say, or we think, the practice is carried on to an alarming extent, and even desired by some employers. " Men willingly believe what they wish to be true ; " and warmth, like darkness, has a tendency to fatten.   These facts were thoroughly well understood by the ancients, if we may judge from their low, ill-built, ill-ventilated, and worse lighted stables—for light is as vital an essential of health as is fresh air. They preferred round barrels and glossy coats to the health of their horses ; and, now-a-days, men who think more of appearances than intrinsic usefulness, foster the same practices.   It will probably always be so to a greater or less extent, for—

> " The tinsel glitter and the specious mien
>   Delude the most ; few look behind the scene."

But my subject is running away with my pen.   I shall have occasion to recur to it in the chapter on " Condition."

CHAPTER III.

STABLE MANAGEMENT.

Hours of work and preliminary process—The winter treatment ; times of feeding and exercise—Hand-rubbing preferable to bandages—No deviation permitted —Removal of offal food—The summer treatment ; times of feeding and exercise—Clothing must be dry—Prevention of griping—Temperature should be even—Necessity of cleanliness—Practical results of my system—Mr. T. Parr's plan and my objections to it—Hours of feeding and quantities of food.

HAVING described the stable, and the necessary requirements to insure the health of its inmates—ventilation and light—it is now the place to treat of the interior routine and economy. The process is not the same in all stables ; though probably its chief features are not often very dissimilar. I must be content to sketch my own system for the reader's information.

The stables are opened at five o'clock A.M. in winter ; and earlier in the summer. At both seasons the horses are first tied to the rack chains, the dung removed and both boxes and stalls cleanly swept out. When this is done, the horses are brushed over and fed, the afternoon horses being watered and done up with hay. The dung is then carted to the manure pit, at a distance from the stable, and the stable-yard thoroughly swept. The boys are then allowed time for breakfast.

In the winter, the horses are exercised at about éight o'clock A.M. for a couple of hours. The limit varies a little ; some taking as much as three hours exercise, whilst the young and delicate go in earlier. They are then thoroughly well cleaned, during which operation a little hay may be given to prevent griping when watered, which is always done before having their corn ; and the latter is given as soon as they are well-dressed and their feet washed clean, tarred, and greased, and their bed put straight for them to lie upon. This usually is about half-past eleven o'clock. They are fed again about twelve o'clock, and done up with hay at one.

The afternoon horses are brushed over and fed between the feeding times of the others and are taken for exercise after the boys have dined, until half-past three or four. The same amount of dressing is given them in every respect as that given to the morning horses before described ; and in like manner after being watered they are fed.

At five P.M. the morning horses are again watered and thoroughly well cleaned, by brushing and wisping them well over. When the legs are cold they should be well hand-rubbed till a healthy glow is produced on all the extremities, hand friction being infinitely preferable to the bandage. By six o'clock, as a rule, the horses are finished, when they are fed, and again at seven. At eight o'clock both morning and evening horses (exercised at their respective times) have hay given them, after the cleanliness of the stable has been attended to and the litter put straight. Their heads are then let loose for the night that they may lie down. The boys have their supper between seven and eight, and usually go to bed at nine.

This is the general routine. It should admit of no variation except in cases of illness, or in wet or foggy weather, when the horses do not leave the stable, unless there be a race near at hand, when of course exercise is a necessity. On Sundays the process is pretty much the same as on week-days ; except that there is no exercising, and labour is in other ways mini-mised as far as practicable. (On exercise in wet or foggy weather, and on the undesirability of Sunday work, I shall have something to say in treating of " Preparation.")

After every feeding, all the corn that is not eaten should be removed and the manger thoroughly cleaned. The offal hay should be treated in the same way. It should be removed, and may be given to the hacks or to the cows. By adopting this method, horses will sometimes be tempted to eat : whilst nothing will induce them to look at, much less to touch, food that has once been blown upon. If horses do not eat they cannot be expected to work ; and it is certain they cannot, in such circumstances, do sufficient work to enable them to compete against others thoroughly exercised.

In summer, the horses undergo a different treatment, which runs pretty much as follows :—

The stable hour is 4 a.m., when they are fed, and after the preliminary matters are duly attended to, the morning horses are exercised from five until seven or half-past, as they may require respectively less or more work. On the return they are done up as has been described in the account of the winter management. The breakfast hour for the boys is 8.30 a.m. ; and at nine o'clock the other horses are taken out to exercise, returning about eleven. The cleaning is finished by noon, when they are watered and fed. At this time the other horses are again cleaned, watered and fed, and all are done up with hay. They will rest until 4 p.m., when the morning horses are again exercised for an hour ; some are cantered once or twice, whilst others are only walked for that or a shorter time. (By

C

this arrangement it will be seen that the horses that are
exercised in the morning rest during the work of those
exercised in the afternoon, and *vice versâ*. (After these have
been well dressed, as described before, the horses are watered,
and fed at six and again at seven; and at eight, as in winter,
finished for the night and fed with hay.

The winter clothing is of course of a heavier description
than that used in the summer. Both sets should be thoroughly
well dried before using, as damp clothing is most productive
of colds : for the prevention of which no stabling should be
without a drying-room. The water that is given the horses
to drink should have the chill taken off to prevent griping,
when it can be safely given *ad libitum* twice or three times
a day.

The stable should in all cases be kept as near one temperature as possible, about 45 degrees Fahr. in winter; and in
summer as cool as can be. All the soiled straw should be
removed as soon as seen, and the stalls and boxes swept clean
every day, and allowed to be bare whilst the horses are out
at exercise; the doors, windows, and air-holes, should then
be kept open, whilst the walls and partitions are freed from
dust and cobwebs. A plentiful supply of clean straw should
be given twice a week—either of wheat or rye: both are
very good but wheat is generally used on account of the
scarcity of the other. Sir Wm. Burnett's disinfecting fluid
I have used for years, and I think no stable should be without
it, in health or in sickness. As a preventive against disease,
a little may be sprinkled behind the stalls and boxes daily.
Its use and efficacy in sickness I shall advert to elsewhere.

My object in this chapter is to show the treatment of the
horse in health, and the hours generally assigned for his
exercise. His gallops and trials will be spoken of later, in

their proper place. I believe the system above given agrees in substance with that to which most horses are subjected whilst in training, as the art is practised in the present day. It is at all events a system that I have adopted and pursued for many years with almost unqualified success, and therefore I can recommend it with confidence to others as being on the whole the best. It, like all other rules, has its exceptions ; and one of these exceptions it will not be out of place to give, although it must not be understood that in doing so I agree with the principles enunciated.

Mr. T. Parr, who is undoubtedly an authority and his opinion entitled to all respect, informs me that he uses no artificial lights in his stables even in the depth of winter ; and that both in summer and winter he gives large quantities of hay, of which he thinks horses cannot have too much, whilst on the other hand oats may in his opinion be supplied too plentifully, and consequently he uses them sparingly.

One consequence of this is that, at certain seasons, the horses in his stable can neither be dressed, watered, nor fed, from about 3 p.m. to 8 a.m. or a little earlier the next morning ; and must in the meantime be not only in a most uncomfortable state of dirt, but breathing a fœtid air that renders them liable to bronchial affections and disease of the lungs, which leave so many roarers ; and to ophthalmia and other disorders of the eye. The times of feeding must be diminished as well as the quantity of the corn given (the most nutritious part of the diet), unless served in very large feeds, which would tend rather to prevent the animals from eating than induce them to eat. The hay too, if given in like unseemly proportions, must have a similar nauseating effect on the horses, preventing their touching what they would, if given in smaller feeds, often eat and enjoy. It is clear the animals under his

care could be fed but twice, or at the most three times, a day ;
a principle which seems to me bad in theory, and one I can
no more approve of than his system of daily giving each
horse a ball.   Yet he succeeded ; and " success is genius."

In sum, I may say that horses should be fed five times
a day, with as many good old oats and hay chaff as they can
eat.   These I think they require and should have, and nothing
more : though in some cases, light or delicate feeders may
have a few old white peas or split beans added to each feed.
In isolated cases this addition may be of service, though I find
most horses do well and even better without it.   Hay may
be given, like corn, without limitation ; for as long as they have
plenty of both they will eat of neither sufficient to hurt themselves.   On the qualities of food and water, a matter
the importance of which cannot be overrated, I shall have
something to say in the next chapter.

CHAPTER IV.

STABLE MANAGEMENT (*continued*).

Value of regularity—A good head lad indispensable—Occupations of the trainer
—Duties of the head lad—Food and its qualities—English oats preferred, and
reasons—Hay must come from good land—Good food the only food—Mr.
Clark on feeding and on soiling, and criticism of his remarks—Feeding in
past times and to-day—Water and its qualities—Mr. Clark thereon—Rain-
water in tanks the best, and reasons—Need of frequent examination of feet
and legs ; use of bandages condemned—Evils of inattention to this—Value of
neatness and regularity.

PUNCTUALITY in the hours and attention to stable management are all-important, for on them rests the ultimate condition
of the race-horse when brought out to run.   All the management in the world out of doors will not compensate for, nor
rectify, mistakes made within ; so where both are not done
thoroughly, evil results must follow.   It is therefore indispensable that the trainer should have a man who is capable of
managing the indoor department as well as of attending the
horses at exercise in the absence of the principal.

If it is absolutely requisite, to be successful, that horses must
be under the charge of a skilful and attentive trainer, one who
knows how much or little work is required to be done by each
and every horse and the best time to give it, (and the proposition will hardly be controverted), it is equally necessary that
he should have a good man at the head of the stable depart-

ment. To him must fall the management of the boys, and, with other duties of less importance, the special one of attending to the wants of the horses; for nothing requires greater attention or more practical ability than feeding.

The services of a good kennel-huntsman are known and appreciated by every master of hounds; whilst to the huntsman he is invaluable. Of exactly the same use a head lad should be to the trainer; for it is quite impossible the latter should feed the horses, before exercising, at 5 a.m., and be constantly in the stables (meal-times excepted) till 8 p.m.; for a portion of his time must be given to other matters that cannot be deputed.

For example, the trainer has his correspondence with his employers on the subject of entries and scratching. For this purpose he must necessarily study the Racing Calendar. It is needless to add that there are many other business calls which consume his time, quite apart from the absences from home to attend the different race meetings, which take up no insignificant portion of it during the summer months. And without an able man at the head of affairs during these absences all would be anarchy with the boys and ruin to the horses.

Such a man is a necessity. He should not only have experience but be absolutely trustworthy, and trustworthy in a special sense. He should be one to be depended upon to carry out the instructions for out-door exercise. In this matter, he should implicitly obey, and no more, the positive orders for the work each horse has to do during the absence of the principal. In the stable, on the other hand, he should know exactly what is best to do, yet only at the instigation of the trainer himself should any alteration be made in the appointed times for feeding and watering;

hay, too, should be given at the regulated hours and at no other.

In the important matter of food, he should be supplied with the very best of oats ; old, certainly, till after March, and later if they can be found sweet, and of English growth. Winter at 42 lbs. per bushel, and black tartarian at 40, are in ·my opinion the best, far better than the thick-skinned Scotch white oats at 46 lbs. per bushel or even heavier, though the latter look to some people. preferable to those I have described, or indeed to any other. I do not object to a few good white oats ; but they must be of home growth of about 42 lbs. per bushel for mixing with an equal quantity of black, such as I have named. But whatever the description given, they should be the very best of the sort or sorts, for it is false economy of the very worst description to buy inferior corn, however low the price. In fact, good cannot be too dear ; whilst middling would be wretchedly so as a gift. To supply the latter shows an utter want of knowledge of his business on the part of any trainer.

My antipathy to foreign corn is so great, that I could never be induced to buy a bushel, or any larger quantity, in my life, knowingly. But I have too much reason to believe I was once imposed on, in the year 1847, in having supplied to me a load of heavy oats, said to be English, which the price warranted, but which turned out to be Scotch delicately kiln-dried ; a process I failed to detect in their appearance, taste, or smell. The result was, they gave the horses diabetes, from which weakening disease it took them weeks to recover: a plain practical proof of their inferiority, and a good reason that none but English should be used. Buy of the farmer in preference to the dealer, and you know you get the genuine article. To

good oats I think little need be added in the shape of
provender besides hay ; though for a spare feeder a few
old split beans may be added to each feed, or, what is
thought by many better, white peas : but as I have said,
I have little faith in the good effects of either and seldom
use them.

The quality of the hay depends more on the land that
produces it than on anything else ; a fact which should
in no case be overlooked.   Hay grown on rich alluvial
soil or well-drained clay is the best ; and that raised on
hungry gravel or poor chalk is the worst.   And though hay
well made from the latter land, retaining all its most attractive qualities, such as colour and smell, may be had cheap,
it should on no account be used : as it contains no nourish-
ment, and is really to the animal very little better than
poison.   But that grown on good land usually let at 3*l.*
or 4*l.* per acre, is by far cheaper, at 6*l.* or 7*l.* per ton,
than the other would be as a gift.   For this reason, and
this alone, I have always had my hay grown on the land
in the Vale of Blackmoor : land I suppose as good as
any in the kingdom, and although draught carriage of
about sixteen miles is an expensive item, I prefer it to
any and all others, and use nothing else, nor have I for the
last thirty years.

I may supplement the above advice with a note from
Mr. Clark, who says: "New hay should not be given
to horses in strong work; it should not be less than eight
or ten months old."   He condemns clover, and prefers
rye-grass to meadow, saying : "It is less liable to imbibe
moisture, and being hard, and firmer than natural hay,
it obliges a horse to break it down more minutely before
he can swallow it, and is easier of digestion."   Now as to

the age of the hay, I coincide with these remarks ; but I cannot agree with his choice, and much prefer the meadow hay such as I have described, when equally well made, to any and all others for horses in strong work.

On soiling, in which I thoroughly believe, for a change in the spring he says :—

" Clover, trefolium, vetches, or lucern may be used, and carrots in winter. Grass in the spring is not only food but medicine, and expeditiously cures disease. It carries off worms and promotes all the secretions, and removes as it were the whole mass of fluids in the body, which it restores to the highest state of perfection of which it is capable." " Sailors," he goes on to say, "from eating dry and salt food are subject to scurvy, and are cured by fresh greens and ripe fruit ; " and adds, " it is the same with horses who are fed on dry food ; they are likewise subject to the scurvy, which in them is called the farcy."

Having said I agree with the system of occasionally giving green food in small quantities as an alterative in summer and carrots in winter, without discussing the similitude existing between the scurvy in the human subject and farcy in the quadruped, I pass on to notice his further remarks on change of diet.

" Malt mixed with the food," he says, "should occasionally be given as agreeable and wholesome. Barley is too purgative, but when boiled is easy of digestion and is given to horses when they are sick or to prevent costiveness." " Oats," he continues, "are generally given to horses in Britain ; but they are apt to make them too costive ; to prevent which a bran-mash is given once a week, or as often as circumstances may require." Beans he recommends, and wheat and barley for a change, but, " new corn like new hay, should not be given."

From the above remarks, it appears horses were fed in olden times pretty much as they are fed now. Indeed with the exception of wheat, barley, and malt, which should only be given in illness, his recommendations leave little to be desired with regard to the food.

The manner and times of feeding and the food itself having been described, it should not be forgotten that equal attention should be paid to watering at stated periods. And here something may aptly be said on the quality of water best suited to the horse.

Rain-water is preferable to all others, and where this cannot always be procured and kept fresh in tanks, well or pond-water, softened if hard with a little wheat flour or chalk, may supply its place. From the use of either so treated I have seen no ill effects. Mr. Clark in his treatise on the horse, thinks water of so much importance to the well-being of the animal, that he has devoted a whole chapter of fifteen pages to its consideration, the salient points of which I think well to give :

"Disease may originate," he says, "from the use of un-wholesome water, and physicians are of the same opinion as regards the human subject; for where the water is bad, disease prevails most. Horses do not thrive well on pit or well-water, as the water is very hard, and causes the coat to stare and stand on end. If taken immediately after it is newly pumped, spring water is likely to partake of all the metallic or mineral strata through which it passes, and is salutary or noxious according to the nature of those substances. River-water is much the same, but it is softer than water that runs underground and better for use. Well- or pit-water is worse than spring; being harder; and the deeper the well the worse the water. Pond-water, under which head may be included all stagnant waters generally produced by rain, when it lies on a clean or clay bottom, and is fresh, answers very well for cattle of all kinds; but in hot warm weather it is apt to corrupt and ferment, which renders it unwholesome and the most disagreeable of any."

As he makes no mention of tank-water, I suppose it was not known, or but little used in his day, or he would not only have named it, but most likely have recommended its use above all others. For in substance he says pond-water (which is rain-water), when fresh, answers well: but does not say so much for any other. And when the rain-water is collected from the roofs of houses and preserved in tanks or reservoirs in large quantities, it keeps better than when exposed to the fermentative influence of the sun. Moreover it is unmixed with the many impure particles that help to contaminate pond-water, and consequently is better; and indeed to be recommended above any other sort. I myself have used it for thirty years with satisfaction, and I know it is used in other large establishments with the same result. I could, were it necessary, quote the opinions of many experienced men to this effect.

So much said concerning the food and drink of the race-horse, my remarks on the internal economy of the training stable may fitly conclude with a reference to one very important matter—the frequent examination of the feet and legs, and the use of bandages.

Too much care cannot be taken in this respect. The legs in particular should be constantly inspected; for unless these be constantly looked to, a horse, to all appearance the soundest of animals, may have received an accidental injury. The injury may be of itself trivial, and if timely attended to may easily be set to rights; whereas, should it

be neglected even for a day, the animal may be irretrievably
ruined.

It is now much the practice to sew cloth round horses'
legs, with the view, I should suppose, of giving support.
But whatever advantage may thus accrue is in my opinion
nullified by the fact that the custom hinders the ready
examination of the parts covered; for a rupture or strain
of the tendon may exist unsuspected. The injury may
not be sufficient to cause lameness until galloped, but then
assuredly it will betray itself; often too late. The harm
done will probably be irretrievable.

The feet also require frequent attendance; for neglect of
them will be followed by serious consequences. The results
of such inattention, however, will be more legitimately treated
in the next chapter.

Let me add that a trite saying, "A place for everything and
everything in its place," is a motto that should strictly be
followed. Its observance economises labour, and gives the
show and reality of neatness to a place. The broom, fork, and
shovel, should have a place assigned them as near the stable
as possible, where they may be kept when not in use. The
dung-barrow may be placed at the back of the stable, or in
some other spot sheltered from observation; as may the
tar and grease cans, stopping-box, and the sand-box. The
saddles and bridles may be kept with the other furniture in
use neatly folded up, in the drying or saddle-room, after
being properly cleaned and dried. The buckets may be
arranged in a row outside the stable walls, and in dry and hot
weather should be kept full. And even so small a matter as
the tightness or looseness of the head-collar is an object of
moment. For indifference to this, as I shall presently show,
may be the cause of the ruin of a valuable animal.

CHAPTER V.

SICKNESS AND CASUALTIES.

Sore backs; their prevention and treatment—The feet; attention necessary—
Thrush and its cure—The legs; signs of disease; treatment—Bandages not
recommended—Cracked heels and cure—Treatment of warbles—Quittors,
sand-crack, and cutaneous diseases are signs of neglect; their treatment—
Coughing and strangles—Treatment of the latter—Cleanliness and air necessary—Colds and their prevention—Sore shins; curious instances—Mr. Copperthwaite on sore shins, and my objections—Swollen joints and ruptures, and
their results—Ringbone, splint, and spavin—Treatment of ringworm—Crib-
biting, &c., are tricks—Lameness; how frequently caused; attention to the
head-collar and stirrup-irons—Roaring; instances of cure.

I HAVE no intention to attempt to write at length upon the
diseases of the horse. The subject has often been ably
handled by veterinary surgeons and other persons duly
qualified for the task. There are, however, certain ailments
the result often of improper or careless stable supervision,
which come prominently before the principal of a large racing
stable; and a word on the causes, often preventible, the
symptoms, and some simple remedies, may not be thought
out of place.

Sore backs, for one thing, are frequently the source of
infinite trouble. These are oftener caused by pressure of an
over-tight roller than by the saddle. With the latter, if the
saddle-cloth be properly adjusted, they will not occur. But

with the roller, the breast-girth passing over the points of the shoulders causes it to tighten, and thus the withers are pinched. With ordinary supervision this should be avoided; and it may safely be said that a sore back is suggestive, if not a proof, of inattention.

But from whatever cause arising, the treatment is simple. A fomentation with a little astringent lotion should be applied to the injured part. This is the best, and, with proper care, an effective remedy. But it is necessary to see that, when at exercise, the saddle does not increase the mischief by pressing on the place. The roller should be discarded in every case of soreness; and a rug alone used, fastened under the fore-rib and before the shoulders to keep it from shifting.

It is very necessary, as I have remarked, to attend to the feet. Neglect breeds thrush. But though this sometimes lames the horse, it is neither a dangerous nor a malignant disease, and readily succumbs to proper treatment. It will be found that a little tow dipped in tar and applied three or four times a week is the most simple and efficacious remedy. The foot when hot may be so from disease, or from defective shoeing in some way, and in either case ought at once to be looked to; for in a state of health the feet are cold.

The legs, on the contrary, should be comfortably warm. When they are not so, weak circulation may be suspected. On the other hand, unnatural warmth is a sure indication of local injury, the precise seat of which may generally be determined by the exhibition of tenderness on pressure. In such cases, bathing with cold water may be used two or three times a day for an hour or more at a time, with cold flannel bandages; but if the suspensory ligament has given way, then consider the first loss the least, and the sooner the patient is disposed of the better; for scarcely one in a thousand ever stands a preparation after.

Bandages, as I have said, I never use except in illness, when dry flannels are the best.   In health I prefer hand-rubbing to anything else, to assist circulation.   The benefit derived from bandages I consider more imaginary than real.   Still, like other fanciful matters, they have their purpose of ornamentation if not of use.   The wavy appearance given to the hair on the legs could probably not be so effectively produced in any other way.

Cracked heels are seldom heard of now, whilst formerly almost every horse suffered more or less from this troublesome complaint, which in very bad cases affected their condition considerably.   The primary, if not the sole cause, I believe, used to be sweating, for the evil has simultaneously disappeared with its abandonment.   But if the heels are left wet after washing out the feet (which is too often the case), it will produce soreness; therefore care should be taken to wipe them perfectly dry.   However, should any horse be so affected, the best remedy is fomentation after the water has been steeped in bran, and strained through a sieve or a wire strainer, and a little of the following ointment applied twice a day: Mix a little red precipitate powder with hog's lard, simmer over a slow fire, and stir till cold.[1]

Just before becoming, or when actually fit, horses are very frequently attacked with "warbles," an irritating and very troublesome complaint, though not dangerous.   It usually appears on the back and sides, and is no sooner cured in one place than it returns in another.   They are very seldom seen in any horses except those in strong work, and in other respects in the best of health.   A little cooling medicine may be given, and an astringent lotion applied twice a day to the parts affected.

[1] Hog's lard, 1½ lb.; powdered camphor, 3 oz.; red precipitate, powdered, ½ oz.

Quittors, sand-cracks, and poll-evil, mange and other cutaneous diseases, I never saw in my stables, and therefore cannot pretend to prescribe for them; but I am convinced they should not exist where proper arrangements are in force. Their appearance, like that of sore backs or crib-biting, is, in my opinion, a sure sign of neglect. When cases do occur, there is but one remedy—to hand them over to a veterinary surgeon; for, if unskilfully treated, the quittors and poll-evil may assume an obstinate form, ending in death; while most skin diseases are contagious, and spread rapidly.

Yearlings when taken up to break, as a rule cough, (probably from the stable being hotter than the one previously occupied); have sore throats and influenza, the latter often the cause of strangles. This disease, many people say, horses never escape, in some form or other (like distemper in dogs); but my experience teaches me to believe just the reverse. Numbers pass from the side of their dam to the grave, after years of racing, and do not have it, or any other disease. They die from accident or old age, but not from sickness. Strangles are however very common amongst young horses, and may easily be detected by a cough, enlarged or sore throat, and discharge of thick mucus, sometimes fetid, from one or both nostrils, often attended with loss of appetite and extreme debility. To blister the throat under the jaw with "Day's" spavin liniment or some other vesicant, is as a rule sufficient to arrest the complaint; if not, the application should be extended down to the chest, when there is no suppuration under the jaw. This will localize the disease and prevent its reaching the lungs. After suppuration takes place, little may be feared if the orifice be kept open, and a little digestive ointment on a pledget of tow be applied after being washed clean with warm water three times a day.

Warm clothing, two rugs if necessary, and even a hood and flannel bandages, should be used. The latter should be removed twice a day, and, before being replaced, the animal's legs should be well hand-rubbed all round. The stable should be kept cool, and the patient fed on nourishing diet; on bran, corn, and linseed mashes, hay, carrots, and above all, grass, if it is to be obtained, though only a little. Malt mashes and barley steeped in boiling water, both form very good changes, and should be given in small quantities. On returning strength, dry food may again be used, though the mashes should not be entirely discontinued until the recovery is complete.

A little exercise may be given in fine weather if only for ten minutes a day, increasing the time with the strength of the patient; a matter seldom attended to sufficiently early. The state of the bowels should be rather relaxed than constipated. The opportunity should be taken whilst the animal is out to open all air-holes and windows, and have the stable thoroughly cleansed and fumigated. I have before commended Sir William Burnett's Disinfecting Fluid as a preventive. In sickness it should be used more liberally: even wetting the sides of the stalls and boxes, and suspending pieces of cloth saturated with it—both often extremely beneficial.

The old horses are not so liable to illness as the younger ones. Still, if after galloping in cold easterly winds they are not soon after cantered or trotted to keep them warm and comfortable, they will cough; and a cold once caught is, like disease in any other form, not easily got rid of; and if attended with much fever would be infectious, and go through the whole of the stable with greater or less severity. It should therefore be guarded against; prevention being better than

D

cure. But in case of an attack, the sufferer should be immediately isolated, or the whole stable may quickly be affected, from its epidemic character. Change of air is an excellent remedy if only for a short distance, and a little time, with careful nursing and liberal diet, will generally be found efficacious.

Most horses suffer from sore shins. There is no guarding against this complaint. It no doubt comes from work, but unfortunately comes suddenly without the slightest warning of its approach. It generally makes its appearance after a few weeks' work, and sometimes before the young ones are broke : some get it at two years old, when about three parts fit to run ; some not till after being tried ; others still later get it from running. But the cause and effect are the same in all, as is the remedy.

Dressing the shins with some vesicant should be resorted to, and a week's rest given and a dose of physic ; after which the horses may be set to do steady work again, and alternately worked and rested till the complaint passes off altogether ; fortunately it seldom returns. A cure may be effected by the first application, or it may want repeating many times at intervals of about a fortnight : during which period only walking exercise should be given. The action of some is so much affected by this complaint that they can scarcely stride over a straw, whilst others go as free and well as the horses that have no signs of it, and its existence in such cases can only be known by the touch.

A remarkable instance of this complaint occurred in *Starter*, whose shins, when a yearling, were very bad, the soreness never leaving him until after he ran for the Goodwood Stakes at three years old. He never went short during the whole of his work ; still the shins were very sore and flinched at the least touch. *Fugitive*, when six years old, after running in deep ground at Egham, returned home with his shins very sore, having lost his action ; indeed it may fairly be said he could not move. He was given up for a few weeks and treated as before recommended, which soon had the desired effect of removing the soreness and restoring his action. This is the only instance I ever remember of one so old being so affected by it in the fore-legs. I never remember an old horse suffering behind from it, although it is not uncommon for young horses to have all four shins sore at the same time.

We have seen there are instances of horses having sore shins from running in deep ground, yet it is generally caused by galloping on hard ground, over which, when thus affected, some animals can seldom if ever move. But no danger need be apprehended from the most obstinate cases. They may leave a protuberance when the soreness is departed, which becomes ossified, but in no way interferes with the action or general usefulness, presenting only an eyesore. This fact leads me to comment on Mr. Copperthwaite's expressed opinion in his work entitled "The Turf and Stud Farm," in which he says

"he has known horses while in training and racing to be shin-sore, and their owners and trainers did not dream of it, and has known yearlings to be rendered totally useless and never to recover their action through this complaint ; and little wonder it was so, for the parties who had charge of them (some of them their owners) could have expected nothing else, taking into consideration that they were, in the month of July, on the hard ground for hours (and cantering about) carrying big men, their legs being little more than gristle."

For my part I certainly have known some thousands of horses of all ages, and never saw one permanently hurt from

sore shins as Mr. Copperthwaite asserts; nor indeed did I
ever hear of such an occurrence as he relates before, nor do I
now believe in the phenomenon. Can one suppose, for a
moment, that the trainer, or in his absence the head-lad,
would not see if a horse went short in his exercise, and would
not seek for the cause by a careful examination of his feet
and legs? Moreover, the legs are felt by the trainer, in the
ordinary way, twice a day, and rubbed oftener by the boy.
Could all this be done, it may be asked, and the excruciating
soreness escape detection, and the "trainer never dream" of
the cause of the total *ruin* of his best horses; watching them,
thus deteriorate before his eyes, with supreme indifference?
I venture to think not; but rather, that Mr. Copperthwaite
has been mistaken in his opinion, as I shall have on a later
occasion to show how greatly he has erred in other matters
connected with this and kindred subjects treated in the same
work. But it is a work more on breeding than on training,
and little is said in it on condition, and that little too much,
either for the sake of the writer's reputation, or his readers'
patience, so far as I am able to judge.

Two other injuries which a horse is liable to, arise from work
—swollen joints, which sometimes are of no consequence; and
rupture of the middle and main tendons, often attended with
fatal results. Rest and blistering are the two remedies,
although I confess that, as a rule, I have little faith in either.
When joints are swollen on the outside they become callous
and do not hurt; but enlargement on the inside of either
fore-leg is generally fatal. Ringbone requires firing, splints
seldom hurt, and yield to the application of biniodide of
mercury or puncturing, and curbs to blistering: or in bad
cases to the actual cautery. The bog-spavin mercurial
ointment will usually cure, and the bone-spavin yields to

firing; but the thorough-pin nothing will permanently eradicate.

Ringworm, that troublesome and very contagious disease, is cured with a preparation of mercury, by rubbing the affected part with a small portion once or twice a day for three or four days. Acetic acid once applied will, in most cases, have a good effect; if not, it may in a few days be again resorted to. The same remedy is a good one to prevent horses from rubbing the hair off the tail, making it sore, and spoiling their looks.

It is only necessary to add that in all cases of illness a plentiful supply of warm clothing should be used, in order to keep the body at a proper temperature. This is infinitely better than the restriction of the supply of fresh air, so essential to the health of all animals.

These are the ailments which commonly come before the trainer; but there are besides injuries the result of tricks arising from careless management, on which I have something to say before concluding this chapter.

On attention to small things, success in great ones chiefly depends. Horses when idle often contract bad habits—crib-biting, wind-sucking, kicking in the stable—by which they sometimes injure themselves. As a rule these things are preventible, and should be prevented.

In treating of sore-backs, I remarked that crib-biting was as easily avoided as they are, by a little attention and proper management. When not feeding or set at liberty, horses should be tied up by the rack-chains, and so kept from nibbling any projections, such as the manger or top-rail of the stall. When this is done, no crib-biters will be found. The trick grows from constantly licking and biting the manger. If it be not stopped, or the horse making the unpleasant

noise removed, in a few weeks the whole of the inmates of
the stable will be equally bad. To my mind there is no
surer test of neglectful supervision than the existence of a
crib-biter, or of a sore-back.

I have mentioned the care necessary in fastening the head-
collar ; for if too tight it is unpleasant to the horse, if too
slack, he may either get loose or his hind-foot become en-
tangled in it. An accident of the kind has been the cause
of many an animal's ruin. The collar-rein should pass over
the roller or through the rings with freedom, and be long
enough to reach the ground to enable the animal to lie at
ease. But if too long, or the log to which the rein is
attached be not heavy enough to keep it moderately tight,
the horse will get his leg over it, and the result, not
unfrequently, be lameness for weeks.

When turned loose to rest in the boxes, the collars should
in every case be removed, to prevent this entanglement. In
the stalls, the bars should be put up between them, so that,
in case any of the occupants get loose, they may be hindered
kicking and savaging each other.

There is another thing to be mentioned. Many a valuable
horse has been ruined simply by getting the stirrup-iron in
the mouth when the boy has left him for a few minutes. To
prevent this, the irons should, the first thing on return to
stable, be drawn up as near the top of the saddles as possible,
and the stirrup-leathers drawn through them ; an effectual
safeguard against such an accident.

I do not know that roaring can fairly be set down either as
sickness or accident; but it is a complaint that cannot be
passed without some notice, and perhaps will more fitly come
as a conclusion to this chapter than elsewhere.

Large horses are, in my experience, more subject to this

disease than the small. It is not only often fatal to the racing capabilities of the animal, but unfortunately it is transmitted to the progeny when the horse is put to the stud. But I have known, in a few instances, horses badly affected with the malady to recover. There is regrettably neither admitted cause nor known cure for it, for the seat of the disease is quite uncertain.

The late Lord G. Bentinck had a grey mare so afflicted killed, and employed Mr. Field, the eminent veterinary surgeon, to trace the cause; but he failed to do so, and said the respiratory organs were natural and healthy, and in fact that there was no malformation or disease, and nothing to be seen that could enable him to account for it in any shape or way. It comes on very suddenly, and is unmistakably defined in a day or two. Horses that have had inflammation of the lungs, or a long illness from strangles, are more subject to it than others that have not been so affected; but some hundreds recover from both these complaints without becoming roarers. Again, whilst some few horses are scarcely affected by it, others, as long as they have it, are perfectly useless for racing purposes; whilst some, the rare exception it is true, recover, and are as good as they ever were, showing no ill-effects whatever.

Brigantine was an extraordinary instance of this exceptional recovery. In the early part of her two-year-old career, she ran successfully and in perfect health. In June she was taken ill, but recovered sufficiently to fulfil her engagement at Newmarket in the July meeting, when, however, she ran badly, and on her return home was found to be an undoubted roarer. The winter passed, and with the spring preparation, as her work increased, the disease gradually diminished, and ultimately left her as sound as the day she was foaled; in time, indeed, to enable her to win the Oaks and the Ascot Cup in the same year. I remember that many years ago Mr. Osbaldeston had a horse called *The-Devil-among-the-Tailors*, which turned a rank roarer, but recovered, and was as good after as before the malady. Some horses, too, have run well as roarers. *Longbow* was a good horse over a short course; whilst *Shadow* could stay any distance roaring like a bull. *Dulcamara* and *Noisy* both returned from Chester confirmed roarers; but whilst there they both ran in perfect health, the latter winning the Dee Stakes easily, beating some of the best horses of his year; but he could never afterwards beat a hack, although both tried and run in public several times.

As to the cause, occult as it is, I feel sure that a sudden change in keep and management has something to do with it. That this is so may be seen with hunters. If they be turned out to grass after a winter's hard work, from hot stables, they not unfrequently become roarers. This is not only my own experience, but I have heard others say the same. This is probably a reason why, as a rule, racehorses are not now turned loose in a box and treated with less care during the winter than the summer months, as used to be the practice. We certainly have fewer roarers amongst our racehorses than formerly, and this I attribute chiefly to more attentive management. Situation, too, may I think have something to do with the malady. At the Cape of Good Hope, I am told, horses never roar; and that the worst roarers if taken there become sound. This is partly confirmed by my own experience. When I consider the number of horses I have had and the few cases of roaring amongst them, I cannot help thinking that the dry and airy situation of my place is either a preventive or an antidote, if so desirable a thing can be found.

CHAPTER VI.

CONDITION.

Predilection for glossy coats—The natural coat of animals—Anomalies of this liking for sleek coats; its evils; the condition-ball and arsenic—Rough coats most often seen doing work—Horses fit when rough: *Hermit, West Australian*—Docking—Public notion of condition; theory and experience—The trainer alone a judge—Deceptive appearances of horses in big and in light condition: Instances: *Catch-'em-Alive* and *Historian; La Pique*—Sir Richard Sutton's treatment of the latter and its uselessness—Personal experiences; *St. Giles, One Act, The Coranna Colt:* Inferences drawn therefrom—Condition for long distances.

IN treating of the subject of air and light, I have mentioned the predilection of certain owners for looks rather than health, and the complacency of those that serve them in satisfying this disposition.

As this fallacy leads to many others, I may well dispose of it before proceeding to touch upon the other points that bear upon that important and interesting part of our subject— Condition.

Glossiness of coat and sleekness have, I have already observed, their especial attractions. The owner is satisfied, and the gazing eye of the wondering multitude pleased. The trainer, who indulges in the practice, is pleased to see his horse, if not "the glass of fashion and the mould of form," at least "the observed of all observers;" whilst the stable

boy is half frantic with delight to observe the cunningly
devised work of his own unaided hands.

Now I, for one, do not say for a moment that a horse is any
the worse for trifling and tawdry embellishments, if legitimately achieved ; just as I would not admit that he would
be any better were he burnished like gold, striped like a
zebra, and his attendant fancifully dressed like a zany. But
there is too much inclination in this direction. Some, perhaps,
would wish to plait or shave the tail and crimp or hog the
mane to complete the picture.

I protest against the practice, because I aver looks are no
test of condition. Bounteous nature has provided for the
comfort and well-being of the animal kingdom warm cover-
ings of various sorts. To the horse has been given long hair,
suitable to his nature, for protection against the inclemency of
winter. We all know that wild animals have a warmer covering
in winter than in summer. It scarcely requires a naturalist to
confirm what every observant person must be familiar with.
Amongst birds we see that they moult in autumn, that the
feathers may be well grown, thick and long, against the ap-
proaching winter. Buffon, in his natural history, from which
I take a few extracts bearing on the point, in speaking of the
beaver, remarks, " It is in winter they are chiefly sought,
because their fur is not perfectly sound in any other season."
Again alluding to the sable, he says, "and yet this (winter)
is the best season for hunting them, because their fur is better
and more beautiful than in summer."

The same principle applies, almost in its entirety, to the
horse. His coat, like theirs, is naturally longest in winter ;
although it can hardly be said to be then more beautiful, nor
is it desirable that it should be so. Deprive him of this before summer, and you do him an incalculable, an irreparable,

harm.   Yet, for a fanciful purpose, he is subjected to all kinds of anomalies: kept improperly warm in the stables; made to take a daily condition-ball—and all for the removal of his greatest possible comfort, and the substitution for it of his summer coat in the depth of winter! Who shall say how many horses are annually lost in this way? And yet, with many, nothing but time and bitter experience will alter the practice. One thing may be safely predicated of it, a fact indeed that has not escaped even superficial observers—the horse with the most glossy coat is least seen in public; that with the roughest, the most often.

But when once the love of popularity, in whatever form, takes hold of the senses, folly is apt to oust reason.   It is difficult to say to what lengths this may not be carried to secure the object of the ambition of the hour, or, it may be lifetime. When its idol is the appearance of the horses, the stable becomes a hot-house, its inmates, sudatory creatures, whose stomachs are made the receptacle of the contents of a chemist's shop.   This is hardly an exaggeration; for it is not possible to tell the ingredients of the condition-ball, or their possibly deadly effect.   We know full well that many a man who has charge of his master's hack or carriage-horse, has been detected administering the harmful balls, or even arsenic in a crude form, to give the coat the desirable glossy appearance in winter as well as summer; with the one inevitable result— the death of the unfortunate animal and the punishment of the man; the latter richly deserved, it must be admitted.

Gentlemen are too willing to judge the condition of their horses from the appearance of the coat.   Were they to ask the desired information from the trainer, whose pleasure, duty, and interest it is to supply it, it would be more satisfactory to both.   And though the result might not agree with the preconceived views of owners, they should still be content in the knowledge: first, that no one is so qualified to advise in such a matter as the trainer; secondly, that no one has so sterling a motive to advise rightly. If this were the general practice, we should see horses looking better in summer, as they would be healthier, as well as in winter.

It will be appropriate here to instance, by way of illustration, a few rough-looking animals which have been brought to the post in absolutely perfect condition—fit, it may be said, to run for a man's life—but which, in appearance, were exactly the reverse, and did not escape the public denunciation.

I will hereafter speak of *La Pique*, a mare of my own, and a case in point. But let us take *Hermit* or *Virago* as examples. What, it may be asked, did he look like the day he won the Derby? or she, when, with consummate ease in one and the same day she carried off both the City and Suburban and Metropolitan Stakes? Or again, how did *West Australian* look when he won the St. Leger at the back end of the year? Why, like a bag of bones covered with hair as rough as a badger's, on which seemingly a brush had never been laid. A hundred similar instances I could name were it necessary. But as with the smooth coat so with the rough—it may be well or ill obtained. In these cases no amount, either of ability or diligence, had been spared to bring the animals to perfect condition. Consummate success was obtained, and yet the eye was not satisfied—they lacked the unnatural and debilitating sleekness at a time when Nature herself withheld it. Surely the trainers did wisely to study the health of the horses before their outward appearance. Yet the capricious multitude and self-confident sportsmen bewailed the lack of superficial gloss, and were, as usual, egregiously mistaken. There was no lack of courage in thus braving, as it were, public opinion ; nor was it, in the result, unrewarded. From their employers, the trainers received well-earned and freely-given thanks ; from the public, an ovation such as a victorious General might be proud of. The public had erred, and had to confess it; being forced to admit that as horses run in all shapes and forms, so they do in every conceivable state of condition, so far as the eye can judge.

To insist at all hazards on a glossy coat is, in my opinion, only on a par with the barbarous custom of forty years ago or more, to shorten the docks of all horses young or old. Usually they were subjected to this treatment during the first or second week after their arrival at the training quarters : the operation being performed by the severance of a few inches of the vertebræ of the tail, staunching the hemorrhage by the application of powdered resin and the actual cautery. Happily for the tortured animal, the practice has long since ceased to exist, as has nicking and nerving, that old and useless veterinary practice ; "more honoured in the breach than the observance." All men now prefer to see the noble animal as formed by nature, rather than in a mutilated shape, disfigured at the hands of capricious humanity.

We have learned something of the essentials, in feeding and stable management, of good condition ; and it will now be well to describe the signs that enable a person to judge correctly of the fitness of a horse to do what may be required of him.

Every one who has seen or takes an interest in a racehorse, talks eloquently, in conventional terms and set phrases, on his condition; a point in which one horse so resembles another, that existing differences often escape all but the experienced eyes. Horses that look pretty much alike are praised or condemned, rightly or wrongly, as fancy dictates.

Now theory, the only guide that persons not intimately conversant with the stable have, which runs so glibly and seems so simple, is found utterly untenable when brought to the touchstone of practice. To my mind, condition is one of the most difficult problems ; one that, however great the genius of persons differently employed, can only be solved by the experienced trainer. There are many gentlemen, owners of horses, most excellent judges of shape, make, and breed, equal in this respect to any trainer ; I may go further and say better than many, but on condition, "they are at sea," and their opinion not of much value. Nor indeed can anything else be expected. They have not the opportunity afforded them of forming a correct idea, and cannot give one : whereas the trainer sees the horses under his charge daily, and knows the work each does, and how he does it ; whether progressing towards or receding from the desired object, which should ultimately culminate in fitness to run. But the owner can know nothing of his horse's every-day performance at exercise, or whether he eats little or much. The utmost extent of his information is limited to seeing a gallop or two, or may-be a trial—the latter sometimes is a test of condition, but not always ; for many are tried thoroughly unfit, and the result is misleading, rather than a clue to the animal's real merits.

It is patent, therefore, that they can know little, if anything, about the material points, and that on such insufficient tests a trustworthy decision cannot reasonably be expected. And if owners of racehorses, with such advantages as they do possess, are often so lamentably mistaken, what must be the value of the dogmatic and oracular opinion of the uninformed public ? I think the general verdict must be mine—nothing.

If this be allowed, it will not be out of place to give one or two illustrations of the difference in outward appearance of

various horses, all of which have been in the highest
condition.

When a horse is stout, or, as many would have it, full of
muscle, looks well in his coat, and has good action, then many
assert he is fit to run.   Most fallacious and untrustworthy
idea; for often the appearance of the horse that is fit is just
the reverse—in a condition, indeed, as I have said, fit to run
for a man's life, yet no one would be bold enough to say so
who feared the laughter of the wiseacres.   On the other hand,
there are few who would not hazard an opinion, and pronounce
to a man, the horse that is sleek and fat, the fittest.   The fact
is, no one but the trainer, who has charge of the animals so
different in appearance, can give an opinion worth having;
the public, on the other hand, would, I venture to affirm, be
wrong in nine cases out of ten.

I will give two examples of the comparatively exceptional
instances of horses being fit when big.   *Catch-'em-Alive*, when
he got out of the van at Newmarket, was condemned as too
big by touts and turf critics, who cynically remarked he would
not have so many looking at him after his race (the Cambridgeshire Stakes) on Tuesday; yet he won, and from sheer
gameness—a never-failing test of condition.   *Historian*, on
his first appearance in public for the Lavant Stakes at Goodwood, was fit and round as an apple, looking to the *cognoscenti*
quite fat, and all said he would see a better day—but he never
did, winning easily, and in the same state won many races
after.

Now let us contrast his seeming fat state with that of a
light bad-conditioned mare afterwards called *La Pique*, who
looked little better than a bag of bones encased in the roughest
of hair.   At the appearance of such a wretch a general outburst of indignation was indulged in, and on all sides she was

voted not good enough for the kennel, which certainly, they
added, was a more fitting place for her than the racecourse.
The fact is, she looked rough in her coat, and was, like many
others, a light-fleshed animal, just the reverse in appearance
to *Historian* and others.   Yet she was well, and proved her
fitness by winning her race, beating a good field of horses in
a Selling Plate, enabling her owners and the stable to win a
nice stake at long odds, for I believe no one else backed her
for a shilling.   There were, if possible, more absurd remarks
made upon her condition after than before the race.   One
was for giving her a little rest ; another would add to that,
sumptuous feeding ; whilst the fortunate Baronet, the lucky
purchaser, knew she was in want of a host of things to make
her fit, and which she should have.   The opinion of the rabble
was expected ; but hardly this confident declaration on the
part of a gentleman of his experience.

The late Sir Richard Sutton placed her in the hands of an
eminent trainer to carry out his positive instructions intended
to improve her neglected condition.   This was done, but to
no effect ; in fact, he failed to make her capable of winning
anything.   The lamented Baronet then tried his own hand at
metamorphosing her ; and I can readily believe that she was
indulged in every sort of luxurious feeding, with rest without
limit ; but to no good end.   Finding himself a victim to his
own credulity, he sold her, as utterly useless, never having
won a race with her.

Now here are animals which, to look at, seemed as diverse
as it is possible to find in nature—both two-year-olds, one
looking really big, perhaps too big, whilst the other was de-
cidedly light, and indeed far too light in the eyes of the public.
The public, indeed (who, having no horses of their own, are
always professing such superior knowledge of the condition

of those belonging to others) stoutly declared in these cases that neither were fit, though their running then and subsequently sufficiently proved the folly of such an opinion and the penalty incurred in uttering it.

Even trainers may be, and no doubt some of us at times are, deceived. As a proof that the public are not always alone in this respect, I confess to having been grievously deceived on two or three occasions. *One Act* misled me, and so did a colt by *Coranna* out of *Eyebright*. As a three-year-old, I thought *St. Giles* fit and tried him, but he was little more than half fit to run a distance of ground, and was disgracefully beaten in his trial ten days before Northampton. Knowing that, as a two-year-old, he had stayed well, I concluded he must require more work than he had had, to make him stay as a three-year-old. I therefore galloped him every day two miles till the Saturday previous to the race, and then tried him, with the same tackle and the same weight, over the same course, when he won just as far as before he had been defeated. He went to Northampton and won the stakes with ease, beating perhaps the best horse in England (*Skirmisher*) according to his subsequent running.

The case of *One Act* is very similar ; the mare having, as I thought, done sufficiently good work for months previously, I tried her, when she was beaten very easily. This I attributed to her condition, or rather the want of it, and set about improving it in the same method—galloping her every day, two and a quarter miles till just before her race at York. I sent her for this as I had done *St. Giles*, and with the same fortunate result. She won the two great handicaps at York, and followed up these successes by winning the Chester Cup in the following week, " looking like a rail." These facts, it may be readily conceived, remain indelibly engraven in my memory.

E

Again, the *Coranna Colt*, just before his intended trial, being, as I thought, fit to run and if anything rather too light, broke his thigh, and was at once destroyed. To my astonishment when he was opened, he was found to be a mass of fat; clear evidence that he was not more than half prepared. Yet, as I have said, his outward appearance betokened that he was thoroughly trained, and if anything, rather overdone. The natural and immediate inference to my mind was that when beaten in their respective trials, *St. Giles* and *One Act* may have been in the same condition; and I concluded that had the *Coranna Colt* been tried he would as assuredly have been defeated. These results plainly indicate how absolutely necessary time and work are in preparing a horse to run a long distance. The practical part of training, the knowledge gained by experience, enables the trainer to give an opinion on the condition of the horses under his charge before any one else; yet, from the many anomalies attending the process, some of which have been explained, even he may be deceived. One horse may look fit, when in reality he is big and short of work; another that is absolutely fit, looks just the reverse, or as some would style it, overtrained.

These difficulties staring him in the face, it behoves the trainer to be ever on the alert; to watch the condition of each horse from the first canter to the last gallop; and how exact and continuous this watchfulness must be will be explained when we come to treat of Preparation.

CHAPTER VII.

CONDITION (*continued*).

Opinions of owners on condition ; Mr. Dixon—Coughs and their various effects—
Lameness and its results—Diverse opinion of two owners—The trainer knows
his own horses—Curious belief in different treatment for handicap, and
weight-for-age races ; the fallacy shown—*Joe Miller, Voltigeur, Brigantine*—
The public and condition—Typical instance of big and light conditions ;
Tame Deer and *Fisherman*—Condition of pedestrians—Fat men—Horses
oftener fit when light than big—Mr. Clark on equine fatness.

I HAVE, in the last chapter, given my own opinion of condition. It will not be amiss in the present to supplement
it with the opinions of other people, of owners and others.
The space devoted to this will hardly be regretted, because
success depends so much upon the condition in which horses
are brought out to run.

I will commence by giving a short account of Mr. Dixon's
experiences. He was the owner of *Blarney* and other good
horses, at the time placed under my care. One of the latter,
Philippa, he had purchased as a two-year-old for £300, after
she had been raced two or three times and easily beaten on each
occasion. In the first race I ran her for, which was shortly
afterwards, she beat *Borneo*, who had been purchased for 1,500
guineas, on whom odds of seven to one were laid. I mention
this to show the quality of the mare when fit to run. The
year following she was tried just before Bath Races, when
she was coughing and easily beaten as one would expect.

E 2

Notwithstanding this warning, Mr. Dixon would run her, and did, and being beaten took her out of training, though she was the soundest mare alive and had many good engagements that year, and by the next might have had many more. He put her to the stud, where she turned out a complete failure—indeed she did not live many years.

Now a cough may be innocuous, or it may be fatal. Horses often cough on leaving the stable, and in it, and after galloping, whilst in good health. At the commencement of exercise horses will often cough, but if, after it, they blow their nostrils no ill-effect need be apprehended. From following others in their gallops a horse will get dirt in his mouth and so a cough ; but it quickly passes off. Again, horses will cough after being watered in the stable ; but it does not hurt them. But on the contrary, if horses cough badly in the stable before watering and feeding, or at exercise shortly before galloping, it is a certain warning, not only that they are not well, but that it is not possible to guess the extent of their illness. Something similar, it may be remarked, can be said of lameness. Swollen legs may prove to be of trifling importance, or end in the total uselessness of the horse so afflicted. I have re-marked on this point in an earlier chapter, and also shown the variety of causes which create lameness, sometimes of little and sometimes of the greatest consequence. But as a matter of fact it should be added that nearly all horses trained for long-distance races, trot lame and yet are practically sound.

It is well to note these things ; for they serve to show how little owners really know of condition, the possible result of lameness, or effect of a cough ; and how greatly to their advantage it would be, if they would listen to the advice of those whose occupation provides them with this information. But there are owners and owners, and a

chapter would not suffice to describe their respective idio-
syncrasies.

In regard to this point, I will briefly give the opinions on
condition expressed by two different owners on the same
animals within the space of a few days. Whilst strolling
round the stables one of them said in great astonishment,
"Why, William," addressing himself to me, "what on earth
have you been doing with so and so, or rather I should say
what have you not been doing? Why, he and the others that
have to run next week are like so many bacon hogs." I
begged to differ in the opinion he expressed, and said that as
far as I knew they were well and fit. This was far from
satisfying him ; whilst his colleague, who happened to come
a few days after by himself, gave it as his opinion that
"the horses were thoroughly unfit." They looked bad in
their coats, were too light and as "dry as a chip," wanting
at least a month's rest and yet had to run the next week.
He added inquiringly "Can they be well?" I replied as
before by saying I thought so. In the result the truth of
my view was amply verified by their running ; though I fear
little to the benefit of their joint-owners, who both came to
the same conclusion as to their unfitness, but, as has been
shown, from diametrically opposite bases.

Such cases are too frequent, and disappointment as
assuredly follows. All opinions cannot be right, and of
three that differ two must be wrong. How is a trainer to
please owners of horses holding these extreme views? To
this one of his many difficulties, I shall have to recur at the
proper place. It is not from ostentation that I say so
much ; but because, if I am to benefit the reader, I must
speak plainly. My experience tells me that if a horse blows
too much after galloping, his work must be increased without

regard to his looks—essentially a very minor consideration. So, too, if he feed badly, his work should be reduced ; whilst it should at all times be apportioned to suit individual constitutions and the state of the legs of the different animals.

These things properly attended to, then, the trainer who knows the daily progress of his horses, can give an opinion worth having on their condition—but no one else can. I may therefore be emboldened to ask, with all the respect that is due to them, what can owners know of these things? They are little better than casual observers, and can only form their judgment on that most fallacious of all tests—the eye ; and by no parity of reasoning can be said to know when, and when only, a horse is fit to run. It is so even with ourselves out of our own stable. I should assuredly find myself lamentably self-deceived, were I to hazard an opinion on the condition of a horse prepared by any one else. It would be the same with the most experienced trainer or the astutest judge of horseflesh, were the one or the other to pronounce on the condition of any animal they had not seen before or for a length of time. Just as in sickness, the qualified professional, the veterinary surgeon, will not trust his own senses entirely, but will consult the attendant before prescribing ; or the physician will inquire his patient's state of the nurse, so should the owner seek his information of the trainer.

But I can give instances of even more extravagant notions on the part of owners than those already cited. On one occasion a nobleman told me (and I have not the slightest doubt said that which he thought strictly true), as the reason he sent his high-priced yearlings to John Scott and the cheap ones to me: " He thought no trainer could train a horse for a weight-for-age race like him," and added, "but I prefer you to all others for a handicap." I argued the point exhaustively with his lordship, but my logic failed to convince him to the contrary. And he believed in his preconceived idea, that when a horse is fit to run for a weight-for-age race there is something lacking in his preparation for a handicap and *vice versâ*. Surely when a horse is fit to run a given distance (no matter what) for a handicap, he must be so for a weight-for-age race over the same course! More, it may be said that many races of the latter kind become and virtually are handicaps, from the extra weights imposed on some and allowances made to other horses by the conditions of these races. I can adduce many proofs, were they needed, that my reasoning is sound; but two must suffice. Let me ask, then, can any one suppose for a moment that *Joe Miller* was less fit to run when he won the Emperor's Vase at Ascot (a genuine weight-for-age race without penalties or allowances), beating *Voltigeur* and most of the best horses of the day, than when he won the Chester Cup, a handicap? Or can any one be simple enough to believe that when *Brigantine* won the Ascot Cup or the Oaks, she was wanting the condition that assisted her to win the handicaps at Newmarket? I need say no more to show the fallacy of his lordship's argument.

But now a word must be said of that irrepressible body the British Public, the first to utter all sorts of illogical assertions, yet limiting inquiries as to the real merits and condition of racehorses to finding fault with those who have the care of them. Owners and trainers alike fall in for their share of the rancour of these prescient sages, who oracle-like condemn "at one fell swoop" and in true stereotyped form, all light horses as starved or galloped to death.

Yet it must be patent from what has been said in the last
chapter, and it is to all conversant with the habits and treatment of the racehorse, that the current categorical con-
demnation of the condition of all beaten horses, is but
an evidence of profound ignorance. As for myself, I have
shown reason enough, I hope, for my conviction that no
trainer would be found guilty of an act so suicidal as
not properly to prepare his horse. His reputation is
at stake, his very existence, it may be said, involved in
the well being of his horses. And if these be ill-fed or
neglected, how can they work? And if they cannot work,
how can they compete with those that do? No, these baseless charges carry their own refutation. No man would set
himself to defeat his own ends; to successfully accomplish
that which each one of us is so strenuously seeking to avoid—
his own degradation and shame. It is sheer nonsense. Horses
have run light and will do so to the end; it is one of the
grand essentials of condition, and few are really fit in any
other state.

But after all, condition is but a relative term, as it may be
viewed by different people. This horse is as widely praised as
that is widely condemned, equally without reason; for do all
we can, nothing will prevent horses in condition being light
in appearance—in some instances to the extent of seeming
neglect—and yet these horses, oftener than not, beat the big
and fat ones. We need go no farther for an example than
the race at Lincoln between *Tame Deer* and *Fisherman;* the
former looking like a donkey and the latter with a coat like
satin, his ribs covered (as it was said at the time) with muscle.
At 3lbs. difference *Tame Deer* won, proving himself on that
day and in their respective condition the better horse at even
weights—yet it was subsequently proved and remains an

authenticated fact that *Fisherman* was two stone and a half the better horse. I may add I never saw the tables turned; a fat horse beating a thin one so vastly his superior; nor do I think any one else ever did.[1]

I think I may fairly assume enough has been said to convince even the sceptical that horses must and do run light from other causes than overwork or mismanagement. But I am prepared to do more: to assert that as a matter of fact there are more horses insufficiently trained and looking too big than there are overdone with work. I mean of course for long distance races, not short ones; for which, as less work will suffice, horses may be run bigger. I am strenuous on this point; but I may remind the reader that I am not descanting on the merits or usages of this or the other trainer; but am contending for a principle in the superiority of which I myself

[1] Turning from the horse to the human being, the condition of pedestrians may be taken as an instance to point my observations. A pedestrian when fit to walk a long or short distance looks starved, more like a skeleton than a man in robust health living upon the most nutritious food without stint. At the time "Corkey" accomplished his surprising six days' walk at the Agricultural Hall he weighed but eight stone : a proof that he was neither fat nor in what is ordinarily supposed to be good condition. Fattest men are not as a rule the greatest eaters, nor do they confine themselves to a diet more nutritious than that of the spare and meagre. The late Mr. Banting could not check his obesity by abstinence in the matter of food. The nobility and gentry live well, yet as a rule they are spare men. In the workhouse or the cottage, on the other hand, we find those who fatten on the poorest of food, and in many cases an insufficiency of that. In my own experience I remember Mr. F. H—— then living at Exeter, a very thin man, to all appearance but half fed, who once at the instigation of Mr. S—— (on whose authority I give the anecdote) undertook to eat a roasting pig for supper— and did it ; a feat that probably would have bothered the renowned Dan Lambert. Yet until the day of his death he remained as cadaverous and as thin as ever, in spite of his appetite. A correspondent of the *Lancet* lately sent particulars to that paper of the case of Mr. W. Campbell, landlord of "the Duke of Wellington," Newcastle on Tyne, who "stands 6 feet 4 inches, and weighs over 50 stone," yet, "his appetite is not more than an average one, and although not an abstainer, he is moderate in his drinking."

implicitly believe ; whose success I have compared with that
of other systems, as have other trainers before me.   This
assurance renders me insistent in recommending it to those
who have not had the same opportunities to test it.

As a fitting conclusion of our subject, Condition, I will
venture to give an extract from an admirable work on the
horse by Mr. Clark (from which I have already quoted at
p. 24 on food) :—

"But the greatest caution," he remarks, " is necessary to be
observed with horses that are very fat.   They require a long
course of moderate and regular exercise before they can be
put to that which is the least violent with safety.   Their
fat, which they acquire by excessive heat, is melted by violent
exercise as it were into oil, and carried into the blood and
causes what is called an oily plethora, which produces a most
violent and sudden inflammation of the lungs, &c.

"The viscidity of the oily matter obstructing the vessels
and preventing the other fluids passing through them,
frequently occasions sudden death ; many instances of which I
have known particularly in those horses which have been fed
with a great quantity of boiled meat in order to fatten them
for sale.   To attain this desirable end and keep him in
robust health in an artificial state we must bear in mind
what he was when wild and imitate it as far as possible.

"Count de Buffon says that very warm climates, it would
appear, are destructive to horses, and that when they are
transported from a mild climate to a very warm one the
species degenerates. "

It therefore may be granted that horses like a medium
climate bordering on cold rather than heat, for we find the same
author (vol. 3 page 38) states that in Iceland, where the cold
is extreme, horses though small are extremely vigorous.

CHAPTER VIII.

THE TRAINING GROUND.

A training ground and its essentials described—Its surface—Extent and shape—
Downhill exercise condemned—Distinct courses necessary for summer and
winter—The trial ground—Methods of restoring the surface—Newmarket
and other sites—Appreciation of situation—A quiet spot recommended and
reasons—Effect of publicity on owners—An instance to the point at
Woodyates.

HAVING learned something of the horse in sickness, and of
what is and what is not condition, we may, before proceeding
to the consideration of the preparation of the horse in health,
give a description of the training ground as it ought to be.
There is nothing more essentially necessary to a training
establishment than a good training ground. The extent,
the nature of the surface, and subsoil, are all matters of the
greatest importance and deserve a strict inspection, when
selecting a spot. The soil should be neither clay nor sand ;
for though the latter may in wet weather afford pretty good
going, in dry it becomes very hard and unfit for galloping.
Unmixed clay is still worse; for in wet weather it is too deep,
and in dry, bakes like a brick, and is very seldom in a state
fit to gallop on and then only for a short time.

The surface soil should be one of a light friable loam
resting on a chalky subsoil, sufficiently retentive of moisture
to keep it moderately soft in dry weather, and porous enough

to prevent its being heavy in wet: such for example are
many of the South Downs in Sussex and those about
Salisbury Plain. The extent should in a great measure depend
on the number of horses likely to be trained on it, and should
always be too big rather than circumscribed; for when it is
the latter, continual galloping on the same track spoils it,
and the horses are more likely to become lame. Moreover
a change of ground is in other ways beneficial for them.
Plenty of scope you must have or you cannot train for a long
course ; besides, the walking ground should be distinct from
the galloping ground. It is necessary to have two or three
pieces of half and three quarters of a mile in extent, and in
addition, space for gallops of a mile, a mile and three quarters,
or two miles, or even longer, straight, is requisite for preparation for long courses. If you have not this your horses
will suffer, as you cannot have them gallop round a circle as
in an amphitheatre.

We are told that pedestrians when in training are made to
do most of their fast work uphill—a clear proof that it is
considered far preferable to running down. It is a system
that cannot be too closely followed with the race-horse.
Horses might be trained by galloping uphill only ; but if
only permitted to gallop downhill would never be got fit.
There is no objection to an occasional steady gallop over
undulating ground ; but the fast work should be done up hill
or on level ground. It is necessary too, that the galloping
ground should be nearly straight, not angular, or the pace
cannot be kept up all the way ; a matter often necessary, and
especially in trials.

In the preparation for spring engagements, the horses cut
up the ground and spoil it for summer use ; it is necessary
therefore to have entirely distinct courses, which should be kept

respectively for winter and summer work; or in other words, for wet and dry weather.   As soon as the March winds set in, exercise may be started on the summer ground; but rather than spoil it, in the event of a wet spring following, return to that set apart for winter.   In this matter it is the weather rather than the season that must in all cases regulate the choice of ground; and if one have to be overworked, let that one be the winter ground.

For trial ground, the best should be selected and strictly appropriated to the one use; although there are occasions, when the ground is dry and little impression made by galloping, when it may be used if needful for ordinary work. When much galloping has rendered the surface of the ground uneven, most trainers have it bush harrowed and then rolled with a heavy roller to fill up the cavities and reduce the uneven surfaces.   I cannot say that it is a plan I am enamoured of.   Repeated rolling improves the appearance of the ground by levelling it, but unfortunately makes it hard, which is the one thing to be avoided; whereas my method, removing the turf by manual labour, levelling, and lightly treading in the turf when replaced, is infinitely better.   In old times the boys in the stable used to do this, but now nothing would induce them to attempt it: so a few labourers in the spring, or as often as is necessary, may be engaged for the purpose; and as a rule they do their work in a satisfactory way.

Newmarket as a training ground is not inferior to any that I know of, and better than most.   It has scope and other advantages to recommend it.   Its worst feature is hardness in a dry summer; but in both spring and autumn it has no superior.   And if, taking all things into consideration, there are other places equal to it, by far the greater number are inferior; places on which scores and sometimes hundreds of horses are trained, in which the nature of the ground precludes the possibility of doing them justice. What is the result of such training? The horses go lame; and those that remain sound must be run about half fit, of necessity courting defeat by horses that are fit—a remark specially applicable to long distance races.

Therefore as horses cannot be trained elsewhere, it is of paramount importance to have a good training ground. The selection of it should be made in dry weather. Then it is in its worst state, and its nature can be thoroughly judged. Bad or indifferent stables may be altered or even rebuilt; but the nature of the ground no process can appreciably improve. As you find it, so it remains; and on it such as it is, you must either work your horses or neglect their condition.

By many the situation is considered the chief object. To make it so, is all very well if the owner race for love of sport regardless of expense. Gentlemen of this mind, prefer having their stables and downs in their own neighbourhood, or failing this, near London, so as to be easy of access during " the season." But those who are bent upon making their horses pay their way, who race with a view of recouping the heavy outlay on the purchase of a stud and its attendant expenses should choose a quiet spot and good ground wherever they may be found; but in reason, the farther from a large town the better. My preference would be for a place thus situated within two or three hours of the metropolis, giving owners ample time to see their horses at exercise and in the stable and return to town for dinner. In such a place there would be perfect freedom of action: no telegraph set in motion to announce your whereabouts on arrival or departure, nor touts to annoy you. Plans could be arranged in peace and the result waited in hopeful expectancy, which would often be well repaid.

As a matter of fact, there are merchant princes, both of the city and provinces, who dare not see their own horses except on the race-course or on Sunday for fear of being recognised; a disability that debars many others from joining in the sport. The late Mr. Graham, the noted distiller, who raced in princely style, was driven from the turf, thus losing the only pleasure of his life in the way of sport, by the annoyance of the attention of would-be friends and the intrusion of touts. As for the latter merciless and wretched spies, many suffer persecution at their hands; for when they assemble in large numbers it is not easy either to control or avoid them. But if your ground be in such a spot as I have recommended, you may and can prevent the appearance of these unwelcome visitors; a fact, if generally known, that might not only prevent secessions from the turf, but induce many gentlemen to keep racehorses who never owned one before.

It is not as though this immunity from espionage were restricted to one or two places. Hundreds of spots, equally undisturbed, could be found, which at a small outlay might be adapted for training grounds equal to any in the kingdom. There is no need to rush into the enemy's camp. As it is, owners more frequently go to the tout than the tout to them. Indeed the rendezvous of this gentry are well known. Therefore avoid them and train in a place "exempt from public haunt," where by yourself, or with invited guests you may have the pleasure of watching your horses gallop, when and as often as you please, without dread of the incursion of the arch-enemy of all racing.

I will give an instance of what was once accomplished here at Woodyates, which I venture to say could not have been achieved at any resort of the tout, although I do not doubt that others who train in quiet spots could record similar doings.

About a week before the Chester meeting, *Starter* and
Our Mary Ann, the property of the same owner, were tried
for the cup, and the latter found to be by far the better of the
two.   The result was telegraphed in cipher to the owner, then
at Newmarket.   He at once went into the ring and did as
follows: On asking ̔ the price of *Starter* he was offered
700 to 100, supplemented with an offer to take 800 to 100·
The owner laid the odds, and being asked to do so again, laid
them again, when the taker a book-maker, obligingly offered
to lay 1000 to 10 against *Our Mary Ann*.   These odds the
owner took, and other bets followed until he had in all 2500*l.*
to 27*l.* 10*s.* laid against the mare—the two animals ultimately
standing in the betting, *Our Mary Ann* 1000 to 15, *Starter*
8 to 1.

Now mark what would have taken place had the horses
been at a public place and the immense difference in results
to the owner.   Immediately after the trial, there would have
been a race to the telegraph office, and the lynx-eyed
fraternity would have telegraphed the result to thousands of
people within a few hours.   When the owner would back
his mare, he would have been offered 700 to 100 and been
told it was a good price ; and should he not like it, the bookmakers would have offered to take 800 to 100 themselves and
have finished by offering 1000 to 10 against *Starter*.

The frequent occurrence of disappointments similar to that
which was in this case prevented, will, I think, clinch my
arguments in favour of quiet training quarters for all that
race either for profit or, it may be said, their own pleasure.

CHAPTER IX.

BREAKING.

Gentleness essential—The tackle described—Other methods, and objections to them —The bit and bridle—The colt ridden loose—Age at which horses should be broke: opinions of Buffon and Cuvier—Best season for breaking—Should be broke as a yearling—Different practices and objections to them—Reasons for breaking early—Examples from foreign horses—Instances in proof of my system; *Antagonist* and the *Nottingham Colt*—Confirmed by the French practice—Big and little yearlings compared—Lord George Bentinck's usage of them—Sir Tatton Sykes's treatment of yearlings described and commended.

HAVING some idea of the ground to be selected, we may now proceed to describe the breaking of the yearling.

> " Those that do teach young babes,
> Do it with gentle means and easy tasks."

The couplet is one worthy to be borne in mind by all who would undertake to train horses. The yearling, when he comes from the breeder's hands to those of the trainer, is (as Mr. Clark observes) often fat. In such cases he requires time, and should only have gentle exercise at first—walking and trotting for several hours daily—and then a dose of physic. After this he may be lounged, and in a few days the breaking tackle may be put on him.

The tackle consists of pad, with side reins fastened to it, bridle, crupper, and kicking straps. When he is familiar with these and lounges quietly both ways (to right and left) a saddle may be added; over which the pad is placed—the

F

crupper and straps remaining still attached. A linen rubber may also then be tied on either side of the saddle. When this ceases to attract the attention of the colt, and he is in other respects quiet, he may be ridden ; the boy being first placed across him a few times in the stable, when by coaxing and gentle handling the colt will soon become used to it, and the boy may sit erect. So much gained, and it requires but patience to achieve it, the colt should be lounged after being led at a walking pace for a short time, and when sufficiently quiet, which will be in the course of a few days, may be turned loose.

Different methods are preferred by different trainers. Some would mount him in the open air for the first time. In this case, great care should be taken not to frighten him. He should be held by a short rein, which gives greater command over him when he plunges, that he may be stopped at once ; for if he gets his head in front of you, nothing will control him, and in breaking loose the shock to the nervous system would be so great that he probably would not recover for weeks. Gentleness and time are two most essential adjuncts in breaking the colt ; for if departed from, and he be hurried in his work or abused in irritable hands, immediately the progress you are seeking to make becomes a retrograde course.

I have seen a plan of breaking yearlings, which to my mind cannot be too strongly condemned. It is to drive them before you ; for what purpose I am at a loss to conceive, and not being curious enough to ask, remain in ignorance. It requires no conjurer to tell us, that, if half a dozen men cannot hold a horse that is bent on escape when close to him, if his head is straight before them, no one man can, at the length of the cavesson-rein, prevent his getting loose whenever he pleases; and this evil is sufficient to outweigh any advantages the system may seem to have. A man leading a yearling should never, until the animal is to a certain extent quiet, leave his head, but have his right hand on the cavesson-rein, holding it within a few inches of the point of the cavesson. If this be done, then if the colt starts from any cause he can be stopped at once. But if, on the contrary, the man be a few yards from him, should he jump forward and kick, which frequently happens, the advantage is entirely his. As well pull at a house with the hope of pulling it down, as think to stop a horse by the same means. The result will be but one: the colt gets loose, the cavesson-rein dangling at his heels to add to the fright already occasioned by the other trappings, and he will likely go for miles before he is secured. I have seen this happen, and necessarily to the great injury if not absolute ruin of the horse. It is clear therefore that a valuable (or for that matter any other) yearling should not be permitted this chance of freeing himself. There are unfortunately too many occasions when ruin may result from uncontrollable circumstances, without adding this gratuitous one.

The bit that as a rule is worn first, is a large snaffle with a few pieces of steel or iron in the middle, and is called a "player bit." The middle part should always be kept in the centre of the mouth: it should not be allowed to remain on one side or the other. The bridle should not be too long in the head, or the colt will get his tongue over the bit, which should in no case be permitted; nor too short to prevent it passing with freedom when moved on either side, or it will cause hardness of the mouth.

When the colt has become perfectly tractable he may be ridden loose, having an old horse to lead him. He should be

made to walk and trot, turning right and left at the will of the
rider, and cantered straight; and when so much is accomplished, the colt may be considered sufficiently advanced to
commence training—before which the tackling should be
removed and a smaller bridle substituted.

With regard to the age at which horses should be broke
and ridden, it should be said at the outset that various and
conflicting opinions are held on the subject. But though the
question is often mooted, I think it is seldom discussed to
a practical conclusion.

On this point the naturalist Buffon says, in speaking
of the horse, "When two, or two and a half years old, they
are mounted, never having before that period been either
saddled or bridled." He is here evidently speaking of the
Arab, for he goes on to say, "Every day from morning till
night all the Arabian horses stand saddled at the tent doors."
Again he says, "At the age of three, or three and a half, we
should begin to dress the colts to render them tractable."
And after giving special instructions for their care and culture,
the author proceeds to say, "They may then be mounted and
dismounted without making them walk till they are four years
old; for before that period a horse has not strength enough to
walk with a rider on his back; but at four years old they may
be walked or trotted at intervals."

If the natural strength of the horse has been here faithfully
depicted, how weak they must have been in the last century
as compared with the horses of the present day!

His description is corroborated in a very striking manner by
Cuvier some fifty years later. In his "Animal Kingdom"
he says, speaking of colts: "At three they are fit to be
handled and accustomed to some management." How totally
altered is the practice of to-day! For we know that they

can not only be ridden without hurt before three years old, but at two, and even as yearlings, when they are trained. There were in fact a few years ago yearling races, a practice happily proscribed. *Schism* ran at Shrewsbury, and others at this age, and as far as I know received no hurt from it.

As to the season at which horses should be broke, a very important subject, our authorities are silent. But common sense supplies the omission, and tells us, that when the ground is soft, then it is fit for this severe preparation. This period may, and most likely will, be in different years at different times between July and September, and even as late as October.

But if the ground be soft enough, in July or soon after would be the best time to ride yearlings loose; or even (if thought desirable) those that are fit enough may be tried before the winter sets in. But in respect to trials the majority would be of necessity in a backward condition, and the following spring would be soon enough—just before the March races, should the colts be wanted so soon. On the other hand, the trials of those having engagements late, may be deferred until nearer the time of running, when a more satisfactory result may be obtained than by trying early as yearlings. Yearlings are broke, I know, as early as June, whilst the ground is hard as adamant—a practice I cannot but think hazardous and one that should not be followed; for they must feel the ill-effects of galloping and plunging in trying to free themselves from the tackling, on the hard ground without shoes or the least protection to their feet.

As to the age when horses should be broke, there is, as I have said, a diversity of opinions; but most thoroughbred horses are broke as yearlings, which I think the best age: whilst some few agree with the practice as given by Buffon

and Cuvier.   The late Lord Jersey used to have the most of
his horses broke at two-years old, and run them at three, and
he succeeded with a small stud.   Whilst Mr. Wreford, and
many others who were equally fortunate, broke their horses
as yearlings (which is the general practice), though some
were not raced until they were three-years old.

As for myself, I am clear on the point.   Whatever the
age at which the horse has to run, he should be broke and
ridden as a yearling.   One good and sufficient reason for this
practice is, that he is then more tractable, and reduced to
submission with less restraint than when older.   If, too, the
breaking be left late, vicious habits may have been contracted
which no training will eradicate.   The late Mr. J. J. Farquharson, of hunting celebrity, used to keep his horses till four and
even five years old running loose in large paddocks, before
sending them to be broke.   But I never knew him possessed
of a good one so treated.   A winner he may have had, which
is all that may fairly be said in favour of the produce of his
stud.   A more savage lot of horses in the stable I never saw,
or on the turf a greater set of rogues.   This experience
should, I think, deter any one from following a plan that
in my opinion has so signally failed, and which may be
said to be the only one tried to such an extent without a
redeeming point.

Those who favour the system of late breaking say : " Our
horses are ruined and prematurely brought to the stud
through unsoundness and the want of stamina caused by early
breaking and running so often."   Such an allegation may be
easily refuted.   For do we not see horses running till ten
or twelve years old, broke at such an age ?   *Historian, Lilian,
Reindeer,* and a host of others, may be mentioned to prove
the absurdity of such a proposition ; for these and many

others on retiring from the turf were sound as on the day of their birth. Now these horses had run over a hundred races each, besides probably an equal number of trials, and it may be surmised could, if required, have done as much more. Their retirement was simply because they were required for the stud or to go abroad : and if evidence were needed of their absolute soundness, it is found in the latter fact ; for foreigners seldom make the mistake of buying any but sound horses—a compliment we can hardly pay ourselves.

In judging of this matter it must also be borne in mind that a horse that formerly ran one race a year, would in the present day run forty or more—doing, in fact, more in one year, than of old was done in a lifetime. We can judge too from horses imported from nearly every quarter of the globe, which we are told were not broke early, nor raced till late in life. Yet these, after receiving careful treatment in skilful hands, are, in comparison to our own early broke ones, deficient both in speed and stamina. The French horses, it is true, are equal to ours ; but why? because they are broke and run early, as ours are. Whilst the instances of the American mare *Prioress* and a few other winners, are only the exceptions to prove my assertion. The Americans have achieved victories, not very many, with other horses, but in two-year-old races only ; and it is a notable fact that after a year's racing in this country, their horses changed their pristine youthful vigour for premature old age—*Umpire* to wit, who did nothing after that age, and there are other examples.

At all events, we have seen nothing in any way to prove the advantage of late breaking ; and I think the two cases I am about to adduce, if honestly compared with our system should conclusively instruct us to adhere to it.

They are the following: The Arabs we have seen do not

break their horses until the third or fourth year; yet they are
always inferior to our own, even in their own country and at
any distance. One remarkable example of this was shown
by a little mare, *Antagonist*, by *Venison*, the property of the
late Mr. Death. She won a few races for him, and was in
1850 sold for £300 and exported to Egypt as a three-year-old.
There, it appears, she was matched against the very best Arab
for a twenty-mile race, and beat him in the commonest canter
under the most adverse circumstances; for not only had she
no preparation for so severe a course, but she had not recovered
from the effects of the voyage. The English mare, half-trained
and unwell, beat the Arab over a course specially suited to
his staying qualities and totally different to anything she had
been accustomed to; and it seems to me, gave the best proof
of the advantage of the system of early breaking.

The second instance, equally conclusive in its favour, is that
of a little two-year-old colt by *Nottingham* scarcely selling
plate form, that I sold for £60 for exportation to Calcutta.
On his arrival out he was matched for two miles (quite
beyond his distance) against the best mare there, and was
beat by a head. But the next day, at a mile and a half, the
running was reversed, the colt winning easily, and being there
and then sold for 1,100 guineas. This statement I give on
the authority of the gentleman who bought the animal from
me, Mr. William Smith, who himself raced and sold the colt,
as related.

Little more, I am persuaded, need be said in favour of
our system, as regards the age at which we break our
horses, to prove it is the most suitable—superior, in fact, to
that of any country or era. But I may remark, as confirmation of my theory, that our only formidable rivals are the
French, (of whom the greatest is Count Lagrange, a most

honourable and unflinching sportsman, deservedly esteemed)
and as their horses race as two-year-olds, they must follow
our plan and break them not only as yearlings, but, I
imagine, about the same time of the year as we do, if not
earlier. So much said, a few additional facts occur to me,
as perhaps of interest to show the proper treatment of the
yearling in the paddock, as also to establish the fact of the
precocity of some horses and the length of time others will
take to reach maturity.

In the paddock small yearlings generally show to the
best advantage, for the larger ones will seldom exert themselves. But this is a poor criterion of real merit. Lord
George Bentinck gave much attention to this subject (as he
did to most turf matters), and paid dearly for his credulity.
He used, as some men do now, to let several yearlings loose
together side by side at the extreme end of the paddock ;
and the one that was first across it, he generally took for the
best, and heavily engaged him. *Foozool*, a compact little
horse, was, from this circumstance, thought to be good, and
engaged accordingly ; but he turned out moderately, and
many he could beat in the paddock, in after life could beat
him, and very easily. *Pyrrhus the First*, to look at in the
paddock, was the slowest of the slow, and all that were with
him then were apparently better ; yet not one was worth a
guinea, whilst he won the Derby.

These opposite instances show the little reliance to be
placed on the galloping of yearlings in the paddock, in which,
it may be said, there is nothing to rouse the indolent ; the
big ones being, as a rule, content to yield the palm to their
light-hearted and ambitious little companions. But at
exercise the real merits may be gauged with some degree
of accuracy.

I may aptly conclude this chapter by describing the treatment of the yearlings in the paddock adopted by the late Sir
Tatton Sykes. Not a few amongst my readers will have
pleasing recollections of strolls with the lamented owner
round the Sledmere paddocks. There, were to be seen in
each capacious and well-divided inclosure, some twenty or
thirty yearlings disporting themselves in the best of pastures
many acres in extent; the colts and fillies judiciously and
timely separated, whilst the foals with their dams evidenced
by their gambols their absolute freedom.

Here, it may be said literally, the yearlings knew no
restraint from the day they were foaled until taken to
the place of sale. The best of corn grown on the estate,
and hay from the surrounding pastures, given in the man-
gers running the whole length of the sheds, was the chief,
if not the only forage supplied to the yearlings. These
sheds are the sole protection against the weather, except in
severe frost, when exercise would be dangerous. On no other
occasions are they kept in the stables, I believe, a single day,
except for a short time before the day of sale, to accustom
them to a little restraint before being led out. There can
be no method equal to this, to my mind, in which to rear
thoroughbred stock; some of the results of it, in my own
experience as a buyer, will be given when I treat of the
purchase of yearlings.

CHAPTER X.

PREPARATION.

Past and present methods of preparation contrasted—Sweating in old days; no longer necessary—My disuse of it—Its evils—Other practices happily abandoned—Other contrasts—Mr. Lawrence on preparation—Alteration in bridles—Sir Charles Bunbury's method—Best season for preparation—Early preparation advocated—The preparation of the two-year-old described—The proper hours for exercise—Alternate rest and labour essential—The preparation of older horses—Danger of excessive work when unfit—Training for long and for short courses—The preparation of the yearling—My own and other methods—Clothing — Exercise in frost — Essential principles to be followed with horses of all ages—Should be commenced in time—Deceptive condition—Appetite—The legs and feet—Final gallops—Precautions against cold—Exercise in wet weather ; and in fog—Curiously fatal result of exercising during fog—Sunday labour not necessary—Pleas for Sunday rest ; anecdote of the late Lord Ribblesdale—Tendency to accept new theories ; the Turkish bath.

WE have seen how the yearling is broken in. It may perhaps lead to a clearer understanding of his subsequent preparation, and that of the older horse, if, as a preliminary, a brief comparison be made of the salient features of the system in vogue to-day and that of some years ago.

For one thing the old practice of sweating—the steady gallop of four miles under the excessive weight of two heavy rugs, a woollen breast-sweater and two hoods—is little heard of nowadays. Indeed the result is so weakening that the principle should have been abandoned long before it really was, especially as it is certain that the evil of it was proclaimed by Mr. Lawrence as far back as the year 1809. His protest, unfortunately, was useless, for subsequently the evil increased, and was carried to so great an extent that no horse was thought fit that had not been thus galloped a number of times.[1]

I may take the credit, I believe, of being the first to discontinue the practice some twenty-eight or twenty-nine years ago. And I have never reverted to it, for in addition to other evils patently resulting from it, there is one in itself irresistible—the great danger of the horse breaking down. I made this unpleasant discovery for myself by laming two, past recovery, that before were sound as a bell. Finding no good accrued from it, I not only abandoned the practice, but denounced it as fraught with numerous unlooked-for and non-preventable dangers.

The work done when I was a boy, some thirty-five or forty years ago, of which I have a vivid recollection, was markedly severer than that of to-day. The sweating, for example, was not restricted to matured horses, but the two-year olds had to go through the same trying ordeal once a-week. And this extreme work was only an addition to that done every day of the week, Sunday itself not being an exception; although on that day the work was minimised, insomuch that a short and slow gallop took the place of the long and fast one. It was in those days customary, before sweating, to gallop the horses the course, whatever it might be, they had to run, certainly up to two miles, whilst the two-year-olds had a half-speed gallop of about a mile; and though they only galloped once a day, the old ones would gallop twice—first about half speed, a mile and a half or two miles, as the

---

[1] Mr. Chifney also thought the work done in his day too severe. A book on pedestrianism, too, I find considered it very trying, and the severest form of work.

case might be, and after walking half an hour, the same
distance as well as they could go.   Mr. Chifney, in his
" Genius Genuine," speaks of horses sweating six miles twice
a week.   For my part, I have never seen it practised more
than once a week, nor the distance to exceed four miles : and
this is surely enough work for the veriest glutton, considering
what was to follow.   For on the hottest day, when there was
not a breath of air, the sweat streaming continuously for half
an hour, the horse would be scraped, wiped dry, and again
started to exercise.   It should be said, in fairness, that the
horses under this severe preparation were as fit to run as any
horses can be, or are made in the present day, and looked as
well.   Yet, in these lenient days, few would like to revert to
so extreme a practice, whilst the danger of laming the animals
would deter the boldest trainer from its adoption, even though
he should think it might be beneficial in some respects.

It was the invariable custom in summer to water the horses
whilst out from a trough near a pond or well, and canter
them afterwards ; a custom plainly at variance with common
sense, and one I unhesitatingly condemn.   The night before
the horse was to run, he was kept muzzled to prevent his
eating the litter.   This is seldom done or needed now.   There
were other usages—minor matters, it is true—in which the
past system differed from the present.   I may name one.   At
the end of the Houghton Meeting (then the recognised conclusion of the racing season) the horses were, in many cases,
turned into a loose box, without exercise, cleaning, or clothing,
being only well fed, and left in that state till the following
January, when they were physicked and gently put to work—
a plan now wisely abandoned ; for the sudden transition from
heat to cold, and *vice versâ*, and from galloping one day re-
lapsing into a state of lethargy the next, has caused many to

be roarers, and been the fatal forerunner of other diseases. This practice was the undoubted cause of *Elcho's* death whilst under the skilful treatment of the late Prof. Spooner, of the Royal Veterinary College, for an enlarged hock.

I have already referred to Mr. John Lawrence's book, "The History of the Horse," published in 1809, and may submit from it certain extracts showing the preparation at that time thought requisite to get a horse fit to run. He confirms what I have said of its severity, the six-mile sweats twice a week, which now, where not happily abolished altogether, are reduced to four miles, and once a week. "The horse," Mr. Lawrence remarks, for one thing, "was purged too much, and shut up from the light of the sun as if it would endanger his eyesight, and kept in the atmosphere of a hot-house as if in training for the climate of Africa, or a hotter place." We happily, to-day, give more, both of light and air, but perhaps few of us to the required extent ; though the difference must be very marked, even as it is. Even in bridles there is a great change now to those in vogue some forty years ago. The majority of boys had then to assist them in managing horses, otherwise uncontrollable, martingale-drawing-reins and saddle-drawing reins. Now such things are scarcely known even by name, and never used. Again, curb-bridles, once con-stantly used at exercise, and in which horses often ran, are seldom seen in our days either in the one place or the other ; though I prefer their use to martingales, so much in request just now.

Sir Charles Bunbury's method of training, we are told, consisted in gentle usage and little work. No one that knows anything of training, I think, would disagree with the former, or approve of the latter system. Nor do I agree in thinking, as some do, that by walking many hours a day a horse may be made fit to run a long course without the aid of galloping the distance, or, indeed, by steadily doing a shorter one. The eccentric and facetious Mr. T. Oliver, senior, used to say he could get a steeple-chaser fit to run two miles, without a gallop, by walking and trotting exercise only; and it is the opinion of a celebrated trainer of the present day, that a horse has only to gallop a mile and a quarter to make him fit to run for a four-mile race. After what I have stated, I need scarcely say this is not my opinion; nor have I seen anything in the running of the horses so trained to induce me to alter my ideas on the subject in the slightest degree.

These are some of the contrasts of methods which years have brought about, and are sufficient, it is hoped, for the purpose of illustration; and we may therefore proceed to consider the process of preparation, as it is carried on in the present day with horses of different ages.

As regards the season of the year best fitted for preparation —all horses should, if possible, be prepared in the spring, without regard to age or sex, as the ground is then soft, and they can be got fit at less risk of injury to the legs than when it is hard. The following is a summary outline of the work to be done in the spring and succeeding months, until winter brings once more the time of rest, putting a stop to all exercise but on the straw bed.

Commence, as I have said, as soon as the state of the ground will permit, minimising the work when it is dry, at which times the horses not immediately wanted to run may be rested, with gentle exercise only. If the drought be of long continuance, a dose of physic may be given before going into active work again. This will keep them from getting too big, and has been the means of bringing many an animal to the post fairly prepared, when so much could not have been

accomplished in any other way. (It is the custom, I should
here observe, to keep horses in the stable the day after the
physic has operated; but if time be of consequence and the
weather fine, I should not object to their being gently
exercised for an hour on that day).

On the other hand, with horses that have to run shortly, the
work must be continuous at all risks. The necessary amount
for each horse varies with the age and constitution of the
animal. A gross feeder would naturally require more than
a delicate one, of either sex; and bad feeders especially
should not be overdone with work. In open weather, if the
two-year-olds (for to them I shall for a short time direct my
remarks), after walking a few minutes feel chilly from a
bracing atmosphere, they should be trotted to assist circulation. When thus made comfortable they may, after walking
some time, be cantered, and this may be repeated at short
intervals; and afterwards they may be galloped about half
or three quarters of a mile, gradually increasing the speed
as they approach the finish of their preparation.

Occasionally they may be set off side by side with an old
horse, and made to go the whole course, as well as they can
all the way; but they must not be abused, or even frightened
by the sight of whip or stick. More should be done with
the handling of the reins and the use of the heels than by
any other mode of urging them to their utmost speed;
whilst just before the finish the young ones should be
allowed to pass the old ones, if they could not do so earlier.
The commencement of the gallop teaches them the way to set
off quickly; an important part of the tuition of all two-year-
olds; and the finish, by passing the old ones, inspires them
with confidence attainable only in this way. This is most
desirable; for if, becoming faint-hearted, they once lose

their natural courage, by racing with those they know to be their superiors, it is seldom regained, and they thus often become rogues, and worse than useless. With regard to sweating, whatever may have been the plea for its practice with older horses, it should never have been used, I am convinced, with the two-year-old.

The hour at which exercise should be taken is important. In winter the weather may regulate it; and almost any time of the day will do, so long as the horses get sufficient— an hour and a half or two hours. But in the summer it is very different; for in hot and dry weather exercise should not be commenced later than 5 A.M., and after an hour and a half or two hours the horses may be taken in, and in the afternoon be again brought out at 4 o'clock for three quarters of an hour or an hour.

The advantages of early exercise are obvious. The ground, in the first place, is much better in the morning. It has been rendered more elastic by the night's dew, and so is conducive to the growth of the feet; and the atmosphere being cooler, horses do their work with less fatigue, and escape the immoderate sweating which, under the broiling heat of a midsummer's sun, with ground as hard as a turnpike road, would be likely to break some down and enervate others, if it did not cause prostration only to be overcome by a long rest. I feel it needful to dwell on this point; to impress indelibly upon the mind of the reader the absolute necessity of adherence to this rule in fine weather. The little extra trouble it may entail should be reckoned as nothing when regard is had to the compensating advantages; one of which, not previously named, is the alternate and more equal division of time allotted to rest and labour.

Now the time of dressing and feeding is included in that

G

of rest.   Thus if you exercise at 5 A.M. the horses rest from
8 until 4 P.M. and from 5 P.M. until 4 A.M., the latter a space
of eleven hours.   Whereas if your horses exercise at 8 A.M.,
they are brought in at 11 A.M. and rest until 5 A.M. the next
morning, a spell of eighteen hours, being an additional rest of
seven hours, or more than the fourth part of a day—a division
between rest and labour in my opinion excessive.   Moreover
by the former practice the stables are opened to receive the
fresh and pure air twice a day instead of once ; whilst your
horses are enjoying themselves inhaling the same on the
breezy downs, an additional incentive to the better enjoyment of their evening repast, when " good digestion waits on
appetite, and health on both."

To this point my observations have had special reference
to two-year-olds.   The older horses will now claim our
attention.

Their work is of necessity similar in most respects, but
there are a few variations which should not be lost sight of.
In the first place, it will be well to remind the reader that
after a long winter old horses get very fat, as indeed do most
others, even fatter than appearance would denote ; and in
this state great care is requisite in commencing their spring
preparation.   The ground then is heavy, and in anything but
a fit state for galloping ; yet the horses are fresh, and the
boys falling off in all directions.   From a long-continued
frost the time is getting on for active work ; and with such
incitement the trainers are often tempted to work the horses
in an unfit state, commencing too suddenly and imposing
tasks too hard, resulting in injury.   This temptation is undoubtedly the primary cause of many a breakdown; but
whether from accumulation of fatty matter inside, or
the want of faster exercise than can be given in the

circumscribed limits of a straw bed, I know not: probably both have their influence. The result, however, is a fact there is no denying; for unfortunately there have been too many proofs, one of which should be sufficient to rout a thousand speculative theories to the contrary.

On the first day on which the horses leave the straw bed for the downs, they should have an hour's exercise in the former before leaving for their canter. This quiets the horses, and helps to keep the boys on their backs; for if taken from the stable direct to the exercise downs, many would get loose, and probably hurt themselves by galloping too far, or by some accident. Sometimes after a week's gentle work the legs will fill. In this case they should have a dose of physic, and indeed any that are very big should have some before doing more work.

When trained for short courses, the amount of work is very much the same as that recommended for two-year-olds; but for longer courses more time and longer gallops would be required to complete the preparation. After the usual amount of walking and trotting exercise, as previously described, they must first gallop a mile, gradually increasing the distance to the required length, whether it be two, three, or four miles. It would be the excess of folly to say how often they should do this, or how fast, as this would entirely depend on the individual horse's condition at the commencement of training, and his constitution. Nor should the state of the ground be totally ignored. All these things can only be ascertained by experience and personal inspection, and unremitting observation of the progress made from day to day. On broad principles only we can say the animal should be made to go steadily a short course for a week or two, till his condition enables him with ease to go faster; then the

G 2

whole length of the course may be galloped at better speed, and on alternate days at half speed, until he is as fit and as well as he can be. The signs of this fitness I shall endeavour to describe in a following chapter.

As a rule, the training of the yearling is commenced by steadily cantering two or three times daily short distances up to half a mile. At this age they should not be allowed in exercise to exceed nor in trial to go less than this distance. I am aware that both Mr. Scott and Mr. Forth were of opinion that a distance of three furlongs is sufficient. But as against their authority there are many that think with me, not least of them my father. He never, that I know of, tried a less distance; and certainly no one tried with greater accuracy or more complete success. It may appear strange, but it is nevertheless true, that some horses as yearlings stay well three furlongs, but never get beyond that distance; just as we see horses which, as two-year-olds, stay the half mile, but never get beyond it when older. But this part of our subject may be more thoroughly investigated in its proper place.

It is well perhaps to say here that the yearling wears no clothing in the stable until January, when he also wears it at exercise. In frosty weather the yearlings are exercised with the old horses on the straw bed, and when the weather breaks up they should go on the downs.

Reverting to the subject of preparation in general, I should not forget to reiterate that unceasing watchfulness is absolutely necessary. From the first canter to the last gallop the condition of the animal must be carefully noted from day to day. Nor does our care cease here; for even in trials, at the eleventh hour some defect may be seen which if speedily rectified may bring the desired success. Appearances are deceitful, and those who trust in them alone will assuredly be

disappointed.   It is the knowledge of the work that horses
have done and of what remains for them to do, and the time
left in which to do it to complete their preparation, that
is essential ; never forgetting that it is safer to stop horses
in their work from prematureness, than to force two days
work into one in order to make them fit.   But although a
dangerous practice, yet in extreme cases, and under uncontrollable circumstances, I would rather have recourse to this
than knowingly run a horse unfit.

No horse should be worked off his appetite, nor indeed
should he be without one, for this only tends to weaken instead of strengthening him.   Rest is here the only remedy ;
not a total cessation of work, but a diminution of it till
the return of appetite, and then the requisite work may be
given, whatever that may be.

The legs and feet of each animal should be carefully looked
to every day, as named under stable management.   If anything is amiss with them, practically your horse may as well
be dead for the time being.   Those with sound feet and legs,
and in other respects well, can scarcely do too much work in
these lenient days of training ; for if horses are not thoroughly
and often extended in their gallops, you may rest assured
they will be so in their races ; and in the latter when near
home and apparently winning they may be often beaten by
worse animals than themselves for the want of sufficient work
in this respect.   A great deal of course depends upon the last
week or two.   At this time they should not be spared in their
exercise, but vigorously galloped.   Sometimes, even the last
few gallops do wonders ; so much so, that by their fulfilment
or neglect you complete or leave unfinished a preparation,
by the result of which you gain or lose a reputation.

I must not omit to mention that great care should be taken

to keep the horses warm whilst at exercise during the cold
and windy month of March, by additional clothing, or walking them at a brisk pace ; or if this be not sufficient a canter
may be judiciously given at short intervals, and after the
gallop another steady canter.   Otherwise they are apt, if
not certain, to take cold and be laid up the greater and best
part of the summer.   These remarks apply with equal force to
wet weather.   If horses are not allowed to dawdle about, but
kept moving whilst out almost to perspiring heat, and brought
in comfortably warm, they will seldom catch cold from being
kept out in such weather, or indeed take any other illness.
On the other hand, as sure as they are allowed to mope about,
or, worse by far, allowed to stand still, shivering, with their
coats reversed, under the supposed friendly shelter of a hedge
or plantation during the continuance of the storm, so sure are
they to cough and have other ailments; brought about, I need
not say, by mismanagement, aiming more at the comfort of
the boys than the benefit of the horses.   This practice should
not be permitted under any pretence whatever.

A striking proof of the harmlessness of exercising in wet
weather may be given in the case of *Joe Miller*.   For three
consecutive weeks it rained incessantly, during which time
he never missed a gallop, nor felt the worse for the deluge, as
was shown by the ridiculous ease with which he won the
Ascot Cup, when a part of the lower side of the course was
submerged.   His victory, indeed, as was abundantly proved
both before and after, was less due to his own capacity than
to the lack of exercise on the part of some of his opponents.

But if no stress of weather, fog perhaps excepted, would
prevent my galloping daily a horse near his race, ordinarily,
in cold, wet and foggy weather, I let the bulk of the horses
remain in the stables, but for not more than a couple of days

at a time. Fog, as I have hinted, I do not like, because, if very thick, there is danger. I can relate a most remarkable instance which happened during a trial at Newmarket on a Good Friday, and which comes to me from the highest authority.

On a beautiful spring morning, after the "dolls and chains" had been removed to allow the horses room to pass through, in galloping "across the flat," just before starting The Two Middle Miles, or immediately afterwards, a most dense fog very quickly came down; the jockeys went out of the course and all fell over the chains and dolls that were left standing, with such terrible effect that some of the horses and jockeys were killed, and others so dreadfully shaken that they never got over it, the surviving horses being rendered useless. I daresay there are trainers and others living who remember this occurrence and may have known both the jockeys and the names of the horses.

And this story brings one to the question of Sunday work. As with sweating so with this practice, I have not taken a horse to exercise on a Sunday this last quarter of a century. Ovid says, "Alternate rest and labour, long endure;" and my dislike to Sunday labour is not my only reason for abolishing it ; I think to do so benefits my horses. Since 1850, up to which time it was on the increase, sweating has gone out of fashion, and so, too, I am happy to say of late years, has Sunday labour.

I may adduce here a few reasons for Sunday rest. First, then, I believe it is essentially necessary that horses in strong work should have absolute rest periodically allowed to them to recruit their wasted strength. Why should the racehorse be the only animal in captivity doomed to perpetual slavery, knowing no rest? He is worked till he becomes as stale as

some unfortunate hack whose only release from the burden of
perpetual toil is death. Agricultural horses, carriage and
other horses, and even the poor and illiterate costermongers'
donkeys, are exempt from work on Sunday; and by such a
benevolent action their owners show themselves greatly in advance of those who gallop their horses on that day against the
dictates of reason and the usages of modern civilized society.

And what after all is the incentive? It is the fashion, that
is all. One does it, and another must follow in his footsteps,
or be thought singular or affected by his neighbours. But
stronger reasons than this should be given for its continuance,
or the objectionable practice should be at once and for ever
abolished. It may furthermore be remarked that the cab
horse, working but six days a week, is capable of doing, and
does, more work than the horse working the whole seven.
This, which I have from a very good source, and thoroughly
believe, should be sufficient proof in favour of Sunday rest,
even if nothing else could be said for it, to induce owners to
keep their horses in the stable one day a week. In wet
weather they are kept in sometimes for days together; a
sufficient guarantee that the one day's rest would do no
injury.

As one instance of marked consideration in this respect I
may mention that the late Lord Ribblesdale came all the
way from the Falls of Niagara to see his horses tried. He
arrived here (Woodyates) late on Saturday night, with the
intention of seeing them tried the following day. But
though he had only that day at his disposal, having to leave
early on Monday morning to return to his ship, which had
merely called at Southampton for forty-eight hours, he re-
frained from doing so, and saw them in the stable only. I
tried the horses on the Monday and sent him the result.

Whilst here his lordship had requested me to put his horses in the Grand Prix of Paris. He had said he saw no harm in running them on Sunday. But this was not my view, as his lordship knew, and consequently he countermanded the entries in a letter in which he said that he concluded on mature consideration, "What might be right for the French people to do in their own country, was not quite the thing for Englishmen to do out of or in theirs."

Personally, I do not work my horses either on Christmas-day or Good Friday ; a matter of prejudice some will say. Still I do not like to do so ; and although, of course, I do not mean to assert that such a thing as the fearful accident I have described as happening at Newmarket on the latter day might not have happened on any other day, it would not at all events have happened when it did, had the horses been in the stable, and probably would not have occurred on a subsequent day. As a matter of fact I have never heard of any other accident so appalling during a trial. I hope I have said sufficient to influence those who practise Sunday labour to abandon it. Cardinal Wolsey is made to say, " And nature does require her times of preservation, which perforce I, her frail son amongst my brethren mortal, must give my tendence to." The lesson should not be thrown away.

One other usage in stables, a modern innovation, fortunately shortlived, and now completely abandoned, I will just glance at in conclusion. We are not altogether free from the weaknesses of our Transatlantic brethren, who, great in ideas, indulge in theories that momently allure only to make the culminating disappointment the greater. Rather than be content with the numerous practical facts at hand for our guidance, to avoid one extreme we rush headlong into another. Sweating being condemned as too severe, we must perforce abandon the practice for one more trying—the Turkish bath. The Turkish bath, in many instances beyond the endurance of the human race, many having succumbed to its enervating influence, has proved to horses little short of annihilation.

This tendency is, as I have said, a national failing. We have Mr. Darwin's theory, arising out of Lord Monboddo's idea. His lordship said over a century ago, "that in some countries the human species have tails like other beasts," and traces monkeys up to men. The wonderful rope trick was known many years ago, though introduced as something new by the Davenport Brothers, and ascribed to spiritualism. The great horse-tamer Mr. Rarey, again, introduced as the greatest novelty and successfully palmed off on us a trick long before both known and forgotten.

These, on their introduction, had their believers ; and the Turkish bath, like other wild and utterly chimerical schemes, found its followers who, only when too late, saw the folly of their credulity. In various parts stables were turned into horse-baths, or places were built for the purpose of carrying out the sweating process with all its adjuncts. There was, however, a strong feeling adverse to such an experiment, and comparatively speaking few subjected their horses to the ordeal. As no benefit followed its use it was speedily given up ; not however until several horses had died and others had suffered severely from the process.

CHAPTER XI.

PREPARATION (*continued*).

The public and their estimate of fitness—The duty imposed on the trainer—Evils of running unprepared—Running "big" and "light"—How Mr. John Scott beguiled the public ; instances : *The Era, Michael Scott*—My father's system and instances—Inferences drawn from the training of the pedestrian—Prejudice of owners for "big" condition—Example in my own experience of "big" and "light" preparation—Severe preparation not necessarily harmful—Evils of "big" condition—Work done in old times—Instances in support of my theory : *Fugitive, Historian, Oxonian*—Successes with my stable in past times ; list of the stakes won, and of the winners ; horses prepared by me and subsequently sold, and prices ; their subsequent performances—Abuse of severe preparation ; horses run too often —Comparison of two- and three-year-old running : *Weatherbound and Dulcibella*—Reasons for my insistence on "light" preparation—Any general rule necessarily imperfect —Farming and training compared.

No trainer, even the most sanguine, can ever hope to bring his horse to the post in a condition to please all parties. His employers are satisfied seldom, and other people never. Before every race they are too big, like a bullock, or too poor, or galloped or starved to death. But the winner in whatever condition is unreservedly praised.

There are two things we as trainers have to guard against : the first is, the displeasure of our employers : the second, the running of our horses unfit—both unwelcome things ; but of the two, rather than do the latter knowingly, I would submit as cheerfully as I could to the former. If you run half fit, you please every one before the race; and if from superiority you win, the victory is attributed to condition, which is highly praised though in reality non-existent. But if you are beaten for lack of condition, the horse will not unlikely pass to another, who, training him regardless of popular prejudice, will make a marked improvement in the animal, and you not only lose your horse and your employer, but above both, and what is most dear to you, your reputation. On the other hand, if you train your horse and suffer defeat, pleasing no one but the owner, some wiseacre buys him with the intention of *making him better.* He makes him *look* better; but when it comes to racing it is decisively shown there is no improvement ; that in fact he runs worse—a result that helps to make your reputation as a judicious and fearless trainer.

I ask, would any sane man run his horse light, when he by any known process could be made to run as well big? Most certainly he would not be so silly. Some may and do, in spite of public opinion, run their horses light for the best of all possible reasons—they know they run so best. There are others that knowingly do the reverse. The great "Wizard of the North," as he was facetiously called by "Argus" and other sporting chroniclers of the day, knew horses could not run when fat. Yet he tickled the popular taste, in short, hoodwinked the public, and made it believe horses run best in that condition, although nothing could be more fallacious than the conclusion thus arrived at. In reality the horses he used to run big, were those that were bad, or were supposed to be so. His good horses he took care to run light as other experienced trainers did. Of two-year-olds, the lightest I probably ever saw run was *Dervish* at Epsom, and of three-year-olds *West Australian* at Doncaster; and yet, in spite of their ragged appearance, they both won easily. The great trainer may have had occasionally his own motives which fatness assisted ; but I conceive the chief one was to please the public—a predilection which in some cases forced him to part with good horses simply because run out of condition.

Two or three cases may be named to show either that he was not quite proof against public opinion or that he mistook the merits of his own horses. *Adamas* was lost in this way whilst running in a Selling Plate to be sold for £40. In the following year he won the City and Suburban and was second for the Derby. *The Era* was also claimed out of a Selling Plate and afterwards won the Goodwood Cup ; whilst *Michael Scott's* running was positively wretched both as a two- and three-year-old. At the latter age he ran seven races and in many carried the lightest weight—mostly in bad company ; yet he was unable to win one, or even get placed whilst in the hands of Mr. Scott. This worst of all brutes then passes into other hands, and within a month commences his successful career by winning the Great North Riding Handicap at Northallerton, and adding six more races consecutively to his list of winnings that year. He therefore loses seven races while at Malton and wins seven after leaving it. He was afterwards sold for a large sum to go abroad.

What would be said if such an occurrence took place with any one that professed to train his horses light? My father always trained his horses light, saying, " Show me a better plan, and I will gladly follow it." But as none was forthcoming, he continued in the same way with the greatest success. In no single case but that of *Toothill* was any horse made better after leaving his stable ; and this exception was clearly traceable to the ground, as it afterwards appeared that *Toothill* could not move on hard turf in such a state as the ground was whilst the horse was with my father. For he won directly afterwards, and whilst in the same condition as on leaving Danebury, for it rained heavily in the short interval before the improvement was shown. On the other hand, the benefit of his system was exhibited in the improvement of *Airy, Pounce*, and many other horses. In no single instance, however, can I call to mind that any horse was made better in the hands of the great Whitewall trainer, who always professed he adopted the same method of preparation. And if he could not show the superiority of big condition over light, I may ask who can? For no one ever had more chances.

I have no faith in a fat racehorse or a burly pedestrian, and nothing will, without proof, lead me to think otherwise than that both are gigantic mistakes.[1] I know my theory and

[1] Man, as a pedestrian, has to undergo great stretches of endurance, his treatment being analogous in many respects to that of the horse, as I have described it. Briefly epitomised, it is thus given by the author of "Aberdeen : "—

"After taking physic twice he commences his training; walks and runs about twenty miles a day. He rises at 5 A.M., runs half a mile at the top of his speed, uphill, walks six miles at a moderate pace, and at 7 breakfast; walks six miles after at a moderate pace, and at 12 lies in bed for half an hour. Then he walks four miles and returns to dinner, immediately after which he runs half a mile at the top of his speed, winding up with another six miles walking exercise before returning home. Thus prepared for three or four weeks he takes a four-mile sweat, running in flannel at the top of his speed the first thing in the morning, proceeding with his usual work after. Added to which he amuses himself by playing at cricket and similar games."

If the violent exercise taken after a heavy meal and the excessive speed of his sweats be excepted, the method of his preparation to render him fit to run is pretty much the same as that of the horse, and where it differs I cannot agree with it. The book further says :—

"It is as difficult to run a mile at the top of one's speed as to walk a hundred : and he is fit, if he can do the first well, to accomplish the latter." Moreover, it says : "It takes some months to complete. Crib weighed 16 st. at the commencement of his preparation, and lost, in five weeks, two stone, being further reduced to 13 st. 5 lbs., having had three sweats in the last month, and walked and run thirty miles a day, besides exercising himself in other ways."

Poor Crib, I think, from such severe work, could have been little more than a

system have been always condemned : not by thinking men, but by those only "who think true what they wish to be so"— the fitness to run of a fat horse.   As do men look in the circumstances of Crib, given at foot, so do horses in the eyes of their owners when first they see them fit to run ; having, be it understood, never set eyes upon them since the day when, enveloped in fat, they left their own stables for those of the trainer.   At this sudden and great change employers often express not only surprise but dissatisfaction ; forgetting or not knowing how necessary the change is—as I hope has been proved by what I have said.   From Mr. Copperthwaite I may glean an amusing anecdote to the point.   He tells us that a friend of his did not know his own horse after a month's training, and said to the trainer, "Why, sir, this is not the half of him !" and added, " I had better secure the remaining half whilst I can ! "   And did so, removing the horse there and then.

It is not often that gentlemen volunteer to instruct the trainer in his business ; yet I have been requested to train my horses big—requests which I may say virtually amounted to positive orders, and as such were faithfully obeyed.   " The late Mr. Scott made a practice of training his horses big, and why could you not do so ?" was a remark once made to me.   "Simply because I know they run better light," was my reply.

On one of these occasions a trial was made.   The horses arrived, as many living noblemen and others can testify, in the most splendid condition, full of vigour, as round as apples, and coats shining like stars.   At Ascot an

shadow of his once great self, yet, from what follows in the narrative (which it is not necessary to repeat here), he appears to have never been better, as success attended his efforts.

opportunity was given to them of showing their supposed
improved form and of displaying their luxurious appearance
in the (supposed) very pink of condition, leaving, as was said,
nothing to be desired to insure the most splendid success,
but a good start and no accident. All seven that ran were
disgracefully beaten, one only obtaining even a third place.
I should mention that I had another horse with me about
whose training there was no order, who won the Queen's
Vase, and it is almost needless to add that before the race
his condition was as much abused as that of the others was
lavishly praised. .

Now all this was not business. It was simply a useless
and costly repetition of an experiment which had signally
failed over and over again to my own knowledge, and had been
tried with the same fatal results by my ancestors. In order to
prevent another *fiasco* I was requested to run the same
horses as I liked at Goodwood seven weeks afterwards. On
arriving there their condition was thought much too light ;
but the result of their respective races will give the most
convincing proof that they were not—and show the superiority
of light or (as I think) well-trained horses over those that are
only thought fit to run when big. One of them won, beating
a large field carrying 8 st. 4 lb., or 6 lb. more than he carried
at Ascot. Another carried off the Molecombe after a severe
race with a mare hitherto considered invincible, and also won
again afterwards. Whilst the third beat a large field for
another race, and followed up her success by winning again.
The other two were placed, being only just beaten.

Now to do bare justice to this most important part of the
subject, and to proceed still further and show not only (as I
have done) that horses are better for racing purposes for the
time being when light, but also that they are not the worse

for it after, and retain their form not merely for weeks or months but years, I will give one instance, which I think should be sufficient to establish the truth of my argument. Three of the horses that ran at Goodwood ran afterwards at Ayr in six races, winning five. Other stakes were likewise subsequently won by the others that ran there. Mr. H. Robinson used to say, "I like my horses to run big with plenty of work." So do I, and I should like to know who does not; but the thing is not possible. What do we work our horses for, but to try and remove the fatty matter? Unless this be done you may as well keep them in the stable, for a "fat," or if the term be preferred, a "big" horse must tire. It is not in the nature of things that he should do otherwise. He is not only a little big to all intents and purposes, which is clearly seen; but he is internally burdened with a weight of fatty incumbrance, his breathing is obstructed by adipose matter which rightly can only be removed by work. Without going so far as to say that after a certain period of preparation is reached before completion, every pound lighter the animal is by that amount he is so much the better, yet it is clearly an approximation to the truth of the principle I advocate; for what does not assist progression retards it. A severe preparation, some will say, is the cause of breaking down many horses that would otherwise stand and run for many races. This is a proposition I am not exactly prepared to admit or deny. *Historian* ran under a severe preparation till ten years old; while others we see are continually breaking down when young under a more lenient system. But, for argument's sake—only admit as a fact that some horses do so break down, yet surely in doubtful cases it is far better for them to break down at home before you have backed them, than in the race, with the mortification of a double disappointment, losing the race and

H

your money, besides the unpleasantness of hearing in various quarters the invidious remarks made as to your horse's condition, and the questionable purposes for which he was started.

But that something beyond my bare assertion may evidence that horses under, as it is called, a severe system, can run many races in one year and for many consecutive years, I shall proceed to lay before the reader a few indubitable facts in support of it. In enumerating a few of the races won by horses thus trained, it must be borne in mind that racing twenty or thirty years ago was very different to what it is now. Then, a £100 plate was thought no mean prize, £20 at head quarters brought a field to the post ; and £50 or £100 added was considered a munificent donation—one to be keenly contested for. Now we have £500 given to many of our races, and even £1,000; prizes which help to swell the aggregate winnings of owners (although to a certain extent the money comes out of their own pockets first, in the shape of three and five guinea entrances to the fund). To win a race in those days, when heats were allowed and stakes were only of a few hundred pounds value, would be something like winning three or four races now, and as many thousands in money. I mention this that a fair estimate of their relative value may be made ; because it was in those early days that many of my victories were achieved. My first racehorse, *Fugitive*, commenced by winning all the three races that he started for at Plymouth and Tavistock, and the total stakes won did not, I think, amount to £200 together.

Historian ran till he was ten years old, and *Schism* till after she was aged, notwithstanding the early age at which she made her appearance in public. *Oxonian* ran till twelve years old, and is still running ; whilst *Vex*, and a host of others too numerous to mention, ran many years successfully, and left off as sound as they were the day they were foaled. They ran various courses, from three furlongs to three miles and five furlongs, two-year-olds winning courses of three miles.   In these they won stakes numbering considerably over 400 (besides others of less significance), amounting in the aggregate to the value, exclusive of the minor races, of over £100,000 sterling.

Heats, as I have before mentioned, and long courses, in those days added greatly to the enormous amount of work horses had to do to accomplish such feats ; yet, as far as I know, no more were broken down than usually succumb to a more lenient treatment in the present day.   That some estimate of the merits of the animals they had to meet may be formed, I summarize at foot a few of the races they won.[1]

As to the performers, I could give a lengthy list; but I must be content to cite a few, and give a brief survey of their performances whilst with me; and I may add that after leaving me, their names were not again included in the list of winners on the flat.   They were disposed of in a variety of ways ; some by public auction, others by private contract, while some few were claimed out of selling races, or bought

---

[1] *Handicaps.*—Chester Cup, Cambridgeshire, Royal Hunt Cup, and Somersetshire Stakes, three times each ; the Metropolitan, Steward's Cup at Goodwood, Great Eastern Handicap, Goodwood Stakes, and Northamptonshire Stakes, twice each ; the Portland Plate, the Cæsarewitch, the Chesterfield Cup, the Steward's Cup at Chester, the Doncaster and the Lincoln Handicaps, and the Newmarket, Lincoln, Goodwood, Doncaster, and Stockbridge Nurseries, the Shrewsbury Handicap, besides most of the lesser Handicaps. Among two-year-old victories may be mentioned the New Stakes at Ascot, and Molecombe and Lavant Stakes, and Mottisfont twice each ; the Findon and Ham Stakes, and Criterion, as well as the following weight-for-age races at three years old and upwards : the Oaks, Goodwood Derby (twice), Queen's Vase at Ascot (twice), Emperor's Vase, Ascot and Goodwood Cups, the Two Thousand Guineas (twice), Royal Stakes, and other races of less importance, including the Yearling Stakes at Shrewsbury.

at auction after winning them. Thus be it remembered, they were not sold as old horses worn out : but as two-year-olds, such as *La Pique* and *Fortune Teller* filly, who, like many others with me, were never beaten ; the rest as three-year-olds and at other ages, sound and in the prime of life, having won a great number of races of most descriptions, including the Somersetshire Stakes, the Goodwood Derby, Cup, and Stakes, Metropolitan Stakes, Royal Hunt Cups, Royal Stakes, and the Two Thousand Guineas. I append the names of a few.[1] Surely out of this list some of them would have improved and done wonders after leaving my hands, if they had been treated on a wrong principle whilst in them ? At all events, if they had subsequently theoretically a better training, not one of them retained his or her form.

I am aware that in mentioning this I lay myself open to the charge of that self-praise which is truly no recommendation. But I trust the reader will not so misconceive what is simply a narrative of events, having for its object intelligibility and not ostentation.

But it must not be understood from my strenuous advocacy of severe training, that horses in my opinion cannot be over-done. I know to the contrary. I have myself trained horses that when fit have been tried so often to ascertain their own form and that of others, that they have been as stale as the proverbial post-horse and as slow as his rider. Yet this proves nothing against the system ; they are but the occasional exceptional cases which go to prove the rule. It is not the training itself, but the abuse of it, in running them so often

---

[1] *Castle Hill, Benefactress, Fortune Teller filly, Philippa, Joco, Sir Charles, Confidence, Valuer, Judge, Starter, La Pique, Miss Williams, Benefactor, Cedric, Conductor, Cedric the Saxon, Pitchfork, Allie Slade, Bugler, Promised Land, Plunkett colt, Leah colt, Albanus, Camelia,* and many others.

when trained and trying them so continually, that deserves
censure, and should be abandoned. *Johnny Armstrong* and
Sultan, the only old horses that I remember ever giving a
high price for, did not suffer from the change of treatment if
they had been previously leniently trained. The former beat
most of the horses of his day at Newmarket ; whilst *Sultan*
won the Cambridgeshire as a three-year-old very easily,
carrying 7 stone 6 lbs.

Facts are more telling than arguments. I may therefore
refer to the horses once under my care, and afterwards sold,
and trained by the most eminent trainers, which never won a
solitary race for their new owners. Of these the names and
the prices paid for them will be found at foot.[1]

It will be to the point to compare, here, the running of
Weatherbound and *Dulcibella* as two- and three-year-olds.
Weatherbound as a two-year-old was a selling-plater, and as
such won two little races. Having been previously beaten
seven times, her selling price was only £40. As a three-year-
old she suffered defeat no less than twelve times, only winning
two little races. When she came to me the same year, she
ran four times, and among her victories may be mentioned the
Cambridgeshire Stakes, and division of the Sefton Handicap,
running well for two other races ; and she continued her
successful career the following year.

Dulcibella's form as a two-year-old was simply wretched.
She was placed last in a field of six at Newmarket, and in the
same hands ran little better in the early part of the following
year—*Cape Flyaway*, a very moderate horse, giving her 17lb.
and no one knows what beating, whilst in other and worse

---

[1] *Promised Land*, £2,350 ; *Cedric*, £1,100 ; *Sutherland*, £1,000 ; *Traducer*,
£1,500 ; *Conductor*, £1,000 ; *Cedric the Saxon*, £1,000 ; *Albanus*, £700 ; *Schism*,
£1,500. All these and many others shared the same fate as *Benefactor*, never
winning a race after leaving me.

company she ran equally badly. Yet this worst of all performers comes to me, and a few months after these wretched
performances, wins the Cæsarewitch in a common canter by
ten lengths, giving weight to both the second and third horses
—conceding to the latter, a four-year-old, 11 lbs. If we consider the way in which this race was won, it may safely be
assumed to be the shortest time race on record, being given
in *Bell's Life* as 4 minutes 1 second.

The reader may think that in this long chapter I have dwelt
too much on the advantage of training horses light, especially
as the matter has already been dealt with at p. 47 *et seq.*
in the chapter on "Condition." There, however, it was
intended to show the difference between horses "big" and
"light"; here, how to prepare them "light," and the results
of the preparation.

But my faith in my system, trebly tried as it has been by
practical results, will, I trust, warrant my insistence on this one
point. I can hardly believe that an unprejudiced mind would
refuse to believe, after the experiences here set forth, that a
horse will run better light than big. There are cases, I admit,
of horses running well when big, and of improving year by
year when so treated; but they are too few and far between
to recommend such a system for general adoption.

I do not say, in spite of all I have adduced, that the
system of training I recommend is perfection; on the other
hand, I do not admit that any other is. But I venture to
submit that it is clearly the best, and if so, it ought to be followed. In truth no one can attain perfection, and for venial
faults excessive blame should not be awarded; for trainers,
however fortunate they may be in individual cases, are fallible
like all human beings. We see an analogy to this in hus-
bandry. The agriculturist who mismanages one field of

many, or treats injudiciously this or the other one of his live stock, is not to be unreservedly censured; because to a certain extent such cases are unavoidable.   But he who from inability or unpardonable neglect, such as want of cleanliness or mismanagement, suffers his fields to become sterile and his herds to be decimated by preventible disease, cannot offer as an excuse that a field here or there is flourishing, or that this or the other animal is in blooming health.

And if in farming, concerning which hundreds of works have been written by scientific men, and for the instruction of whose followers colleges have been built, so many acknowledged difficulties present themselves; what must be the difficulties that beset the trainer!   In our profession we have no learned treatises; no lectures on condition; no teachers of the subtle art.   It is a sealed subject, never discussed; one on which nothing beyond a mere passing word has been written.

Under such circumstances, to lay down clear rules is a task neither easy nor safe; and infallibility cannot be looked for. Amongst trainers, then, the one who makes the fewest mistakes is most to be commended.   No judge or general, no layman or divine, is perfect in knowledge.   Knowledge is in fact progressive and progressing.   The man who at a given time knows more than at the same time in the previous year, is in a fair way of attaining the knowledge he not only covets but deserves, be his merit or his station ever so humble or so exalted.   "Reason," we read, "is progressive; instinct is complete.   Swift instinct leaps; slow reason feebly climbs."

CHAPTER XII.

PREPARATION (*concluded.*)

Horses differ in constitution—Treatment must be varied as necessary—Horses should not be run in public too often; evils of the process—Fitness; its signs indicated; only to be achieved by perseverance; anecdote of the late Mr. R. Stephenson—In-and-out running considered, and examples—*Jester* and *Charon:* their performances explained; the lesson to be learned therefrom—The American system of training—Contrast of distance and pace—Extra clothing —Proofs of its inferiority in rarity of their victories here—*Prioress* at New·market—Mr. Ten Broeck and Mr. Sanford—Condition of *Preakness* when at Epsom.

THE trainer's difficulties are numerous and great. No rule can be laid down with mathematical precision that will enable him to overcome them. We must be content therefore to accept general rules, and apply them as far as may be practicable in varying cases. In a stable of fifty horses or less, it may be said that no two of them will thrive on exactly the same treatment. When it is so, it is the exception. They differ in many ways: in constitution, in temper, in variability of health, in soundness and in appetite, as well as in other things; and each individual case should be carefully studied and treated accordingly. This special treatment applies to the time and manner of feeding (the change of hay, corn, and green food) and in other ways attending to their comfort in the stable, and to the regulation of the work given to each animal in his exercise. Nor is this all. Physic is undoubtedly an essential in training; yet were all horses physicked alike, the lives of some would be endangered, whilst others would be hardly affected.

In some horses the urinary organs are so defective that it is necessary after severe work to give them spirits of nitre in the water; for without it, not only would the animals suffer great pain, but inflammation would set in and death follow. Again, of two horses, one will probably be predisposed to constipation, the other to relaxation of the bowels; to treat both alike would be tantamount to killing one of them. There are other differences of constitution and temperament in different animals too numerous to specify, which can only be discovered in each individual by a practised eye; and these should be dealt with as the particular case indicates. Moreover the time at our disposal is short. Horses, like company, are continually coming and going, whilst each season brings its addition of yearlings. One mistake is often sufficient to produce disaster. "Break but a link in the chain and it is useless," is an aphorism to be borne in mind in connection with training, and not less the one that tells us "One man may lead a horse to the water, but twenty cannot make him drink;" which latter applies with equal force to edibles, for "Druid" tells us in "Post and Paddock" that John Scott could never coax *Voltigeur* to eat.

The treatment of preparation would be incomplete without this caution against a conclusion that it is to be achieved by following any dogmatic rule. There is another point on which a word of advice should be said—the frequency of running in public.

I am not an advocate of doing this too often, and when I do run my horses I like them to be fit. It is perilous to do otherwise even when you think you have something in hand;

for others may not only think so too, but have it.   The result
is that, if half prepared, you are beaten through reliance on
your own horse's superiority and the inferiority of your
opponents'.   There are some trainers who purposely start
their horses only half prepared, that they may race themselves
into condition, and even back them when in such a state; and,
in the result, they often lose their money, as they richly deserve
to do.   If you bring your horse fit to the post, you probably
win the race, and most likely a large stake in bets in addition.
After one such victory you can afford to wait; it is worth half-
a-dozen that may be won with half fit animals that you cannot
back with confidence.   For let your first victory be what it
may, you are sure to have the unwelcome assistance of the
public whenever you want to back your horse again.   Another
reason why I like to run my horses fully prepared, is, that a
severe race does not affect so prejudicially a horse so trained,
as it does one only half fit.

There seems little more to be said on the subject than
briefly to explain some of the signs of this desirable fitness.
One clue is, when it is found, at the finish of his gallop, that
the horse's nostrils are distended comparatively very little,
that he blows little, does not heave at the flanks, and quickly
recovers his former state of composure.   Excessive sweating in
gallops or races is no proof of unfitness; for often those that
sweat most profusely are fitter to run than those which, after
galloping, are scarcely wet.   But, after all, there is nothing
like a trial to arrive at a horse's exact state of fitness; for,
if he tires, then he will probably require more work, but
if not, may be considered fit—and the issue may be taken
as his correct form.

It is said of the late Mr. Stephenson, of engineering celebrity, that when making a reservoir he was told after it was

completed that it leaked; to which he replied, "Puddle." This was done, but with no effect, and recourse was had to him again. He again replied, this time somewhat peevishly, "Puddle, puddle." In the end, by following his laconic advice, the defiant nature of the work was satisfactorily overcome. I can only recommend any one aspiring to train a racehorse to keep this anecdote in view; for gallops added to gallops will often complete that which less work would have left undone.

This, I think, must conclude my direct reference to the subject at present under consideration. But before proceeding to another, it will not be inappropriate to glance at two matters cognate to it; that interesting puzzle, in-and-out running; and, secondly, the system of preparation favoured in America—from both of which inferences may, it is hoped, be drawn that may help us a little.

On the former head it may be allowed, at the outset, that horses are not always in the same condition of health. Could we correctly ascertain the state of their health, at given times, we should be much assisted in coming to a fair conclusion as to their real merit, and should satisfactorily conclude the reason of many, otherwise unaccountable, defeats. It is equally certain that horses may and do improve, in a manner which no amount of vigilance can detect or skill account for. Moreover it is an indisputable fact, proved beyond all manner of doubt, and intelligible enough to any thinking man, that horses get ill unobserved by the most observant of all observers; and whilst so, that no man can calculate to what extent they are affected by such illness.

I will illustrate this by the instances of two of the most remarkable horses I think I ever remember in one year, and emphasise their performances by contrast with those of others.

Jester was one of the most wonderful horses of his day in respect to the improvement he made between his two and three-year-old form. As a two-year-old he ran no fewer than fourteen times, mostly in Selling Plates, without winning. As a three-year-old he started a new career by winning at Winchester, after being beaten at Epsom. He won a second race at Winchester; and the third time at Ascot, where he was claimed for £1,000. At the same meeting he won another race, and was sold for £4,000. Yet this wretched plater could have been had as a two year-old over and over again at Selling Races for less than £100. The real mystery here consisted in the fact that he was undoubtedly run out of his course—a short distance instead of a long one—and in all probability was never tried privately; his sterling merit being only shown, when in public he proved he was, over a distance of ground, about five stone better than over a short course.

In this case condition had nothing to do with the wonderful alteration, as he remained in the same hands, and therefore no doubt received the same treatment one year as he did the other. It is certain, also, that he would not have been run unfit in Selling Races, for fear of losing him, if his merits had been known beforehand. Neither the trainer nor the public discovered the improvement he had made at three years old, until his public form showed it. No, not even that lynx-eyed individual, the tout, who daily saw him at work; or, if this latter gentleman did, by some strange oversight he forgot to mention the astounding fact to his numerous patrons, even in his stereotyped form, as "going well and strong, and pulling up sound." So much for the valuable services of such fellows.

We now come to the performance of the second horse

referred to—*Charon.* In him we have a similar case of improvement from two to three years old, except that he did show pretty good form in some of his two-year-old races, having beaten *Hesper*, *Julius Cæsar*, and other fast horses. He was in the hands of the most talented men, who had the whole of the winter and part of two summers, to discover his latent merit ; yet the commencement of his three-year-old racing was so wretched, he was pronounced a " selling plater," and as such was started at Goodwood and won, when he was claimed by one of the shrewdest and most popular gentlemen on the turf, and within a few weeks placed the next race he ran for to his new owner's credit. He was "sold again," as the Cheap-Jack says, for a sum comparatively small in relation to his real worth ; and after passing through the hands of well-nigh all the talent, fell to one who, if his discernment had been equal to his luck, and had led him to try the horse privately over a distance of ground before making his merits public, would not have missed a fortune without adding to his reputation for astuteness. In his hands he eclipsed all former doings, winning several long-distance races, and was sold for 1,750 guineas. Nor did his victorious career end here, for he did his noble owner good service by beating *Jester* and the winner of the French Derby, besides many others.

Here, again, the secret seems to have been that the horse's form was over a distance of ground, and no one appears to have been aware of the fact till too late. At his first effort on a long course every one was fairly electrified ; he was only beaten a head by *Thunder*, and as *Lily Agnes* was behind them, it proved that the old horse was not out of form. We are all very wise after a mistake has been made, and see then what should have been done to prevent it ; though in reality we would probably have done the same thing, or something worse. Had the precaution been taken with *Charon* to try him privately over a long distance before running him publicly over a long course, he would, like *Jester*, have been one of the most valuable horses of his day ; for the two great handicaps at Newmarket, and many more, would have been entirely at the mercy of one or other of the two.

It may well be asked, what was the cause of this astonishing change ? Was it simply that a trial over a distance of ground was wanting to develop their merits ? Was the previous bad running the result of illness or defective management ? Or did time, and nothing else, work the wonderful change in the two ? The facts are set forth. The reader may be left to form his own deductions as to the curiosities of in-and-out running, and the fallacy of form, as shown in public running, and occasionally in private trials. One thing I may say in support of my preference for light over big condition, which was manifest to every one who saw *Charon* at Doncaster. He was extremely light, and being a light-framed animal, his slender form looked most attenuated. Yet he was fit as a fiddle, and, in any other condition, probably would not have been so.

As regards the system of training favoured by our Transatlantic cousins, it would not, if Mr. R. Ten Broeck's be taken as an example, be a bad one with a little modification. So far as I can learn, his plan is to walk his horses many hours daily and gallop *long* distances slowly. The time devoted to walking I certainly think excessive, for as many as six or seven hours a day are spent in this way. Also in regard to the long distance gallops, four miles, which are done at a very slow pace till about the last half mile, when the speed is increased to its utmost stretch, I must add, with all respect to Mr. Prior, a most worthy man and excellent trainer, I think the distance may, in most cases, be curtailed beneficially, and the speed advantageously augmented and kept at a more uniform rate. The clothing, again, is superabundant, and I should think such a load, in hot weather, must tend to weaken the horse. One thing is quite certain. If the Americans do not use too much, we use too little, and the knowledge of the happy medium would be of service here, as well as in the work done and the way of doing it. We appear to do fast and short work, while they do long and slow. If we made ours a little further and they made theirs a little shorter, probably both systems would be improved, whilst, in other respects, the plans of each might be adhered to. There is one thing pretty clear ; the American horses, in spite of all the long work they do, have never stayed better than our own. This has been shown on many occasions, but never more clearly than in three long distance races, the Goodwood Cup and Stakes, and the Cæsarewitch, under favourable circumstances as regards weights. These I won, beating them very easily with *Promised Land, Elcho,* and *Dulcibella.* Nevertheless, the victory of *Prioress* in the last-named race, after running a dead heat with *El Hakim* and *Queen Bess,* with a large field behind her, is evidence that the American system is not a bad one.

But that, as compared with our own, there is something defective either in the system of training, or in their management, or in some other way, may, I think, be reasonably concluded from the fact that, with a fair opportunity of exhibiting their prowess, they were compelled to beat a retreat ; our horses showing themselves better than theirs, in my opinion, over any course. Mr. Sanford has not, up to this point, done much good with his little team, and if he have no better horses than, so far as we know, he owns at present,

I fear he will have to follow in the wake of Mr. Ten Broeck, and seek victory against native horses in his own country.

I have never heard anything said for or against his mode of training, and therefore conclude it must be much the same as our own. But this I do know : the horse he ran at Epsom, *Preakness*, was bigger than ever I saw an English horse turned out to run in good company. The animal may have shown the result of the American system of training and Mr. Sanford's idea of condition, but certainly was not prepared, according to my notion, for a two-mile course.

Of other foreign horses, most are trained after our fashion whilst here. Indeed, as a rule, the preparation is entrusted to English trainers, and consequently could hardly be otherwise.

CHAPTER XIII.

HINTS ON PURCHASING.

Purchase of old horses—Those best worth buying—Value of a trial; other considerations—The best seasons to buy—Legs and hocks: uncertain durability of; cases of indifferent legs standing severe work—*Wapiti, Virago, The Deformed*—Curbs, spavins, and their results—*Defender's* thorough-pin—Unsound horses best sold—Horses should stand well—The foot and its size; signs of speed—Moderately-sized horses preferred—Large and small horses and examples: *Camerine, Touchstone*—The first railway-van—Durability of small horses illustrated in the case of *Joe Miller* and his performances—Exceptional instances of the same in large horses; *Rataplan, Fisherman*—Contrast of the running of small and large horses as two- and three-year-olds and examples: *Parole, Heroine, Wild Dayrell, See Saw, The Earl,* and *Crucifix*—Roarers—The earliest yearling race—Inferences to be drawn from the preceding—Reasons for trial before parting with large horses—Observations on warranty; curious instances—Chronic lameness of horses in strong work.

In offering some observations on the purchase of horses, it is my intention to endeavour to describe the sort most likely to repay the purchaser. In buying old horses—that is, those whose form is known in public—regard should not be had to their performances only, but also to their soundness and the condition in which they were run. Nor is this all: their breeding, size and shape should be considered, and also the prospect they offer of becoming good brood mares or sires at the stud should they break down. A well-bred, good-looking mare, or horse, that has run well, would be worth more lame than a

I

moderate performer, indifferently bred, would be worth sound,
the difference in value between the two varying in instances
from £100 to £1,000.

If a private trial be given, the result should mainly determine the animal's worth. Yet there are other things besides
those already mentioned that should not be omitted from the
calculation—the animal's engagements, and the probability of
his winning the whole or a fair portion of them; and the state
of his legs in reference to their capability to stand many pre-
parations. A horse that has shown form at two years old, and
lost it at three without apparent cause, may be of very much
more value than one that can win small races at the later age.
For in the latter case no improvement could be looked for ;
but in the former a return to the two-year-old form may be
expected, and your hopes realised in a valuable purchase.
Mares, it should be remembered, often run better at the back
end than in the spring of the year. We have had many extraordinary instances of this, particularly with the three-year-
olds, at York and Doncaster in August and September. The
best months in which to buy three-year-olds that have lost
their form are June, July, and August, with the hope of their
returning to it in the autumn. For general purposes I should
always prefer a small horse to a large one—one that stood
well on his legs, having moderately-sized feet, in preference to
large ones. But no one is judge enough to decide whether
this or the other horse's legs will stand one preparation, and
much less, many. Yet this fact should not deter the exercise
of our judgment in the selection of those which seem most
likely to do so.

On this point I will give a few illustrations to show that legs
which have appeared the best have gone first, whilst those
which have looked the worst have stood longest. The case

of *Cracovienne* is a remarkable one to the point. To all appearances she was the soundest mare in the world; but she broke down standing in a loose box, and from the severe effects of this breakdown she never recovered, and after baffling all veterinary skill had to be put to the stud. On the other hand, *Wapiti*, *Vauban*, and *Virago* were so bad on their legs that their most sanguine admirers scarcely hoped to see them many times at the post, if at all. As it turned out, *Wapiti* was the best mare of her year, and was never beaten. It is true she never ran except as a two-year-old; but the other two I have named won many and large races as three-year-olds over very trying courses, astonishing every one, and not least their trainers. As Mr. Copperthwaite justly remarks: "Some legs last longer than others, and in many instances doubtful-looking ones prove the best."

All that has been said in relation to the leg applies with equal force to the hock. The worst-looking hocks, with spavins and curbs, often stand the test of work, whilst the perfectly-shaped ones will give way with little or no warning, and never get right again, treat them as you will. No one would like to buy horses with malformed hocks and legs except at a greatly reduced price. But when they can be had cheap I should not mind buying them, if I did not think the defects too bad, and liked their appearance in other respects. The *Deformed* had her four feet twisted in so much that her toes nearly touched each other as she stood; and her knees were so far apart that one might have wheeled a wheelbarrow between them without touching one or the other. Yet shaped like this she could not only run, but well, and won many races. Like *Wapiti* and *Virago*, she was a beautiful and very fine mare down to her knees, but dreadfully bad below.

In hocks I should not much object to a spavin or a curb;

I 2

for though I have seen many horses with them, very few ever were hurt by either blemish. Nothing, however, would induce me to buy a horse with a thorough-pin; for I have never known one so affected to stand a thorough preparation, no matter what, or how numerous the remedies that were tried.

I remember well the late Lord George Bentinck buying *Defender* of Mr. Isaac Sadler for 2,000 guineas (a large sum in those days). On his arrival at Danebury his lordship asked my grandmother (Mrs. A. Day) to look at him; and she said he had a thorough-pin, though perhaps it was not fully developed, adding that he would never stand a preparation. At this startling and unwelcome announcement his lordship immediately sent for that eminent veterinary surgeon the late Mr. Field, who after examining the horse said he apprehended no danger, and that he thought the defect would yield to mild treatment; if not, that a seton would effect a cure. This and many other remedies were tried, but to no purpose, and the horse never ran afterwards, and was put early to the stud.

When horses break down they are best sold or given away for other than racing purposes; because not one in a hundred ever stands afterwards. *Soapstone* was an exception, and so was *Misdeal;* the latter was fired, but the chances of standing with a crooked sinew are too remote to be worth a trial.

Horses sometimes are lame from big joints, and if the enlargement be on the inside, it is, as I have observed before, as a rule, fatal; but, if on the outside, with a little rest and blistering, the joint generally gets right, though the enlargement remains. *Capote* and *Maid of the Vale* had such legs; yet both stood, and won lots of races. A fair-sized foot is preferable to a very large or extremely small one; for the former of the two is better suited for cross-country purposes than for

flat racing, and the small foot is often the result of contraction
brought on by disease. As horses sometimes get lame from
diseases of the feet, it is best to purchase those only that
appear sound in this respect, and without malformation,
unless a proportionate sum be taken off—a concession many
demand, as before mentioned. For the stud, or running, I
should prefer moderately-sized horses—about fifteen hands
one or two inches high, standing straight on their legs; but if
bent either way at their knees, forward rather than backward,
as in the latter case they are more liable to break down. The
toes should stand straight on the feet: but if they be
turned either way it is preferable to buy horses whose toes
turn out, which is an indication of speed, rather than those
whose toes turn in, which indicates slowness.

A really good big horse is probably better than a really
good small one; but as a rule you may get fifty good small
horses for one good large one, and the former will and do run
well after the latter has been put to the stud. *Bay Middleton*
and *Elis*, two exceedingly good racehorses, were both failures
at the stud, having left the turf early ; whilst *Venison*, comparatively a pony, was good at both. His son, *Joe Miller*,
was also a pony ; and *Dulcibella* and *Weatherbound* very
little bigger.

A good big horse may beat a good little one over a short
course, or even at a mile or so ; but I think at three or four
miles a good little one would beat the best big one I ever saw.
Camerine was perhaps, in her own or any other day, the best
four-mile mare, and *Touchstone* probably the best long-distance
horse. The former, after winning a race over the Beacon
course (four miles), ran through Newmarket on to the Bury
hills (the other side of the town) before she could be stopped.
Neither of these horses stood, I should think, over fifteen

hands and an inch, and *Venison* was still less. *Venison's*
performances were extraordinary. He was beaten only twice
at three years old, by *Bay Middleton* and by *Touchstone*—who
was a year older—and it should be remembered he travelled over
1300 miles on foot, running long distance heats in twelve races,
including many Queen's Plates. We may well ask what he
might not have achieved in these days of railway locomotion.
In the same year, *Elis* was sent in a van to Doncaster with
The Drummer. They were the two first horses conveyed in
this way to a race-meeting; and I believe the van was the
first made for such a purpose, and was, as may be imagined,
a heavy affair in comparison even with the improvements on
it which were in general use until the cheaper and more
expeditious railway horse-box superseded them.

More particularly to illustrate the durability of small horses
over big ones, I may mention that *Joe Miller* was not specially
prepared to run a long distance on one or two occasions only,
but was so trained over and over again. His first race as a
three-year-old was for the Metropolitan (two and a quarter
miles), which but for an accident he would have won : for he
beat the winner, *Stilton*, and forty-one other horses, in the
easiest possible way just afterwards for the Chester Cup.
He was then prepared and run for the Derby and Ascot Cup
(Emperor's Prize), winning the latter, two and a half miles,
never having been headed from start to finish ; a proof of the
method to make running, it may be observed, which may
be of service to us later by way of illustration. And besides
being prepared for other races, he was made use of to try
Weathergage and *Hobbie Noble;* the former winning the
Cæsarewitch and the latter running second for the Cambridgeshire, and indeed would have won it, as those who
saw the race know, had he not been ridden to a standstill.

Some years after doing all this, *Joe Miller* retired from the turf as sound as the day he was foaled. To set against this experience are the instances of *Rataplan* and *Fisherman*, both large horses that achieved wonders. But they are the only two of the kind that I can remember to have run so often and so well over a distance of ground.

Little horses as a rule seldom improve much after their second year; some I think are never better than as two-year-olds at half a mile. *Parole* and *Heroine* are, I think, instances of this. The latter won very easily the yearling race at Shrewsbury in 1856 (the first on record, if I am not mistaken), and the former a small race at Brighton as two-year-olds; but though *Heroine* was a winner afterwards, they neither of them did anything later really worthy of notice. Large horses, on the other hand, improve often when much older, and even until they are aged. *Crucifix*, a long, leggy and slender mare, was good, it should be remarked, as a yearling, and also later. But *Wild Dayrell* when tried as a yearling so conspicuously failed that he was sold; whilst both *See Saw* and *The Earl* at the same age were positively wretched, and indeed did not improve much as two-year-olds till late in the year. These three were not only large but heavy horses, which may make the difference in the two cases, and account for the badness of the colts as yearlings and the goodness of the filly at that age. "What's in a name?" The then Lady Grosvenor thought there was much in one, for she said to Lord G. Bentinck, "You have an admirable mare, but I don't like her name." To which he replied, "When she is beat, Lady Grosvenor, I will change it." But as she never was, she retained it; and after running was known by her famous title at the stud. The inference from this is that small horses are at their best as two-year-olds, and the large, later: a very important consideration in either buying or selling.

There is another matter in reference to the size of the horse that it will not do to ignore altogether ; large horses are not only more liable to break down, but more often become roarers.

The performances of small and large yearlings in the paddock have been referred to in Chapter IX. ; but the purchase of yearlings is a subject of so special an interest, that I shall not attempt to deal with it now, but reserve it for the next chapter. We may however, I think, conclude from what has been here put forward, not only that small horses are best as two-year-olds and the larger ones later, but that small yearlings, if bad, may be got rid of with little fear ·of parting with a good one. Large horses ought to be tried a distance of ground before being sold as good for nothing ; as indeed should the small, unless they are wretchedly slow. A horse that has speed should always be tried over a distance of ground which may prove to be his forte before being parted with even for a good sum. So much said, it appears that with some observations on warranty, this portion of my subject may be brought to a conclusion.

It is very seldom a warranty of any sort is given with a racehorse, age and pedigree always excepted. I have known but very few people who ever asked for, or gave one, as to soundness. Though I have sold hundreds of horses I never remember warranting one sound, and have seldom been asked to do so. When *Oxonian* was sold for £1,200, it was conditional that the veterinary surgeon should pass him sound. He was examined and returned, though really one of the soundest horses alive, and the following year, after doing "the state some service," was sold unconditionally for £1,100 to the gentleman that had before refused him. He has since been running some eight or ten years, apparently as sound as ever. I doubt if one race-horse in a hundred would pass a strict veterinary examination ; for if nothing else would condemn them, all horses that are trained go short, wanting the freedom of action noticeable in carriage and other idle horses. A veterinary surgeon cannot well pass them in such a state, though there may not be, for racing purposes, the least thing amiss with them.

I have seen and known several curious cases in selling horses. I once sold a thorough-bred horse for a hack for £15, certainly as far as I knew, one of the soundest horses in England, and a few days after he became a confirmed roarer. My grandfather once sold a horse for a small sum, and was asked by the purchaser to allow him to remain for a few days ; to this he assented, but jocosely remarked, "If he die in the night he dies yours." This had so great an effect on the purchaser that he went home and sent for him next morning ; but on the arrival of the servant the horse was dead. My brother-in-law had a young hunter, and sold him to a gentleman for £80 if he passed the veterinary examination. This ordeal he was subjected to, and on account of an incipient spavin refused. I was asked to look at his hock and did, but failed to detect anything amiss with it. The late Professor Spooner was called in and passed him sound in every respect, and the gentleman took the horse, and as I never heard of anything being wrong with him after, I imagine he remained sound.

A few days before *Joe Miller* ran for the Ascot Cup, whilst trotting in the paddock he went very lame. This so astonished his owner that he begged of me not to gallop him ; but I assured him he was never otherwise when in strong work, and I took no notice of it. He was satisfied; the horse galloped, and won after. Many horses can scarcely walk when they first leave the stable, and some do not regain their proper action until they have had a good trot and a canter or two. After such experiences who would venture to give a warranty of soundness with any, even with those apparently free from every defect?

CHAPTER XIV.

THE PURCHASE OF YEARLINGS.

Difficulties of judgment—Fallibility of good looks—Hints on buying : attendance on sales ; opportunities at Doncaster ; necessity to try paces before purchase— Failures of high-priced yearlings : *Maximilian* and others ; exceptional case of *Promised Land*—Instances of successes of low-priced yearlings : *Brigantine, Schism, Blue Rock*—Judges of yearlings and their reputation ; Lord George Bentinck, my father, and *Mendicant ;* her performances as a race- horse and her appearance as a yearling—Instances of yearlings rejected as undersized : *Sweetmeat, Venison, Joe Miller, Musjid*—A high-priced failure : *Glenlivat*—Prices in past and present times contrasted : absurdity of prices now given at public auctions ; contrary examples of out-turn of reasonably- priced stock ; Mr. J. B. Starkey's purchase of *Viridis ;* my purchase of *Elcho* for Mr. Gerard Sturt and his achievements—Fashion and its influence : how yearlings are bred to be sold, and how they should be bought—Value of blood ; produce of old mares often good : examples, *Crucifix* and *Caractacus* —Predilection for fat yearlings, and resulting disappointment to owner and trainer—My preference for light yearlings ; where such may be bought, and instances : *Starter, Judge,* and *Steward*—Progress of light and big yearlings contrasted ; prevalence of sore shins with the latter—Excellent result of Sir Tatton Sykes's method of breeding ; rarity of disease amongst his stock ; their successes and instances—Points that should be looked for—Reason of Sir Tatton's successes ; " like begets like "—His disposal of colts and fillies ; account of a visit to Sledmere and purchase of *Palmistry*—Private and public breeding-studs contrasted, and reasons for the successes of the former— Results of paying high prices, and examples—An unfashionably-bred winner : *Jester*—Horses run in all shapes—Inferences to be drawn ; the best yearlings to buy—Engagements of yearlings : hints and arguments ; current errors ; early trials recommended, and reasons—Dictum of the Marquess of Anglesey.

THE subject I have chosen for this chapter is one of great difficulty. Perhaps in racing nothing is attended with more trouble and less satisfaction than the purchase of yearlings.

This, I think, will hereafter appear. As " all is not gold that glitters," so the best-looking yearlings are often the most worthless. No rule can be laid down by which to guide an intending purchaser with any degree of certainty as to selecting the best and refusing the worst. Experience is the only sure guide; yet a few hints may be thought neither presumptuous nor out of order.

In the first place, then, I should recommend the would-be purchaser to attend all the yearling sales, or in any case those which usually commence in June and end (at Doncaster) in September. There are sales too at Newmarket so late as October which may be attended with profit. But for many reasons I should purchase if possible before then.

There is no better opportunity to buy, in my opinion, than at the Doncaster September sales. There is always a plentiful supply of all breeds and sizes at all sorts of prices and, very often, cheap. Before buying anything I would always see the animal in action. If I could not see all his paces, I would at least see him walk ; for if he does that pace well, he will generally gallop well. Many a good-looking, fair-sized yearling by a young, well-bred stallion unknown to fame at the stud, and out of an equally well-bred mare, may be had there for about 100 or 150 guineas ; whilst fancy-bred ones fetch fifteen or twenty times these sums. I have seen year-lings sold for 1,000 and 1,500 guineas apiece, or double, which were not worth sixpence for the purpose for which they were bought. Indeed I think the highest priced yearling ever bought, *Maximilian* (he fetched over 4,000 guineas) is not good enough, to judge from his public running, to win a Selling Plate at the lowest allowable rate, if he ran for one. Even roarers have been bought for as much as 1,000 guineas apiece. However, this is an error any one may fall into ;

for there is no method of detecting the existence of the defect before purchasing, unless, indeed, surreptitiously through the attendant.

For one, *Promised Land*, I gave this price; or rather I should say, I gave Mr. Robinson £500 for half of him, and he was a fortune to both of us. I have bought many cheaper ones, such as *Brigantine* for 150 guineas; and indeed, had always an objection to paying long prices in so risky a matter. Amongst good bargains in yearlings, I may mention *Schism* for twenty guineas, bought at Doncaster at public auction on the sale of the late Lord Clifden's horses. She won me many thousands of pounds, and her victories included the Queen's Vase at Ascot, and the Somersetshire Stakes at Bath. I sold her afterwards for £1,500. But the very smallest sum I ever gave for a yearling was ten guineas for *Blue Rock*, who won me many races, including the Great Eastern Handicap at Newmarket, and Cup at Shrewsbury. On the occasion of his winning the former race, he slept in London, went down to Newmarket by train in the morning, and returned to his stable at night without sustaining the least harm.

It is a very common expression that Mr. So-and-So is a first-rate judge of yearlings, and on every fortunate purchase his praises are sounded everywhere, though little is ever said of his mistakes. The late Lord George Bentinck was always looked on as one of the best judges of his day; he certainly bought many good, and it may be added, many bad ones. My father, with whom he then trained, bought most of his lordship's yearlings for him. One of his purchases was a filly by *Touchstone* out of *Lady Moor Carew*, which was bought privately of Mr. Whitworth for 300 guineas. It appeared that his lordship had previously seen and condemned her as too light, without legs sufficiently strong to carry even so weak a body. He refused to have her, and no doubt there was much truth in his opinion. Yet she was racing like and evenly shaped, and if nothing else she looked like going fast; so my father had to keep her, and afterwards sold a moiety of her to Mr. Gully. This wretched-looking under-sized "weed" that the astute nobleman would have nothing to do with, was *Mendicant*, the best animal of her year; the winner of the One Thousand and The Oaks, besides many other races. She was better than *Pyrrhus the First*, the winner of that year's Derby, of the truth of which assertion there can be no doubt, for they belonged to the same owners and they said so. Here is a remarkable instance of two acknowledged judges disagreeing as to the latent merits of one of the best yearlings in the world; one being in raptures with her looks and blood, whilst the other disliked one if not both. The sincerity of their declarations on this point was supported by their unwavering faith in their judgment; the one rejected and the other bought her.

With this case before us, how can we trust the judgment of any individual? *Sweetmeat*, I am told, did not fetch £100 as a yearling, and many a noted good one has been sold for half that sum. *Venison* was so small that the late Lord Lonsdale would not send him to the sale with the rest of his yearlings; and he was afterwards purchased privately by my father. *Joe Miller*, in the month of July, looked more like a foal than a yearling. *Musjid* returned to his paddock after having been seen by all the best judges at Doncaster, for the want of a purchaser at 150 guineas; at which sum the late Sir Joseph Hawley bought him some time afterwards. *Glenlivat* was bought for 1,000 guineas, a high figure in those days, but he only won once by walking over, after running a dead heat with

Hetman Platoff, who broke down in the struggle for victory at Warwick.

In those days, some forty years ago, it was considered an extraordinary sale if anything fetched 1,000 guineas; but now it is a poor sale if many of the yearlings do not reach four figures, their lucky and brave purchasers receiving deafening plaudits for their skill and indomitable pluck in securing the coveted prizes. This is no romantic picture, for as a matter of fact I remember a few years ago seeing yearling after yearling sold not only for 1,000 guineas, but 2,000 guineas each ; reaching as much, in one case, as 2,400 guineas. Nor must it be concluded that a few picked lots only went for high figures ; for some forty, I think, realised at this sale an average of 500 guineas apiece. Just after one of these sensational flatcatchers had been disposed of to some unfortunate individual, a nice little filly, but rather upright in her fore pasterns (a dwarf to the giant that preceded her), was led into the ring, and nearly led out again without a bid, as Mr. Tattersall had ordered her back and called for the next lot, when a couple of hundred was offered for her and she was knocked down at that figure. The late Mr. J. B. Starkey was the bidder ; and the impression was that the purchase was made, not by a particularly good judge, or an astute trainer, such as had bought the high-priced yearlings, but by a genial gentleman, who, having shared in the host's hospitality, felt it a duty to bid for something. However, he bought the best animal at the sale, and though this is not saying very much for his bargain, it proved a really good one, as the yearling ran a very good mare—the well-known *Viridis*. Now there were present at this sale not only all our home purchasers of note, but foreign judges buying for their respective governments or private clients ; yet not one of them selected the right horse; to do so, was left to a gentleman up to that time, not celebrated as a purchaser of yearlings. So much for the judgment of good judges.

Mr. Gerard Sturt (now Lord Alington) asked me to buy him two yearlings, if I liked any, of Sir Tatton Sykes, at York. He had but one restriction to make, and that was : he would have them out of mares that had bred a winner, no matter of what, or how few races. I bought him *Elcho* and *Prince Imperial* (as they were afterwards called), for 100 guineas each. The latter was claimed, in a Selling Race at Doncaster, and the other won the Doncaster Nursery, Good-wood Stakes, and the Metropolitan, beating *Asteroid* and *Caractacus*, the Derby winner of the same year, giving him 2 stone 5 lbs. He was a little horse, but stayed well, an additional instance of the goodness of little horses. I would much prefer having three or four yearlings for 1,000 guineas than pay that sum for one; and there are many good-looking ones that may be had for 200 guineas each or less. But such is the rage now-a-days for fashion, that dwarfs or giants, legs crooked or straight, are alike quickly bought, at any, even enormous prices, often to their new owners' sorrow.

I do not for a moment say that you should disregard particular breeds, such as are distinguished as having pro-duced runners. I say rather: "Buy them if you like their appearance, and you can do so at a reasonable rate." But rather than give extravagant sums for fashionably bred weeds, or overgrown brutes without legs or anything but flesh to recommend them, I would buy something to look at, out of a young mare, even if by a young stallion. For many so bred turn out well. On the other hand, I have seen many fashionably bred yearlings fetch large sums, that after the fall of the hammer were never heard of again, except at the stud; and there only as great failures as they had proved in racing.

Nor should yearlings out of old mares, hitherto failures at the stud, be totally disregarded, for at times such old mares breed good ones. Of such produce we have examples in the following: *Crucifix*, who was sold by the side of, and with her dam, for sixty-five guineas ; *Caractacus, Hero*, and *One Act*, all good animals, whose dams before had produced nothing— indeed, had figured for many years before at the stud as useless breeders of a more degenerate race than themselves.

It is now the fashion to have yearlings sent for sale, walked only from the stable-door to the rostrum, like so many fat beasts at Smithfield or some other cattle-show. Breeders see, and for their own purposes take advantage of, the prevailing taste for large animals ; and by having their yearlings well fatted are sure of a market. Let them but be fat, and it does not seem to matter what they may be like in other respects. The kind of feet and legs they have, or how these are set on, the really essential point to a buyer, is not of the slightest consequence ; for if good judges refuse to buy, there are plenty of others eager to take their place.

Thus it comes about that year after year trainers have sent to them large, heavy-shouldered, slack-loined, little-legged brutes, that would fall over a straw, with instructions to prepare them for their engagements. And whilst it may be taken for granted that if horses cannot walk well they are not perfect in any of their other paces, yet if these incapables are not metamorphosed into good-looking animals by the following year, and do not win many races, the trainer is reproached. The blame is laid upon his unskilful treatment or total neglect ; whereas the fault is with the purchaser, in buying great unwieldy brutes, without a single quality to

K

recommend them but lumps of fat. It is forgotten that a man can only work to the best of his ability with such tools as are supplied to him.

Now a good useful-looking yearling, with plenty of bone and strength in proportion, may often be bought for a moderate sum of a breeder who prefers to sell at home, who does not stall-feed, and whose yearlings have their liberty in the paddock from the day almost of foaling until the hour they are sold. A case of this sort I may give that happened to me some time ago. Whilst looking over Mr. Harrison's breeding establishment in the North, I saw three rough-looking colts galloping in his paddock, and in reply to my inquiry as to their price, was told they would be sold at York that week; but as I could not stay for the sale I made a conditional offer for them of £500, supposing they were not sold. They were put up, but not sold; their rough, hardy appearance, telling against them side by side with other yearlings got up for sale, as I have described. After the sale I received a telegram: "Horses not sold; please send for them." I did so, and the three were *Starter*, *Judge*, and *Steward;* either of the first two being worth double what I gave for the three, both proving to be the winners of many races. These colts had no glossy coats and very little flesh; but they were perfectly healthy, and their health and appearance the result of play in the paddock, where they galloped a great part of each day.

Colts like these, when put in training, improve just as fast as the fat ones go back. The fat ones become thin, whilst the thin ones become comparatively fat, and in the following year the latter are in much better condition, with muscle more fully developed than the others which previously *looked* so much better. Nor can anything else be expected. The simple fact is, the thin ones have to a certain extent been training themselves for months before coming into the trainer's hands; whilst the others, debarred their freedom, have had their growth prematurely forced by art, at the expense of nature, and are like hothouse plants,—drawn up, weak, and slender. This condition, to my mind, is the predominant cause of sore shins, which have so much increased of late years—not only in extent but severity,—and can very seldom be got rid of under several months and sometimes not for years. This tendency is another and powerful reason for buying yearlings brought up in the enjoyment of early exercise in extensive paddocks.

A more striking instance can scarcely be adduced to show the truth of the above remarks than the way the late Sir Tatton Sykes's yearlings were brought up in the Sledmere paddocks, as I have described in Chapter IX. His method is, as I said, the natural way of rearing thoroughbred stock; and my opinion is that if Sir Tatton had not kept too closely to his own sires, he would in the race for supremacy have beaten many of his more fortunate neighbours, who sent their mares to different stallions. As it is, he was fairly successful ; for in addition to a host of winners, he bred *Grey Momus* (winner of the Two Thousand and Ascot Cup) and *Black Tommy* (second for the Derby). I have myself good cause to remember he was also the breeder of *St. Giles, Elcho, Companion,* and *Greyling,* which, with many other winners, I was fortunate enough to buy of him. Moreover, to the best of my belief not one of the many scores of yearlings so purchased had a contracted or diseased foot, all standing well on their legs, and with substance. Not one that I ever remember broke down or had sore shins. And whilst this is a most remarkable fact, it is not the only one ;

K 2

for I may add that (whilst with me) not one of them was ever lame from ring-bone, splint, curb, or thorough-pin. In other respects, too, they were more free than most horses from diseases of every kind ; I never lost one by death, or had a roarer amongst the whole.

So satisfactory a result, it will be admitted, is worthy of attention ; and it may be asked, How was it brought about ? The answer is, through exercise unrestrained, not forced, aided by a plentiful diet of good hay and corn and soiling their natural food.

With these experiences, we may dismiss all fears of the result of rough appearance in yearlings without a second thought. The lesson we learn is to look well to the method of their treatment since foaled, and we shall not go far wrong in our selections. That which is wanted is muscle, not fat. The one implies strength, the other physical debility, burdening their tender limbs with an unnatural weight they cannot sustain, making some crooked and others weak.

Further to account for Sir Tatton's breeding so many sound horses, it may be said he scrupulously attended to the shape of the ancestors, and chose only those standing well on their legs. If by chance a yearling stood a little back in his knees, or the least upright in his pasterns, the Baronet would be the first to call your attention to the defect by saying (as he always did), " He does not stand quite pretty on his legs;" and if such a one were not sold, he would give him away rather than breed from him—so great was his aversion to those that did not stand well. It is open to other people to breed sound animals if they will only follow his most excellent example, instead of breeding, as most do, from any crooked-legged, deformed brutes, if only they have a brother's or sister's fame to recommend them favourably to the public notice, forgetting that "like begets like." A condition worthy of note in Sir Tatton's sale was the total absence of the fillies. These were kept to breed from; and those not good enough for that purpose were disposed of for hacks. His colts had always a reserve of 100 guineas placed on them. But if they returned to Sledmere unsold, no reasonable offer was ever refused. *St. Giles, Greyling,* and *Companion,* were bought of him in this way at sixty guineas each after returning from the sale at York. All were winners: the former perhaps one of the best horses of his day over a distance of ground, as he was most certainly the finest.

Sir Tatton professed never to sell brood mares; nor, as I before said, yearling fillies. But he was always exceedingly kind to me, and sold me three brood mares with their foals, all the mares being served again by *Andover,* for 300 guineas. One of the foals, as a yearling, I sold for 500 guineas. The mares I thus bought were *Palmistry,* the dam of *St. Giles,* and two young mares out of her dam; and when Sir Tatton told Snarry, his old stud-groom, of the sale, the latter said, "Sir Tatton, you have sold one of the best mares you have." "Never mind, Snarry," Sir Tatton answered, "Mr. Day is a good customer, and I would rather sell and repent, than keep and repent."

On this memorable occasion I asked him another favour, which he also readily granted. It was to sell me a foal. I was commissioned by the late Lord Ribblesdale to give 300 guineas for *Brother to Centurion,* if I liked him. I did, and bought him for twenty-five guineas; which the generous old Baronet begged me to give to my uncle Samuel with his compliments; which was done.

In concluding my remarks on the yearlings bred at Sledmere, I may say that Sir Tatton was hospitable to a degree. A capital lunch and a "pitcher of ale" was always partaken of before going round the paddocks ; and the very last time I traversed them in company with Sir Tatton, then about eighty years of age, he stopped suddenly and turned round saying, " I hope, Mr. Day, I don't walk too fast for you." To ease his mind on the point I walked beside him, whilst trudging through the remainder of the paddocks, agreeably discussing the breed and merits of the several occupants.

I cannot account in any other way for the superiority of horses bred in private studs over those bred in large breed-ing establishments, than by the advantage of air and exercise the former have over the latter. The defunct Rawcliffe and others may be cited as instances of gigantic failures, while the following private breeding establishments may be pointed to as so many successes: those of the late Lord Jersey, the Duke of Grafton, and Mr. Thornhill ; and later we have that of Mr. Wreford, whose great success was equal to that of the preceding, carrying everything before him in his day. Again, if I mistake not, Mr. Bowes has bred no less than four winners of the Derby, a thing unprecedented in the annals of racing. And if reference be made in addition to the late Sir J. Hawley's and Lord Falmouth's studs, it will be sufficient to show the difference that exists between horses bred for racing and those that are bred only to sell, and the superiority of the former.

We see the advantages the companies enjoy in the enor-mous sums which they give (as occasionally, too, do private individuals) for stallions and mares (as much as £12,500 for a horse, and 3,000 guineas apiece for mares). It cannot, there-fore, be said they start on a bad foundation ; yet with all these "appliances and means to boot," they are unsuccessful in the attempt to breed the best horses. For this there must

surely be an assignable cause ; and if it is not wholly attributable to the want of exercise, as I have before suggested,
it may be found in the different quality of the food, or in a
combination of both.

But to return to the more immediate subject, the purchasing
of yearlings — it may be concluded as pretty certain that
large horses fat will sell, when small and poor ones will
not, except at a reduced and inadequate figure.   Now as the
latter often turn out the best, common sense leads one to
choose them in preference to the others.   People are to be
found that will give £1,000 or £2,000 for anything, however
shaped, that is brother or sister to a Derby winner, who would
not give £100 for one much better shaped, less fashionably
bred—and more likely, so far as experience teaches, to turn
out much better than the high priced one.   How many
could I not point to that have been sold, like *The Rover* and
Maximilian,[1] for fabulous sums, that have proved utterly
useless, never having won a race.   On the other hand, of
unfashionably bred ones, *The Hero* was sold for £150 and
turned out the best horse in England.   *Elcho* and *St. Giles*
were as indifferently bred, and sold for 100 guineas and
60 guineas respectively, both really good horses over a distance of ground.   Even as I am writing, we have an extraordinary instance of the superiority of a badly bred horse
over those of good pedigree.   I allude to the breeding of
Jester, who is, without doubt, the most unfashionably bred
horse in the world : his sire, *Merry Maker*, could not go
fast enough to beat a hack, and his dam was a mare whose
parentage was not thought worth preserving—in fact he is
not proved to be thoroughbred.   I have before mentioned
his victories, which need not be repeated here.

[1] Since this was written *Maximilian* has proved a winner.

Surely enough has been said to convince the most sceptical that little dependence can be placed on the breed of any horse, and that as they truly run in all shapes and forms, so they do in every variety of breeds. *Bay Middleton* was the largest and longest horse, as well as the best, I ever saw at a mile, and *Joe Miller* the smallest and shortest. Again, *Promised Land* was just the opposite in shape to *Crucifix* — he, short and strong, having the very shortest neck I think I ever saw ; whilst *Crucifix* had the longest, and altogether appeared the weakest mare in the world ; yet both were equally good.

I will not multiply instances, but bring my remarks on the purchase of yearlings to a conclusion by saying that, all things considered, it is best to buy those that are out of young mares and dams of winners, and by stallions that are the sires of winners, if only of little races : that is supposing you cannot afford to give large sums for the most fashionably bred ones, which may pay for purchasing, if they are properly shaped as well, and have any pretensions to size.

Only next in importance to the purchase of yearlings is the engagement of them, a reference to which will here fitly find a place.

Here again opinions often totally differ. Some engage the best-looking horses only, whilst others, holding opposite views, engage only the best bred ones. Some again engage their horses often ; others, but seldom. Adopting a different mode altogether, some, irrespective of looks, or breed, engage all heavily alike.

My ideas of engaging horses are summed up in a very few words. The good-looking, if well bred, I would engage heavily ; and the worst, as far as looks and breed are concerned, the least, or rather not at all. My reason for acting

in this way, would be chiefly because I should know that no
one would be able to oppose me with better looking, or, from
their breeding, horses more likely to run ; whilst many would
bring into the field horses which, comparatively speaking,
would be brutes.   Were I induced to break the rule, it would
only be to put a well-bred colt or filly of moderate looks in
the Derby or Oaks.

Now, how very seldom do we see horses engaged in this
way.   Rather do we not notice continually the reverse
adopted ?   We see the breeder of, say half a dozen yearlings,
or the purchaser of a like number at indiscriminate prices, no
matter what their breeding or looks, engage them all alike in
the best stakes against the most fashionably and best bred
horses in England.   It is quite true one or other of them
may be good.   But he must be a bold and sanguine man to
expect success as the result, that engages horses after this
fashion.   Since the introduction of the small entrance fee,
stakes that formerly had but a few subscribers have now
many, and in most races some good horses are generally
to be found entered.   What then is your chance of winning
but a very poor one with a "weed" or an unfashionably
bred colt or filly?   Moreover, many of the yearlings that
are thus heavily engaged, have been well tried before the
day of closing the stakes, whilst others are receiving an
allowance that yours may not be entitled to.   Under such
a load of disadvantages, who can hope to win with anything
but the best, or nearly the best, of his year ?

But the yearlings being engaged in the hope of winning
something, the temptation to run often follows as a necessary
consequence ; and by doing battle against superior animals
your own becomes stale, and unable to win other races in
which, having different opponents, there would be chances in

your favour. It is found in the result that thousands of pounds have been paid away in travelling expenses and stakes to little or no purpose.

Now if these, or indeed any other animals, had been tried, as yearlings, and not engaged until tried, the worthless would not have been entered, whilst the good could have engaged with a fair chance of success against all comers; and that which in the one case would have been a losing, would have been turned into a winning account at Old Burlington Street.

It may be thought that the engagements of yearlings might more appropriately be noticed under the head of trials than under that of purchases; but as there are important stakes, the entry for which must be made before the young ones can possibly be fairly tried, the subject (which however important does not claim a chapter to itself) is better treated now.

But in this matter of trial before engagement, I should point out how many opportunities are given for it in the present day; there being a greater number of stakes closing after time for a fair trial has been allowed, than, before, there were races of all kinds. It should therefore be borne in mind that before a trial, breeding and good looks are everything; but after, these go for nothing—the only animal that is valuable, then, being the one that has given undeniable proof that he is so. The veriest brute to look at may, by trial, be discovered to be a nonpareil; whilst the best-looking may be found to be the worst horse in creation. These are both excellent reasons for early trial; for you can then fearlessly engage the horse that has acquitted himself well, to your heart's content. The late Marquess of Anglesey used to say, " The next best thing to finding a good horse is the discovery of a bad one ; " which I thoroughly believe. And therefore

I would try all as soon as fit, that the bad may be discarded, and the rest properly engaged; but until tried, be chary of engaging for the reasons above enumerated.

Some of the anomalies connected with sales with engagements, I shall have occasion to notice later in my suggestions for certain alterations in current practices on the turf.

CHAPTER XV.

TRIALS.

Immense value of trials—Difficulties of the subject—How short trials and how long
trials should be made—Unsatisfactory trials; false pace —The best method of
trying—In doubtful cases try again—A good pace essential—Disappointments
in races in which running is made, accounted for; how the pace should be
made; instances at Goodwood and Newmarket— Points to be noted in trials
—Mistakes in trials; hints thereon; a second trial advised—Illustrative
trials : *General Hesse* and an Arab, *Crucifix* and *Iris, Rising Sun* and *Twilight*
—False pace and its results—My success in repeated trials—The pace in trials
and in races.

WE have seen how horses should be purchased and brought
to that condition which, in turf phraseology, is called " fit to
run ; " and now must discuss the subject of trials, the only
true method of ascertaining if this desirable condition be
achieved.   Nothing can be of greater value than a correct
estimate of the merits of the animals you possess ; for by it
you engage and run them, lose or win fortunes, staking your
reputation on the accuracy of your opinion.

On reaching this stage of our journey in search of knowledge,
it might be thought and hoped that the most difficult obstacles
had been vanquished.   But it is hardly so.   It has been aptly
said,

" Errors, like straws, upon the surface flow ;
 He who would search for pearls must dive below."

And so with trials, it will be found that no era of ease and
pleasure has set in ; that which, to the uninitiated seems easy
of accomplishment, the experienced knows to be not only
difficult but often totally impracticable.

We hear of most wonderful trials in private ; but we never
see them repeated in public. The cause of this I will
endeavour to explain.

In a trial certainty should not be looked for. It is a matter,
to a limited extent, of opinion and judgment. Nevertheless, a certain approximation to the truth may be arrived at
with a tolerable degree of accuracy.

In short trials, old jockeys are often requested not to bustle
their horses the first fifty yards, but to let them get well
"on their legs" first ; particularly the old ones. The advice
is necessary and often attended with good results ; but, unfortunately, it too often happens from over-cautiousness that
not only fifty but 150 yards are got over in this way, and
then only is the pace made good ; a mistake by which the
course is so much shortened. Again, in some cases, it occurs
that the young horse overpowers his rider, and the old one
never fairly gets on his legs. The result is in both cases,
although the causes are different, precisely similar, viz :—
failure. Pretty much the same may be said of long courses.
In a two-mile course it often happens that the first half mile
is traversed at a slow pace to enable the horses to get well
together, and on their legs as it is termed, being steadied
down hill and round turns ; after which they do the
remainder at their best speed.

This is the sort of trial that many rest satisfied with, and
upon which they build their hopes of success ; and when
beaten in public they wonder at the difference between the
running then and the running at the trial. The horse is

condemned as a rogue, particularly if tried again in the same way with the same result as before. In this manner many horses that subsequently have distinguished themselves over a different course, have been injudiciously parted with, as useless, for a mere song.

Running like this very naturally appears to those who suffer through it, quite unaccountable. But a little reflection will clear up the seeming mystery, and set things in their proper light. The simple fact is, that having tried two miles at a false pace, and then run the same distance in public at a true one, you have based your calculations for a race of two miles on a trial that has been only a mile and a half; for, under the circumstances, that is all your two-mile trial has in reality amounted to. The result of the running of most horses (except when gross error has been committed) will tell you this; for over and over again we see horses that have been well tried by experienced men, look like winning the race some distance from home, then tire and be beaten. Now what can this be but the fault of the false pace in the early part of the trial? for we often see these supposed good stayers win races on a shorter course.

Whatever the length of the trial, whether half a mile, two miles, or any other distance, all without exception that are in it should be given every chance to win. Should it suit the old ones to wait, or the heavy weights to make the running, let them do it; but in each and every trial have a good pace from one post to the other, no matter how long the distance. Trials conducted on any other principles than these are sure to lead to error and disappointment. Under any circumstances you cannot be too careful. If there is the least doubt about the accuracy of a trial, I would, after the lapse of a day, try over again, and watch the last more intently if possible than the first ; to prove beyond misconception where the error, if any, existed, and to provide, when found, a remedy in future. I should always give preference to the last trial, unless, in it, anything happened likely to upset one's calculation.

It is in the nice discrimination of the pace at first and during the whole length that your judgment is shown, and an opinion obtained that is worth having. Horses may get upset in running a short course by getting off cross-legged, or in other words, by being bustled at starting. They are in this way quickly disposed of, and a false trial is the inevitable result. In such cases, the remedy is to try over again and abide by the last trial.

Trials should always be run as nearly as possible at the pace which you may fairly expect to see in public. We know that short courses are always run at top speed from the starting post to the finish ; and this being so, on what ground can any one, in the trial, justify waiting until the old horses are on their legs as before mentioned ? Again, you may always insure a good pace in a long race by making it, or hiring others to do it for you ; but you can never say it shall be a slow one. Therefore, it imperatively behoves you in trials to have a good pace all the way.

I may here mention an interesting fact, which is the cause undoubtedly of unsatisfactory performances in long-distance races. It is the waiting too long for, or more strictly speaking perhaps it should be called, the lying back too far from, the horse that is detailed to do the work. As a rule the distance between the two is some eight or ten lengths. It should never exceed two or three lengths ; for if you concede more you are virtually making not a fast, but a waiting race of it. You know that your pioneer is much worse than the one he is started to assist, and cannot hurt him, go as fast as he will ;

therefore when once the horse that is set to do the work is fairly exhausted, the other should carry on the running : or how can his condition and gameness tell? The two best paces I think I ever remember seeing, were in the Goodwood Cup and the Cæsarewitch. In the first *Schism* started to assist *Promised Land*, and *Prioress* to do the same office for her stable companion *Starke*. The American mare started at the top of her speed, but was not fast enough to make the pace which *Schism* did, *Promised Land* lying a length from the second horse until a mile from home, when he took up the running, was never headed, and won in a common canter. In the Cæsarewitch, *Killigrew* made the running for a mile, when *Dulcibella*, who laid second until passing the ditch-gap, took it up some 100 yards ahead of all the rest and won in a trot. In another case, for the Emperor's Vase at Ascot, *Joe Miller* took the lead and was never headed.

But this is a matter connected rather with the race itself than with the trial—to return to which I should observe that there are, in long courses, many fortuitous circumstances worthy of note. One horse, for example, may get an advantage at the start ; this is usually little thought of, nevertheless the lost ground has to be made up by his opponents. Others, again, may lose ground at the turns, or lie out of it, or be ridden to a standstill ; in point of fact, from any one of these causes, the winner in a trial may be the worst of the lot, and the trial a farce. The mistakes made in trials are not only marvellous, but of everyday occurrence. I cannot see why they should be so. If you take for your trial horse one that has lately run in public (which should always be the case), so that his form at the time may be accurately known, and have another to gauge his running I can hardly see what mistakes could occur; yet, as a matter of fact, as I have said, they do occur, and far too often and inexplicably. The state of the ground, for one thing, should be carefully considered in its effect for or against individual animals. Neglect of this may upset the rest of your calculations. For myself, I have very seldom seen horses that have been properly tried, fail to exhibit the same form in public—rogues only excepted. I can only, therefore, conclude that when mistakes are made, they are assuredly assignable to some cause, and may be traced either to the want of foresight on the part of the trainer, or to an opinionated owner, or to an unskilful jockey. It often happens that little *contretemps* take place in trials and races that the jockeys alone know of, and of which they seldom speak, unless questioned on the subject, which, if known, would explain seeming contrarieties. It is often seen in a race of twenty or thirty runners, that two-thirds of the number of horses that have been highly tried and pronounced by astute judges to have an excellent chance, are literally "never in it," being beaten by some veritable outsider. In such cases there must be something wrong, and a thorough investigation is necessary. Were the case mine, I would do as I have already described in the case of an unsatisfactory trial—I would try over and over again until I had satisfied myself as to the source of error, and then take precautions against a repetition of it.

In illustration of the suggestions contained in this chapter, I will describe two or three trials of which I was an eyewitness.

The first took place here in the presence of a nobleman, one of the cleverest and most experienced men on the turf, between *General Hesse*, a speedy old horse, and a half-bred Arab, over the T.Y.C. The latter, with only a boy up, beat

L

the old horse, steered by one of our most accomplished jockeys, and very easily too. For some reason, probably because of the ease with which the trial was won, I doubted its correctness, although the noble earl was satisfied, and the jockey had no excuse to offer for the result. However, for my own satisfaction, it was arranged that the old horse should be left with me to try the other with again, neither his lordship nor the jockey being able to stay or take part in the proceeding. A few days afterwards, in a second trial in every respect the same as the first, the *General*, with a stable-boy on his back, entirely reversed the earlier result, beating his opponent as easily as before he himself had been beaten, and confirming my suspicions that all had not been right when the grey had won too easily to please me.

Watching this trial very narrowly, as I did, and seeing nothing in it that I thought I could alter, I felt sure it was correct, and that the first one, from some unaccountable mistake, must have been wrong. I communicated the result to his lordship on seeing him at Ascot, but he could scarcely believe it, and still considered that the first trial with a jockey up must have been the right one. The jockey, when told of it, was of the same opinion. The *General's* opponent and quondam victor ran, and was, as I was sure he would be, last. Had prudential tactics not prevailed, there would have been no second trial in this case; the first would have been implicitly relied upon as correct. We should have lost our money, and the blame would have been mine; a sufficient reason, on the trainer's part, to make "security doubly sure," by trying a second time when the least doubt exists.

To account for so extraordinary a change as in this case within so short a time, is, I candidly admit, beyond my power. The probability, however, is that *General Hesse* got off cross-legged in the first trial, whilst the contingency was guarded against in the second. Such is the glorious uncertainty which racing can, as well as the law, claim for its own.

A similar case occurred with *Crucifix* for the Chesterfield at Newmarket. A false start occurred; but the race was run, and the mare was easily beaten by *Iris*, to whom she could have given two stone, if not more. It was run over again, when *Crucifix* won as easily as her opponent had done in the first instance.

One other example I will refer to. After *Petra* had won the Steward's Cup at Chester, Mr. Copperthwaite asked me if I would try his horse *Rising Sun* with her for the Derby, asserting that his horse could beat his old mare *Twilight* at even weights; to which I replied that "anything that could do that must be a good one," and suggested that they should be put in the trial, not at even weights, but at seven pounds, as we had better err on the right side, and not impose too severe a task on the young one. This was done, and the young one was easily beaten. Certainly a stone would not have brought him near an animal he had just before beaten at another place at even weights. In fact this was a complete reversal of the other trial at the same distance, and, like most other trials, the last one was the most correct. The fact is, the young horse was beaten from the severity of the pace, as he certainly went fast for a mile and then tired. Had a false pace been indulged in he might have won again. Mr. Copperthwaite's idea of trying would preclude any possibility of having a good pace (a thing he would think so much against the young one) whilst under his control or joint management at his training quarters. In sum, his horse's earlier victory was sufficiently explained by the system in vogue with its owner.

It will be abundantly seen that, for myself, I believe in

L 2

second trials in all cases of the slightest doubt, and most strongly commend their adoption to others. A few days should intervene if possible; and all else that is necessary is, that the animals should keep well, and the ground admit of the performance. I know that second trials are considered by many to be too severe, and are therefore condemned. But the practice is one I have the greatest faith in. I tried it with *Dulcibella* and *Weatherbound*, before their respective races at Newmarket; also with *St. Giles* and *One Act*, as I have already described, and in no single instance have I had cause to regret it.

We all know that horses must gallop. There is no disguising this fact, say what we may; nor can there be any objection to their doing so without their clothing, or without knowing the respective weights of the boys: and this is in reality all the difference between a good gallop, such as they must have near the time of their running, and a trial. But I go further, and say it is better that they should gallop now and again free from the incumbrance of a heavy suit of clothing, and with a boy on their back a stone or two heavier than you have any reason to suppose he is. Indeed, it is folly to suppose any one would do otherwise who had at heart his own interest, and that which is not only inseparable from it, but is his first duty—the interest of his employers.

CHAPTER XVI.

TRIALS (*continued*). ·

How yearlings should be tried, and instances : *Parole* and *Crucifix—Schism's* performance as a yearling—Early trials recommended—The best method of trying the two-year-old, and examples—The trial of older horses—Private trials and public form ; uncertainty of the latter exemplified in the case of *Promised Land, Europa,* and others—Trials proving ultimately more trustworthy than public form, and instances : *Cossack* and *Hermit*—Defeats accounted for; instanced in the running of *Fisherman,* and mistakes of jockeys —The case of *Lady ·Elizabeth* and her detractors discussed ; the mystery accounted for; analogous cases : *Green Sleeves, Macgregor, Gamos,* and others.

IT will be seen from what has gone before that I am an advocate of early trials. I have already observed that some horses as yearlings stay well three furlongs, but never get beyond that distance ; and that some horses stay the half-mile as two-year-olds, but do not later improve upon this performance—facts that should be an important guide.

Thus, with yearlings, try half a mile, and you will be able without additional risk or expense to know more of their real merits, and be a better judge of what they are likely to be, than if you tried them only three furlongs. *Parole* I tried this distance only, and paid dearly for my first departure from an old-established and excellent rule. She won easily, but could never get beyond that distance ; though she won a little race at Brighton and was claimed, and I think never won after.

Crucifix, who was never beaten, was tried in September half a mile with *Seth*, a four-year-old animal (having fair speed and the winner of many races) at two stone and won easily. In fact, I was up myself, and think if I had carried another stone I should have won, as the mare did not show the least symptom of tiring; and it may be taken for granted that the pace was good, as my father rode the old one, and was second, the two others tailing off a very long way. *Crucifix*, the next and following year, won thirteen times, including the Two Thousand, One Thousand, and the Oaks; clearly showing, not only that a half-mile trial did her no harm, but, in the most indubitable way, that it gave conclusive evidence of her superiority, which a trial over a shorter course might have left in doubt—the latter a most unsatisfactory mode of procedure.

Formerly yearlings were not only tried, but run in public; and I remember winning the yearling race already mentioned as the first on record, in 1856, at Shrewsbury with a filly by *Neasham*, out of *The Maid of Saragossa*, beating six others. And *Schism*, as already named, the year following was only beaten a short head for a similar race, which she ought to have won with consummate ease, as her jockey lost more ground at starting than he could ever recover in so short a distance. A remarkable fact in this instance, and one worthy of record, is that she was a leggy, overgrown, half-furnished sort of mare, sixteen hands high at the time, and the least likely animal to run such a course that can possibly be imagined. Yet this race, in which she carried 7 st. 4 lbs., did not hurt her, as she ran successfully for many years afterwards.

Nevertheless, there are many professed judges who object to any trial at all until the horses are three years old; before

which age they would not have them run. Others, again,
think that two years old is the best age. Yet, I think,
after what has been shown here, that there can be no
valid objection to trial as yearlings, or to the adoption
of my principle ; which is :—Try early, and discard the
animals that are found wanting, keeping only those that
show actual merit, and those that, having breeding, soundness, and size to recommend them, give promise of improvement with age.

And so with the trial of the two-year-old : as the half-
mile is recommended for the yearling, I advocate a
longer distance for the older horse. If the two-year-old
that stays the half-mile, as I have said many can do but
no more, had after or before winning in public at that
distance been tried three-quarters of a mile, his non-staying
powers would have been discovered, and much useless
expenditure of money saved, by not engaging him in a
host of races beyond that distance, no one of which he would
have the ghost of a chance of winning.

Furthermore, if I wished to try a good two-year-old
early in the spring, I should ask him to beat a first-class
speedy three-year-old, five furlongs at two stone, and in
the autumn, three-quarters of a mile at sixteen or eighteen
pounds; and if the young one won, I should expect, and
most likely find, I had a good horse. I know *Lady Elizabeth* beat *Julius* ten pounds, and I also remember *Vulture*
gave *Grey Momus* two stone and beat him in a canter
in the autumn, and the next year he won the Two·
Thousand and other races. *One Act*, the week before
Sultan won the Cambridgeshire, could beat him that distance at twenty-two pounds, and most likely would have
done so six furlongs at eighteen pounds : and though

neither was first class, both could and did win good races. Indeed one of them was about as far from "the top of the tree" as the other, and so they answer the purpose of illustration as well as better horses.

I should also expect to see a good three-year-old beat the best four-year-old in May at sixteen or eighteen pounds, a mile, and a mile and a half at twenty or twenty-one pounds, and in the autumn at ten pounds. I think many horses are never better for courses up to and under two miles than as three-year-olds in October and November. *Dulcibella* and *Promised Land* were never so good after that age, though they were both very sound animals, and ran many times subsequently.

Having discussed the trial of the yearling, and of older horses, it may be well before entering into our next topic, to glance at private trials in contrast with public form; the latter, the great test of a horse's merit with the majority of the lovers of the turf.

The staunch attendant at race-meetings will on all occasions look for the winner in public form. He diligently searches his " Ruff's Guide," or " Racing Calendar," and from one or the other, it must be allowed, sometimes finds what he looks for. But the owner or trainer believes implicitly in private trials; and these, if properly and ably managed, are the safer guides. For in racing to obtain knowledge, you run with too many; whilst in trials, with only a few: and added to this, which I think is an advantage, in the latter you have the undoubted benefit of secrecy. Before running you can by trials, gauge collaterally the merits of horses that have run, whilst no one else has any knowledge of the merits of your own horses until they have appeared in public.

To show how often public running is incorrect, if not actually monstrous, I will comment upon certain examples ; but first, however, will state that I have seen very many instances of horses that have been well and properly tried, being backed on their first appearance in public, and winning.

Promised Land, at Goodwood, beat a horse that before had not been beaten, and the latter (*North Lincoln*) was most certainly, at the distance, the best horse of his year. This would seem a contradiction, were it not added that he was conceding five pounds (for previous victories) to his conqueror. *Lord of the Isles* did a similar thing, at the same place, by winning the Molecombe Stakes ; as did also *Banditto*, who after being beaten at Ascot, in his turn defeated *Europa*, who until that time, like *North Lincoln*, had been without an equal. I think that on this race there was more betting than I ever remember on any race of the kind before or since : the patrons of the Danebury stables relying on public form, on which *Europa* was a long way ahead of her opponents ; whilst we based our assumptions solely on private trials, which led us to believe the Ascot running was all wrong, and the form of our horse better than that publicly shown by *Europa*. The accuracy of our conclusion was proved to the very letter by the result.

Wild Dayrell may also be quoted in confirmation of the truth that trials, when carefully carried out, are the safest guides. For he won the first time he ran at Newmarket, and the following year he won the Derby.

To these could be added endless instances of the trustworthiness of home trials, verified by the performances of the same horses in their public races : but let those already given suffice ; and let us turn to the other side of the picture,

and show a few cases in which the best horses have been
beaten in their races after winning their trials.

At many places we have seen horses running with a great
reputation derived from home trials, easily beaten in public ;
yet afterwards reversing the result in the most decisive
manner: proving beyond all doubt that the race, and not
the trial was wrong — though no one detected or could
account for the error.

Cossack was beaten for the July Stakes ; and this was
undoubtedly a mistake, for he won the Derby afterwards.
Hermit was likewise beaten at Newmarket as a two-year-old,
and the following year he also won the Derby. In neither
of these cases could any one see where the error existed ;
the public believed the two-year-old races were right, whilst
the owners believed in the trials and knew the races were
a farce. It was abundantly proved, by their subsequent
running, that their trials were right and their races, when
beaten, were all wrong. So far therefore I think trials may
more safely be trusted than races.

Public form is often so contradictory that little reliance can
be placed on it ; for have we not seen horses win one day
and be beaten the next in the same company, without the
semblance of cause for the transposition of places ? I may
add that hundreds of instances might be found, if only the
finding would repay the trouble of the search. But a few
will be given to emphasize the untrustworthy character
of public running.

I have seen the same horses win easily one day that have
been beaten a long distance the next in the same company, at
the same respective weights, over the same course and with
the same jockeys up. Who is to account for these extraordinary performances ? Such races, like others before

mentioned, become the more perplexing the more they are studied ; and even to the *cognoscenti* are little better than enigmas.   It is not, I feel sure, possible that any one should give a satisfactory solution why the races so opposite in results ended as they did, or say which of the two results was the right one, or if both or neither were correct.

There are instances again when defeat of highly-tried horses may be accounted for ; as, for example, when *Nimrod* beat *Fisherman* and *Marionette* at Stockbridge in 1859.   The owner of *Fisherman* gave me £25 and paid *Nimrod's* stake (£10) to make running for him.   This the rider of *Marionette* also knew, and *Fisherman* and *Marionette* waited together so far behind that they never could get up and were easily defeated, both being about two stone better than the horse that was enabled to beat them through the circumstances described.   A singular case of this sort took place not many years ago at the same spot, when odds of fifty to one were actually laid on a horse which waited such a long way behind his stable companion, a mare, that he could never catch her, and so was defeated by a head.   These are mistakes occasioned by the want of foresight and common prudence on the part of the jockeys : and who knows how many other mistakes are made by them in a different way in large fields, that are not detected ?

I have elsewhere said that horses are not always well though they may appear to be in the most perfect health ; and others in their races meet with disappointments which if known at the time would account for much of their in-and-out running.   But surely there must be at the bottom of all this extraordinary and inconsistent running, some all-powerful cause (which, though unknown, is certain in its effect) that time may help to unravel for us.

The instances I have given are so numerous, and I trust
so much to the point, that I think nothing more will be
required to show that public running is not the infallible
guide that many hold it to be; but rather that owners of
horses and those having the opportunity to watch them
in private trials, have the better groundwork to rely upon.
But I cannot conclude all reference to the topic without
calling to mind the circumstances of the celebrated, or as
some may be inclined to call her, the notorious, *Lady Elizabeth*, and contrasting her running as a two- and as a three-
year-old ; performances in the one case so extremely good,
in the other so wonderfully bad. It may be well at the
same time to cite one or two other remarkable cases which
will supplement what I have already said in Chapter XII.
on the mysteries of in-and-out running.

As a two-year-old, *Lady Elizabeth* ran thirteen times
winning twelve races, her only defeat being by *Green Sleeves*,
when carrying ten pounds extra in the Middle Park Plate.
Undoubtedly her best performance was in a match T.Y.C.
against *Julius* at ten pounds difference (equal only to an
allowance of seven pounds if sex be considered) when she
won by a length ; her opponent having only just before
won the Cæsarewitch, a long course, which, as staying was
not, in my opinion, his forte, makes the victory the more
remarkable—for she met him at his own distance, which
was the T.Y.C. or at most a mile.

As a three-year-old she could beat nothing. She ran four
times, and was never even placed. Her first appearance in
public in that year was for the Derby, her starting-price in
the betting being seven to four. No sporting man is likely
ever to forget the sensation caused by her ignominious defeat.
Nothing like it had been known for years, or has been known

since. All kinds of sinister reports were circulated. She ·
had been poisoned; she had been pulled; she had been
trained to death. Nor were these all; for amongst innumerable insinuations then in circulation too base for repetition
here, it was pretty freely said that every man in the stable,
as well as every friend of those in it, had made a munificent fortune by rascality at the expense of the ever-
confiding and credulous British public; which had been
unblushingly and grossly victimised, and as usual left to
grumble and bear it.

But when we come to the facts of the case, we find that
nothing was ever put forward to show that the mare was
either improperly treated or neglected in any way. And I
think that we have a right to assume that there was no
ground for the complaints; but rather that credit should be
given to those in charge of her for assiduity in everything
that skill or experience could suggest for her well-being, and
that the whole mystery may be summed up in these few
words: no robbery took place, nor was one ever contem-
plated; the mare had simply lost her form—she was not so
good as a three- as she was as a two-year-old.

Nevertheless, although I myself and others whose veracity
cannot be doubted, may assert that she lost her form or her
temper, I am aware it is not easy to make incredulous people
see the matter in the same light. Therefore, for the benefit
of these unbelievers, I will add a word or two more. If any
one actuated by dishonest motives, or the inordinate love of
gain, took advantage of the opportunities to his hand in the
Derby, it is yet impossible for the boldest of these declaimers
of the sins of others to assert that any sordid motives could
influence the mare's running in subsequent races; and in
these it was equally bad. This fact should be of itself

sufficient, even if other proofs were not forthcoming, to silence those so ready to impute evil motives to others.

But what after all, it may be asked, was there so very different in *Lady Elizabeth's* running to that of hundreds of others of which nothing is heard afterwards? The reader who has done me the honour to follow me so far, will have read of instances as confounding, which have been adduced for the purpose of illustrating other points in connection with the racehorse. But a few more may be given.

Look at *Green Sleeves*, who as a two-year-old was the only animal that ever beat *Lady Elizabeth*. She was, if possible, worse than her opponent at three years old; and had she not been beaten for the One Thousand, would have had as good a right to favouritism for any race as *Lady Elizabeth* herself. *The Maid of Orleans* was another example of a mare that, excellent as a two-year-old, could beat nothing afterwards. Then for an instance of later running upsetting the earlier in an exactly opposite way, we have *Formosa*. At two years old she only won three races out of nine, being beaten by a mare (*Europa*) that had been beaten at Goodwood by *Banditto;* but as a three-year-old completely turned the tables on those that had beaten her before —winning the One Thousand, the Oaks, and the St. Leger, and running a dead heat for the Two Thousand. After such victories as a three-year-old, can her earlier performances be said to be a whit more explicable than the running of the other mares whose best form was their earliest form?

Take another case; that of *Macgregor*, who after winning the Two Thousand, started for the Derby at nine to four (as he had a right to start, if any horse be entitled to such a price). He was not placed, and so far as I recollect, never won afterwards. *Hester*, again, for whom even money was taken for the Oaks, was like *Macgregor* unplaced ; and she was a good mare as a two-year-old, and even at three won the One Thousand.

Lastly, there is *Gamos*. In 1869 this mare, then a two-year-old, wins six races out of the eight she runs for. In the following spring she is, at Bath, beaten so easily in the very worst of company, that her jockey has to pull her up, and she does not pass the winning-post. Yet in the next week, in the hands of the very same jockey, she wins the Oaks! Surely this case will be allowed to be the strangest of all I have mentioned ; yet it was but a day's wonder, whilst the cases of *Lady Elizabeth* and some others have been in the mouths of the racing-public for months. With such examples, one must think that racing with them, like kissing with others, must go by favour.

CHAPTER XVII.

JOCKEYS.

Difficulties in obtaining good jockeys—Necessity of reform of the light-weight scale—Evils of having boys in the saddle in short and in long courses—Audacity of the boys—Heavy jockeys wanted—Temptations in their path; lavish gifts to children—Results of extravagance—The simple remedy, to pay a fair wage—Value of an able and experienced jockey—Remuneration in days gone by; the Duke of Grafton's gift; my own experience; incident at Welbeck Abbey—The work of a jockey in the past and present contrasted; wasting in the old days; luxury *versus* deprivations.

THE difficulties of the trainer do not end when he has had the happy fortune to secure a good horse, and to bring him fit and well to the post; for then comes the all-important and difficult-to-be-answered question, "Who is to ride him?" In times gone by, in the days of Chifney and Robinson, there were men of talent in the profession who rode scientifically. To-day, with a few brilliant exceptions, the charge often heard that our jockeys are "a host of butcher-boys" is unfortunately not very far from the truth; for they are for the most part precocious lads who neither know their own business, nor will submit to be taught it by those who do. If you have weight to spare, you may chance to secure the services of an experienced jockey; but the chance is a very slender one, and more often you have to put up a useless boy, and bear as best you can the inevitable defeat.

Of all the reforms needed in turf matters, the revision of the light-weight scale is the most urgent. The necessity of this is not more keenly felt, or its adoption more earnestly desired by any, than by the older jockeys and by trainers. The result of the riding of the pigmies who are now put up, is but a series of mistakes from first to last, as owners must have learned to their cost.

At the start, boys (for I allude to them—the light-weights of the present day) are generally left at the post or get badly off, and ride their horses to a standstill before half the distance has been gone over, in the vain hope of regaining their lost ground. After the race the youngster has the audacity, with smiling face, to tell you he was first away to a very good start; at any rate he will never admit being further from the first horse than a length or two. It may well be asked how is the trainer or his employer, who has not himself witnessed the start, to know the merits of his own horse or of those of other people, when condemned to accept the statement of these urchins? What possible chance has your horse in a race, T.Y.C. or six furlongs, with twenty or thirty runners, in which the loss of a few lengths would seriously jeopardise your chance in the hands of an experienced jockey, if with a mere boy up, treble that distance be lost? The horse would in reality be very much better in his stable. These mishaps not only occur daily, but will never cease to do so, so long as boys are in the saddle.

It is unfortunately not much better in long distance races. It is true that in these the start is not so all-important. The lost ground may be made up, and your hopes momentarily raised at the prospect of success: yet before the lad's assistance is needed, it is apparent he is too tired to urge his horse to his utmost speed; he loses a race he ought to

M

have won, and you receive the heartfelt condolence of your friends on your bad luck. If, nettled at the result, you venture a remonstrance, the youth, with a confident audacity, will lay the blame upon the horse, and will add with supreme indifference, "If I had not minded what I was about, I should have gone the wrong side of a post or two, I was shut in and run against;" and will wind up by affirming with the utmost complacency, "I managed to keep him straight, and made a good effort to win at the proper time." If this be not the excuse, he will probably look you in the face and declare that your horse was not fit, and that beat him.

This is the result of trials and months of watchfulness at home. Your calculations are upset by the woful exhibitions of these pigmies when your horse, in primest condition, comes to run in public. And nothing that I can see will alter this lamentable state of things, until the scale of weights be raised, when the services of men may be secured in lieu of those of boys.

It must certainly be said for these unfortunates who ruin themselves in the destruction they thus deal broadcast on others, that they are but boys. A portion of the blame is their own; but another, and the greater part of it, falls to others. Lord Byron says :—

> " The youth who trains to ride or run a race,
> Must bear privations with unruffled face."

It would be well if this couplet were borne in mind by employers, friends, and backers; for often the lads, intoxicated with the success that in reality they have done so little to achieve, will, at the invitation of fortunate backers, drink champagne and smoke cigars, until the indulgence in these things becomes a confirmed habit. Then they forget themselves, and lose their position by leaving, with the joy almost of a manumitted slave, their masters, who often are their only real friends.

The lavish gifts to jockeys who are really no more than children is one of the gravest errors of the present day. We remember, as one early instance of this, how Captain Scott, looked up to and worshipped as a modern Crœsus, used freely to reward boys on the least success, whether that success resulted from merit or accident ; a misguided bounty as ruinous to the lads as it was to himself. Even grown men are not always proof against the fascinations of prosperity ; for we see instances, happily few I grant, of jockeys winning more than one Derby and other great races in almost unbroken succession, and thus rapidly amassing large fortunes, only to fall beneath the weight, consigning themselves through intemperance and negligence to wretchedness and to the poverty from which they had so lately emerged.

Gentlemen would do well to think twice before placing such temptations in the way of boys. If gifts be made to the deserving, let the money be given in proper keeping until the lads are old enough to appreciate the value of the present ; when it would be of service to them, and its donor remembered with gratitude.

"The world," it is said, "has not yet learned the riches of frugality." It is to be feared that movement in this respect is rather retrograde than progressive. I am bound to say, that in my opinion much of the misbehaviour of our light-weight jockeys has its rise in the extravagant presents made them by owners of winning horses—at least tenfold what they merit or indeed should receive. Latent presumption is thus turned to impudence, exhibited to any and to all who are not in a position, or, as a matter of principle, decline to pay on the same absurd scale.

"Then you will plainly understand that the next time I ride for you I shall know what to do." This, or a similar impertinence, rises at once to the lips of these tiny boys when addressing men who are not only their masters but old enough to be their grandfather.

But the remedy is simple, if it is not likely to be adopted. Pay them fairly but no more, and they would soon learn that "civility gains esteem." Indeed, for my part, I see no reason why even an old and valued jockey, much less a mere lad, should be paid so much in excess of his real deserts : he takes no trouble, has no anxiety, never probably having seen the animal he rides until a few minutes before the start, and in a few minutes afterwards, is presented with £1,000 or even double that amount for riding, be it ever so badly. Some may, and I know do say, that such sums are given to encourage acts of honesty; and that smaller payments would have a contrary effect at a subsequent period. Now the truth is, that whatever power a jockey may possess, or however brilliantly he may exercise it, so long as he receives the regulation fee, he is well and fairly paid for his services; and I should have little faith in the honesty of a jockey whose moral rectitude "stood on such slippery ground" as the expectation of gratuitous and in reality unearned money.

I think no right-minded or liberal man would for a moment object to pay for talent, real or supposed. As a matter of fact, most owners do so, by the salary given for a call for the services of this or the other jockey, sometimes even to boys ; but any payment beyond this is an act of generosity and should be so considered. But when a jockey rides in your trial and works himself night and day to reduce himself to the proper weight by wasting, and faithfully keeps your secrets, then a present, and a substantial one, would be but a well-deserved compliment, which it would be a meanness to withhold.

But I have already avowed my appreciation of the services of an able jockey.   It is to those who are better described as unformed riders than as jockeys, that I particularly refer.   To such boys the gift of a small sum might not only be welcome, but amply sufficient to foster honesty and frugality.   If this were to be the practice, we should see an end of the ruinous dissipation indulged in by these mites—the result of lavish gifts accepted without thanks.

If we turn to days gone by, we shall find things very different, and in their results very much more satisfactory.   When boys as jockeys were neither wanted nor known, men used to look upon a five-pound note for services well and truly performed as an acceptable present.   What would the jockeys of to-day think of a present offered to them like the following, and for similar services?   After winning the Two Thousand, the One Thousand, and the Newmarket Stakes for the Duke of Grafton, the jockey was requested to attend at the lodging of Lord G. Fitzroy (the duke's brother) who wished to make him a present.   His lordship, after descanting on the jockey's virtues as a man and his ability as a jockey, finished a diatribe of about half-an-hour's duration by taking from his writing-desk a purse, and saying, "In the duke's name, and for him, I present you with two new five-pound notes on the bank at Bury St. Edmunds, and beg you will take care of them."   This was rather a different method of appreciating or rewarding talent than is customary now, and yet they had honest jockeys, and good ones too, in those days.

Judging from my own experience, I do not think rich gifts were often presented then to jockeys or for some years after ;

for the first and only present I ever received, was £5 for
winning on *Bracelet* at Newmarket, although I rode the winner
of the Ascot Cup, and of very many other weight-for-age
races, and handicaps, on *Chapeau d'Espagne, Ratsbane, Airy,*
and others. But I should add that Mr. C. C. Greville very
generously gave me fifty pounds for riding *The Drummer* in
the trial with *Mango,* after the latter had won the St. Leger.

A present once made me for riding a trial deserves to be
mentioned, more for the nice manner in which it was given
than for the value of it. It was at Welbeck Abbey, where
with my father and Mr. Flatman I had gone to ride a trial for
the late Duke of Portland,[1] who requested all his servants to
attend in the park to see it, his grace being judge. When
everything was ready we started, all "sporting colours,"
as if it were for a race, and when over we partook of some
refreshment, during which time his grace sent a letter and
enclosed each of us a £5 note, whilst to me he said "he
was satisfied with the way I had ridden, and he hoped I
should make even a better man than my father."

If we come to compare the work done in old days by jockeys
with what is done to-day, we shall find as great extremes ; and
it may be added, parenthetically, in the work done by stable-
boys as well. It was once no uncommon sight at Newmarket
to see, daily, ten or a dozen wasting jockeys returning from an
eight-mile walk, thoroughly exhausted. Now such a thing is
scarcely known, and never done, except with a few of our
oldest men. Jockeys then were seen riding over Newmarket
·Heath, with a light saddle tied round their waist, in their
boots and breeches, and carrying their own saddles to the
scales, and saddling their own horses. Now most of them ride
in carriages to the course dressed as gentlemen in the very

---

[1] Written in 1878.

height of the fashion, and having their horses saddled for them
What would such jockeys think of riding from Exeter to
Stockbridge on a small pony with their light saddle tied round
their waist after the races, and arriving at the latter place in
time to ride there, and to start for Southampton races, the
next in order, in ample time to ride ?   Mr. Montgomery Dilly
and my father both did this when boys, for two consecutive
years.   Old Mr. Forth, as a boy, I am told, used to rise from
his bed and walk wasting during the night, in order to keep
himself light, besides doing his daily work.   And when my
father trained, he often wasted by walking on the Downs
during the time the horses were taking their exercise ; which
is much more tiring than walking on the road.   And yet
with all his riding and with 100 horses under his charge,
he had no one to wait on him, neither valet, amanuensis,
nor clerk. Similar cases might be given by scores ; but I
think enough has been said to show how great is the change
for the worse, not only as regards the physical capability,
but the inclination to exert themselves, in the jockeys of the
present day.

.

CHAPTER XVIII.

JOCKEYS (*continued*).

Examples of the diverse running of horses when ridden by boys and by men :
Fräulein, Valuer, Dulcamara, and *Noisy*—Disastrous results of putting up
boys—Recalcitrant jockeys—Declarations to win : instances of disobedience ;
at Shrewsbury ; *The Cur* and *Collingwood* and Mr. Rolt's retirement ; Mr.
J. B. Starkey's disappointment with *Viridis* and *Land Tax ;* the Duke of
Hamilton's better fortune with *Lollipop* and *Midlothian ;* copy of letter to
Sporting Gazette on the Wrekin Nursery at Shrewsbury, with suggestions.

I WILL now give a few instances of horses running with
boys on their backs, and compare the running of the same
animals with men in the saddle.

Fräulein, running at Goodwood in the Steward's Cup, with
six stone four pounds on her, was not placed ; but running afterwards for the Doncaster Cup, beat *Marie Stuart,* and won other
races at other places in the hands of men, showing about
three stone improvement. Again, we see at the same meeting
(Goodwood) that *Valuer,* running with six stone four pounds
on his back, was not one of the first twenty ; and yet he was
always better than *Historian* at even weights. He ran no better
at Newmarket with similar weights the same year, which was
some twenty-eight pounds worse than his real form—a fact that
was afterwards publicly proved by the many races he won
when carrying two stone more in much the same company.

Again, I think I make no mistake in attributing the
defeats for the Chester Cup of *Dulcamara* and *Noisy* (the two
best horses that, in my opinion, I ever tried) solely to the

incompetence of the boys that rode them. *Noisy* was beaten with five stone four pounds on him, and won the Dee Stakes with eight stone seven pounds in the hands of a man in the commonest of canters, and beating such horses as *Lord Alfred, Lady Tatton, Corœbus*, and other good ones at even weights the same week.

I think it is clear that such riders can only enrich the bookmaker, who has the chapter of accidents in his favour; and that to their employer, who is obliged to stand or fall by the solitary object of his choice, these performances mean nothing but ruin to all but millionaires.

There is another difficulty with jockeys in our day which has yet to be described. We have seen that the urchins put up to ride have not always the power to do as they should, even when they have the desire. But there are other cases in which riders can and ought to do their duty, but when, by the wilful disobedience of the legitimate instructions of their employers, they render racing no longer a science, but a game of chance on a par with hazard, and make the opinion of the tyro equal to that of the sage. Happily such cases are few; but that they do occur with both boys and men, there is evidence as ample as there is certainty that, with the latter at least, such a thing should never be.

I allude to races in which "a declaration to win" has been made.

If an owner runs two horses in a race, he has a right to declare with which of the two he will win; that is, supposing that the one he selects can beat all the other horses in the race except his stable companion. On such occasions, we sometimes see the jockey who is riding the other horse come and win, when the animal concerning which the declaration has been made is second, in open defiance of positive

instructions, and possibly to the ruin of his employer. Such
a case happened at Shrewsbury in 1871, and produced some
spirited letter-writing : Admiral Rous taking one, and in my
opinion, the wrong side; whilst Mr. Chaplin, with his usual
acumen, ably advocated the right.

I will now name one or two other cases ; not, be it understood, that they are the only ones I could put my hand upon,
but because they will suffice to show that the instances are in
themselves too frequent, and something of the immense injury
that such occurrences may produce. The first I remember
seeing was with Mr. Rolt's two horses, *Collingwood* and *The
Cur*, at Goodwood in 1847. He declared to win with *Collingwood*, but George Whitehouse beat him on *The Cur* by a
length, and nothing else near. The incident caused, as one
might expect, a great deal of excitement and much angry
feeling at the time, and led to an investigation on the subject.
The jockey's explanation, that he mistook the colours of the
rider of *Collingwood*, was accepted, and so the matter ended.
Mr. Rolt lost large sums by the result, and to this may be
attributed his retirement from the turf, which took place soon
after. Mr. J. B. Starkey had a similar case happen to him with
Viridis and *Land Tax*. The latter was backed for many and
heavy sums, whilst no one had backed the other for a guinea.
The owner made the usual declaration to win with *Land Tax*,
who beat all the rest in the field but his stable companion, the
latter winning easily. This fatal action of the jockey's not only
caused Mr. Starkey's secession from the turf, but, it is to be
feared, brought about the ruin of an honourable and estimable
man ; for he went abroad, where he died a few years after.

In contrast to such fatal performances, it must have been
truly gratifying to his Grace the Duke of Hamilton to win as
he did, his orders being obeyed to the very letter in the hands

of a jockey who not only knew his business but did it, when on *Lollipop* he allowed *Midlothian* to win, though the latter might have been beaten as easily as the selected horse was beaten in either of the disastrous instances named.

I shall conclude my remarks on this subject by giving *in extenso* a letter of my own written in 1871, which I trust may be thought to deal in some measure with so serious a matter.

To the EDITOR *of the* SPORTING GAZETTE.

SIR,—To the many remarks the extraordinary running for the Wrekin Nursery has called forth, may I be allowed to add a few, which I trust will be found pertinent? An owner of horses has so many difficulties to contend with, that few men can tell where they commence, and none where they may end. Suffice it for me to draw attention to a few adverse circumstances that may happen to any owner. Even with the start, or rather I should say no start, or at the least a bad one, your hopes may be frustrated. Your jockey may come in short of weight, he may carry too much without declaring it, or be too late in doing so ; he may go the wrong course, the wrong side of a post, or, in racing phraseology, he may " come too soon " or " too late," and so lose the race he ought to have won. These, though casualties none can foresee or prevent, are, nevertheless, very annoying when they occur, and enough to deter many from racing that would otherwise do so. But when jockeys wilfully disregard their legitimate orders, then no censure can be too severe, and correction should in every case be administered at once ; for, if not openly condemned, it would tacitly be offering a premium for insubordination and dishonesty. There is generally some sinister motive for acts of disobedience on the part of refractory jockeys—I do not say it is so with all, but with many—which requires strong repressive measures to prevent its repetition.

Such races as the " Wrekin " happily are not of frequent occurrence. Still, we hear of them too often. Look at the race with Mr. Wreford's two, many years ago, at Stockbridge ;

then we have *The Cur* and *Collingwood* at Goodwood ; and of later date, *Viridis* and *Land Tax* at Stockbridge. But why multiply instances? Enough, I think, has been shown of such disgraceful exhibitions to induce the authorities to take the matter in hand, and make a rule more stringent ; so that in future, if any owner runs two horses in a race, and declares to win with one, should the other come in first (provided they are first and second), he should be placed as the last horse in the race, and the stakes and bets be awarded to the second, or "declared" winner, and so render to the owner that which he is justly entitled to, and will always expect, at the hands of an impartial and all-powerful tribunal—his rights. The offending jockey should in every case be heavily fined and suspended.

This modification, I think, would meet the exigencies of the case better than by doing away altogether with the custom as it now stands. It would be a great injustice to owners who may have two or more horses in a race if they are not allowed the privilege of declaring to win as heretofore ; for the best horse may be *hors de combat* from a variety of untoward circumstances, and if fortunate enough to win with his worst, it would afford him a little consolation for the disappointment with the other. Moreover, it would help the entries and strengthen the fields, and so in both and other ways act beneficially on racing in general.

Yours obediently,
AN OWNER.

With these observations on declarations to win, the consideration of the performances in the saddle of to-day may fitly terminate in this place ; although when we come to discuss weights, and, later, to offer suggestions for remedies of current practices, the evils of the prevalence of light-weight riders will again come before us. These two chapters, it is trusted, may suffice to show how desirable it is, before sending your horses to the post, to have secured the services, if it has been practicable to do so, of an able and upright jockey.

CHAPTER XIX.

THE RACE AND ITS RESPONSIBILITIES.

The different race-courses; effect of their shape and slope. Mr. Copperthwaite on
the Derby Course; incorrectness of his deductions—Fitness of the horse the
sole essential—Examples from the Epsom and Ascot courses, and inferences—
Running in wet and dry weather; effect of deep ground; instances: *Joe
Miller*, *Speed the Plough*, and *Oxonian*—Racehorses across country: *Emblem*
and *Emblematic*; *Joco* a failure—Ownership—Erroneous popular view of the
duty of owners to the public; Admiral Rous's evidence on scratching, &c.
before the House of Commons; fallacy of the view exposed—Conflicting
public judgment of horses and its fallibility; instances: *The Hero* falls lame
and wins after, *Bird on the Wing's* illness, *Hermit's* reported accident—The
real reason why horses are not seen oftener at the post; "forestalling"—
Owners and their friends; value of secrecy; how secrets are revealed and
fatal results; exposure of letters—Eminent racing tacticians and their errors:
Admiral Rous and *Weathergage*; Mr. C. C. Greville's career; anecdote of
the latter; ultra self-confidence the reason of only partial success—Registered names and their publicity; current evils of the custom and suggested
remedy—The anonymous letter-writer; instance of his malpractices at
Whitewall.

ALTHOUGH it is not my intention to describe the race itself,
an event which has been graphically delineated by many pens,
there are some points worthy to be noted by owners and trainers,
even when the horse on which all hopes are centred is fit to
run, and the services of a good jockey have been retained.

A thing of great importance, but one which is often overlooked or too lightly considered, is the state of the ground,

wet or dry, and how differently horses are affected by running over it in its different states ; and yet another thing not to be omitted from the calculation, the superiority of one horse to another over different race-courses of the same length.   With regard to the latter, the shape ought not to be totally ignored : whether it have sharp angles or be straight, whether the ascent be steep or gradual, or the gradient of decline be little or much, or whether it be wholly a flat course.   By carefully considering these things, advantages may be gained that would not appear to a superficial observer.·

When speaking of the external conformation of the horse, how often do we hear that he has a back that will carry him up the hill, but that his shoulders will never allow him to come down it ?   Without defining the reason, which I think is very obscure, we know, as a matter of fact, that some horses do run better over one course than another even of the same length. One animal may have pluck and stamina enabling him to run over a severe course, whilst another may lack both, and yet be better over an easy one than the former.   And this will happen though both may be trained alike, and there be nothing to indicate from external appearance why one can stay and the other cannot, or why the one should show to better advantage over one course than another.

It would seem to be Mr. Copperthwaite's opinion that train-ing has something to do with this matter ; although it should be said that his observations on the point bear as much or more on the subject of severe training—a subject on which, it has been already shown, I think he is mistaken.   Therefore, before giving instances of the different running of horses over different courses, I shall briefly notice his remarks.   "No doubt," he says, " the Derby course is about the most severe and trying in England."   Here I disagree with him, for I think it is one of the easiest, or one which circumstances often render so.   In proof of this I may say, that generally the horses only canter up the hill, which is a fact shown by their being all together at the top, and then they run at a good pace the last three-quarters of a mile down hill.   " The consequence is," he further adds, " that more valuable horses are broken down from this cause when training for this race than from many of the others put together.   Such a horse will never stand a Derby preparation.   Why?   Because he is frequently galloped to death and broken down."   Such reasoning to my mind is diametrically opposed to common sense.   For it appears to me that to say a horse is fit to run over one course a given distance, and not over the same distance on another, is little less than sheer nonsense.   It is just as absurd to allege that it takes more or less work and requires it differently administered for preparation to run over opposite courses of the same length as we find them here in England.   Horses cannot but be fit, as I have elsewhere demonstrated, and when fit to run one course must be fit to run any other, provided only it be the same length.

But to return to more directly consider how horses are differently affected by running on different courses, I may say that probably the two most dissimilar courses in England are Ascot and Epsom, over the last three-quarters of a mile.   The one is all up hill, and the other all down.   *Conspiracy* may fairly be said to run at least sixteen pounds better over Epsom, than any other course.   Of this we have public proof, whilst other horses do the same at Ascot.   *Sir Charles* won the Royal Hunt Cup there very easily, owing to his preference for the course, for he never won before or after, though he often tried elsewhere ; and by a strange oversight he never ran there again.   He left me shortly after the victory because the owner did not win money enough on him, and I was not therefore the cause of his subsequent mismanagement.

These instances have a lesson of their own. There is evidently a something in particular race-courses that alters the running of some horses; and what that something is, it is incumbent on the trainer to ascertain, if he can do so, before engaging them. There are certain methods which readily suggest themselves. Horses could be tried up hill with stayers, or down hill with speedy animals; or might be galloped across the flat at Newmarket or the reverse way of it: whilst on other courses, similar opportunities might be found, which would give some clue to the probable performances of the animal on this or the other race-course.

As for the state of the ground itself, this is not less important: for it has often more to do with the success or defeat of racehorses than many suspect or would be inclined to believe. Some horses cannot run on wet ground; others, when it is hard; some again can go well on either: whilst others are best when it is neither wet nor dry, but simply what is called "good going," though as a rule it should be said the majority are most at home when it is either one thing or the other.

Joe Miller could run when it was hard or soft, and of this power he gave two remarkable instances by winning the Chester Cup with the ground as hard as a brick, and the Ascot Cup (Emperor's Vase) when the course was partially submerged, as has been related; he also ran equally well when the ground was really good going. *Speed the Plough,* a very moderate horse, won the Criterion Stakes, beating the best horse in the world, when the ground was very heavy going. It should be noted that wet ground tells most hardly against the horse least trained. *Oxonian,* though very sound, was ten pounds better on wet than on dry ground; which may account for his many defeats on hard ground when success seemed certain.

It is very likely, indeed, that the truly wonderful improvement some horses make running across country over their previous performances on the flat, may in a great measure be assigned to the state of the ground; the summer racing being mostly over dry ground, and the winter or steeple-chasing over wet. *Emblem* and *Emblematic* were not good enough to keep in training over flat courses, and were certainly non-stayers when thus run; yet, four miles over the heaviest ground in the kingdom they were winners of the Grand National Steeple-chase at Liverpool, though at the time they ran, respectively, neither looked strong enough to carry a saddle over such a course, let alone the rider. However they did, and beat the bulk of the finest, and strongest, and best horses of the day. Indeed we have direct proof that many of the speediest horses on the flat, which in racing could not stay a mile, some of them not half the distance, have stayed in steeple-chases, getting well over their four miles across country. It is surprising to see these little weeds with heavy weights on them, beating all the best weight-carrying horses that can be found, under circumstances seemingly so favourable to the latter—literally running through mud.

Again, we see thorough-bred horses that stay well on the flat, and seem the most likely to make good steeple-chasers, turn out the very worst. *Joco*, the slowest and very gamest horse I think I ever trained, winner of the Metropolitan and other races over long courses and dry ground, and strong enough to carry twenty stone to hounds, was the worst across country. He was sold to Mr. Heathcote for a steeple-chaser; but was found whilst schooling so inactive and lost so much

N

ground at his fences, that he was not fast enough for a hunter;
and was sold again in consequence.   This Mr. Heathcote
told me himself.   One would have thought of all horses this
would have been the best to have carried a heavy weight
through deep ground a long course ; but it was just the reverse—a good hunter could beat him, and I have no doubt
many of Mr. Heathcote's did, or he would not have parted
with him.   From all that has been said, I think it is a duty
to look well to the state of the ground and the shape and
features of the race-course ; and before parting with any horses,
to give them a chance over different courses and different
lengths, as well when the ground is wet and sticky, as
when it is dry and hard.   To do so, at least, will be to have
done all that is requisite to deserve the success that fickle
Fortune so often denies her votaries.

Another consideration is the relation of owners and trainers
to other than their stable and immediate friends.   " The duty
of owners to the public " is a phrase in every mouth ; and it
will be not irrelevant to this portion of our subject to inquire
as to what this duty consists in, and contrast the reality with
the inordinate conception of the responsibility so widely held.

"I will be master of what is my own," is a principle that
the masses, if they had their way, would not permit to be held
by gentlemen who spend large sums of money frequently more
for the pleasure of the multitude than for their own.

For my own part, I believe that the owner of a stud has,
in common fairness, just as much right to do what he likes
with each and every one of his racehorses, as he has to deal
with his hack or his hunter, his flocks or herds, so long as he
violates no principle of honesty ; and that if he cannot protect
himself in any other way against those who forestall him, he
is justified in defeating their ends by not running.   The great

bone of contention between those who keep racehorses and
the public, is and always has been that of a spurious
ownership ; the public erroneously thinking that every horse
brought out to run, nay, from the moment of his appearance
among the list of entries, becomes, and for ever remains, virtually the property of the British public, and that he should
be run to suit their pleasure and for their own peculiar
advantage.   I need scarcely remark that I differ with this
presumptive dictum, agreeing with owners in thinking that
as long as they " pay the piper," they have a right to " call
the tune," and if forestalled in one race, may run for another.

Nevertheless such a belief prevails, and hence a perpetual
warfare is waged by the two contending parties, to the injury
and annoyance of both.   That the public are wrong in thus
interfering with and appropriating other people's property
is, I think, pretty clearly shown in this matter of forestalling.
It is a usurpation of authority which owners resent, and are
compelled in self-defence to meet, by the exercise of their
undoubted right to scratch their horses.

But let us hear as to ownership what the late Admiral
(when Captain) Rous says in reply to certain questions put to
him on the subject of betting.

These questions epitomized would run somewhat as follows :

" Have the public a right to complain when owners do not
run their horses as they (the public) expect, and they lose
their money ? "

" Should a person have backed a horse that in his opinion
has in some way or other been prevented winning, has the
person a claim, under such circumstances, to recover his
money ? "

Again : " Supposing this horse could have won, had his
backer such a right ? "

To the second of these questions, the gallant Captain replies:—

"Not in this instance. In the first place, if you choose to back another man's horse, you do so at your own risk. I have hardly ever known an instance of gentlemen losing their money on the turf, especially those not much on the turf, when they do not conceive that they have lost their money rather from roguery of others than from their own stupidity; they had always much sooner make out the rest of the world to be rogues than that they themselves were fools."

To question number three his answer is:—

"He might have reason to complain, yet I would afford him no redress, for he has no right to bet on that particular horse; no man can say that another's horse can win. He may imagine such a horse can win, but I defy any man to say certainly, such a horse could win and such a horse could not win. Some people think that racing is reduced to a great nicety; they imagine that horses always run the same, and they can calculate to a nicety what horse can win; but I never met a man yet who was able to judge of the transaction; and not only that, but the more persons are conversant with horses, the more they will know of the uncertainty of racing. I have tried one horse one week, and he has been beaten a quarter of a mile; and then perhaps two weeks after, in consequence of having a couple of sweats, he has won a second trial on the same racing terms."

To prove the absurdity of any one being able to say any horse could win that had not done so, he goes on to say:—

"Yes, even for the jockey. I have often made matches on the representation of the jockey, that if he had not done so and so he could have won, and in nineteen out of twenty cases I have found the jockey wrong; any man who follows the advice of his jockey is sure to be ruined."

These extracts are taken from a book called " The History of the Horse," and the evidence was given before a Committee of the House of Commons on gaming, 1844.   In the same work there is the evidence of other gentlemen on the same subject which is hardly worth repeating here, as I think the Captain's is sufficient for the purpose; for as it is an expressed opinion clearly and unmistakably in favour of a man doing as he likes with his own horses, no argument worth hearing is left in favour of a contrary idea.   Indeed I think I may go so far as to say, a man could not, in doing what he likes with his own horse, do an act of injustice to another ; though many non-owners are continually declaring themselves aggrieved, whilst in truth no one has a share in their wrong but themselves.

But it is not only the act of scratching that is found so much fault with; but also the condition of horses that run, both before and after any race on which there has been much speculation.   One party is found affirming the animal is the pink of condition, whilst others loudly assert he is not fit to run for a saddle at a country fair : and after the result, be it what it may, from one party or another, the poor owner comes in for a round of abuse, as though he were the veriest rogue in creation.   "If a favourite," they argue, " does not run, he dies from the effect of 'milk fever,' or succumbs after much vitality to metallic influence after the last guinea has been got out of him."

Now there may not only be no word of truth in any of these statements, but most certainly those who so glibly make them have not a scintilla of knowledge to guide them.   They judge from appearances, and must of necessity condemn in error.   " After So-and-so " (one of the first horses introduced into the betting) "had met with an accident he was, to the owner's praise, honourably struck out," argues one. But another says, and with possibly greater propriety: "If he had been left in, he would have run and won, as his lameness was not of a serious nature; and why was he struck out and not left in on the chance of his recovery?" Thus you may strike out early with the most honest intention, or leave in to the last moment actuated by the same laudable principles, and circumstances over which you may have no control, render either or both right or wrong, and you are blamed for breaking faith with the public in either event.

If I take a case or two in point it will most clearly illustrate the fallibility of public opinion, and the unreasonableness of expecting horses to run when the public think they should, in ignorance whether they are lame or otherwise unfit to do so. The first case I shall allude to will show the impropriety of deciding too hastily, and how desirable it sometimes is to hope against hope, and not strike out until the last minute.

The Hero, after being backed for the Goodwood Cup down to a very short price, one day after galloping pulled up lame. Off went the touts, running or riding to the telegraph office, and wired to their employers the startling information, probably in their own emphatic and terse language: "He's a dead 'un, get every guinea." The horse did not make his appearance, either from necessity or stratagem, for a day or two; and then was, as they say, "restricted to walking exercise," and was looked on as virtually out of the race. After being driven to long odds he was reinstated in the market, "of course only for hedging purposes," argued they. Great dissatisfaction was expressed on all sides. It was affirmed that all chances of his winning were hopeless from the very time of his accident, and that he should then have been struck out in an honourable and straightforward manner. But the owner thought otherwise and left him in, and he won.

Now suppose for a moment the horse had been struck out, and being engaged in other races at the same meeting, had won one of them. It would have been said immediately, a more outrageous and infamous robbery had never been more ingeniously concocted or carried out with effrontery so unblushing ; that he had been backed by the public for thousands upon thousands at all sorts of prices, and that the stable, having got the last guinea out of him, had made him go lame and had struck him out, knowing he was as well as any horse could be. His subsequent running would have been pointed to as proof, with the positive assertion that he could have won the Cup just as easily, had he been sent for it. It would have been added that horses often pull up lame from leg-weariness which soon passes off, and that this had been the real cause of his apparent break-down ; and the whole would have wound up with the triumphant and significant remark, " That the man in the street knew that it was so, and that the secret of his having been so suddenly struck out must ever remain a secret to all save those engaged in this profitable but dishonest transaction." And what was it all ?   Simply a clear case of leaving the horse in though he had lamed himself, on learning which the public, forming their own wise conclusions, clamoured to have him struck out.

Again, I give an instance of a like nature. Exactly ten days before *Bird-on-the-wing* had to run at Doncaster, her owner came to see her, and at five o'clock in the evening (stable time) she was taken ill, apparently in excruciating pain; but at the very time, our veterinary surgeon, Mr. Snow, passing quite accidentally, was called in to see her. He said she was suffering from acute inflammation of the lungs and was dangerously ill, and prescribed, besides medicines for internal administration, blisters for both her sides, and bleeding, as well as a sheepskin over her loins, and gave orders that she was not to leave the box for a fortnight. Now had this been known "outside the stable" what would have been the result? Why, an outburst of indignation because she was not immediately struck out; and the affirmation that if anything could have induced an owner to strike out early, this was the case in which to have done so. But "whilst there is life there is hope," and here hope was realised beyond expectation. I had my suspicions that the mare was suffering from colic, and not from inflammation; so the bleeding and blistering were delayed and only the sheepskin used, and a little turpentine given internally, which had the desired effect, the recovery being as sudden as the attack—as is often the case in spasmodic affections. The day after, the sheepskin was taken off, and she took gentle exercise, and afterwards resumed work, notwithstanding the injunction that she was not to leave the stable for a fortnight. She ran at Doncaster, beating *Sally* and others in the Park Hill Stakes, making the whole of the running; and the same day, decided the Doncaster Stakes, without running for it, with Lord Derby's *Longbow*.

Now had the mare had a relapse near the time, and so could not have run, the whole thing would have been denounced as a swindle. The charge would have been strengthened by the opinion of the veterinary surgeon, that of an able man, and one that doubtless the circumstances within his knowledge justified him in forming; and once more it would have been placidly concluded that she had been left in for the purpose of obtaining money from the public.

There is no more remarkable case than that of *Hermit*, in 1867, and one which will be in the memory of most of my readers. On this occasion it was implicitly and almost universally believed that a catastrophe had befallen him. A few days before Bath races (the week fatal to many a Derby favourite), the canards so industriously circulated as to the real cause of the deadly opposition he had met with, were to the effect : that he had broken down, had broken a blood-vessel in his head, and I know not what; but that, to a certainty, he was *hors de combat,* and on the eventful Derby day would be an absentee, as his forlorn price of 100 to one clearly fore-shadowed. The astute believers in this state of things wanted to know what was the good of keeping the horse puppet-like dangling before the eyes of an enlightened public after the last guinea had been got, and there was no chance of resus-citating him, and added that now, if only for appearance sake, he should be struck out. But Mr. Chaplin (the owner), that straightforward gentleman and fearless sportsman, ever as anxious to please and serve his friends as himself, thought and did otherwise, and decided to run the horse that all might see how false the rumours were. He ran and won.

Instances like these could be multiplied *ad infinitum.* But they are enough. They show clearly the incisiveness of the gallant Admiral's remark already quoted : "Losers would always much sooner make out the rest of the world to be rogues than themselves fools." Racing men are as anxious to run their horses as ever the public are to see them run; and for the best of all possible reasons, namely—it does not pay to keep entering them without doing so. The cause of so many absentees is, not dislike on the part of the owners to bring their horses out, but the action of the public who prevent the owner obtaining a reasonable price ; for he, under such circum-stances, prefers scratching to running his horse to his own injury. The public complain, but the remedy is in their hands and in their hands only. Let them follow and not take precedence of owners, and we should then see larger fields at the post, and the pleasure and profit of all enriched by this forbearance.

These, then, are the relations between the owners and the public as they are, and as they should be.   Let us now turn to see how the former stand towards the many who claim, often, with little reason so far as action or motive is concerned, the title of friends — friends who are so ready to dictate what should be done with the horses, without reference to the trainer's judgment or expressed opinion.

" Secrecy is the soul of all great affairs," so says the adage ; and there is no business, trade, or profession of any sort, that so strictly requires reticence as racing does.   But unfortunately the gentlemen that commence racing are generally young and inexperienced ; whilst those of riper years are acquainted with the habits of their old and business-like friends, and assume that the same caution characterises their young and thoughtless acquaintances.   Secrets ooze out in many ways, and often by means least suspected.   Thus it happens that all connected with the horse may be wrongly and ungenerously blamed, when the owner of the animal has himself inadvertently supplied the information.   He has in strict confidence revealed the matter to a friend, and no sooner is this done, than it is. repeated to another—in the same strict confidence it may be, yet equally to the annoyance and injury of all concerned.

The late Lord George Bentinck used to say, " If you really want anything thoroughly well known, write it to a friend in strictest confidence and its proclamation will be complete." So it is with racing.   Plans are laid with the greatest care and secrecy, only to be upset.   They are disclosed as a great secret and retold in the same manner, and so become the property of hundreds, although through the process the confidants have been restricted to sincere and trusted friends.

The same thing often occurs through the thoughtless exposure of letters. They are left lying about, and the best arranged schemes are defeated through the advantage the unscrupulous will take of the habit. To prevent such a thing letters should be carefully locked in some place of safety, if not destroyed as soon as read ; or better still, whenever possible, really important business between owner and trainer should be transacted verbally—a plan I certainly recommend to all who would not have their schemes nipped in the bud, as unfortunately too many are nowadays. Sufficient attention is not, as a rule, paid to little matters, the neglect of which not only causes disaster, but brings censure on innocent persons.

But if this source of disappointment be mostly attributable to the action of the novice on the turf, to the older and experienced sportsman some share of blame attaches in other things. Polonius tells us :

> " It seems it is as proper to our age
> To cast beyond ourselves in our opinions,
> As it is common for the younger sort
> To lack discretion."

If it be true that his wisdom is the wisdom of old age, what he would teach us here finds confirmation in racing matters. For we see, from some cause or other, that the most eminent men on the turf, full of experience and practical knowledge in all matters relating to turf lore, are patently not the most successful.

In excelling wisdom, among turfites, I should think stood foremost the late Admiral Rous and Mr. C. C. Greville, a gentleman of unbounded experience, honour, and ability. Yet we find these astute judges not reaping the advantages of their talent and position so fully as one would expect.

Though the Admiral never kept a large string of his own,

yet he managed for the Duke of Bedford who had a fair-sized one. Also, as is well known, he made all the principal handicaps, or the most of them, for a number of years, without winning any of note that I remember. Yet he did not lack the materials for achieving success, having, besides many others, two such good horses as *Asteroid* and *Weather-gage.* The latter, after leaving the hands of this consummate master of weights, in spite of him, won the Goodwood and Cæsarewitch Stakes, besides other good races ; although but a few months before, under the guiding hand of the Admiral, he could not win a Selling Plate at Northampton and was, on his return to Newmarket, disposed of privately for £40.

Mr. Greville, considering all things, may be said to have been equally unfortunate ; for he not only kept a large string himself, but was confederate with the then Duke of Portland, and was also consulted on the management, if he had not the absolute control, of one of the largest establishments in England. Yet withal, he failed to carry off many of our best trophies. It is true he won the St. Leger with *Mango,* and among other of his victories may be mentioned the Goodwood Stakes, over which I believe he did little or no good, and the Cæsarewitch Stakes, which may be said to have been, at one and the same time, his greatest *coup* and the most gigantic mistake.

On this memorable occasion he unwisely intrusted his commission to one Perkins, a man of straw (as many commissioners are) who, after receiving the money, as might have been suspected, decamped with the whole of it without paying a shilling of the losses, which had to be paid afterwards. This affair Mr. Greville took so much to heart that nothing could drive it from his memory ; and one day, whilst looking over the Admiral's stud, in reply to a question thrice repeated, " What do you think of the colt?" gazing intensely on him, he suddenly exclaimed, "Who! what, Perkins?"—an incident that caused much laughter among the assembled guests, in which the chief actor did not join. Indeed, I do not ever remember his taking part in any hilarities.

Nevertheless, Mr. Greville was deservedly much liked by all classes of racing men, as also was the Admiral. But I think that he, like the latter, placed too much reliance on his own unaided efforts, and thought about as lightly of the trainer's opinion as the Admiral did of that of his jockey—of whom he used to say if he had followed his advice, he would have been ruined over and over again. It is quite certain from the Admiral's own account, that he ignored the advice of his jockey, and as he generally made his matches impromptu, his ill-success could not fairly be attributed to the faults of either the jockey or the trainer. I may add, that, so far as I may be permitted to judge, I am of opinion that this self-confidence is prevalent with far too many gentlemen in the present day; and with the same probably unlooked-for and yet inevitable result—the loss of money and the severance of friends.

In respect to the question of secrecy, some as we know prefer to race in assumed names; but I think that very few who do so can thus hide their identity. The late Mr. Graham, who changed his registered name perhaps oftener than any other person, was as well known by the last as the first, a few days after registration. But my impression is that the object of registering a name was not so much to hide the identity of an individual. I believe the practice originated chiefly from a desire to prevent the recurrence of such a thing as that one man should run the whole of the five horses that started in a race in five different names. It was thought that registration would cause the ownership of each horse to be defined when

necessary. The attempt was a praiseworthy one ; but I fear
it is powerless to grapple with the evil it would crush, that a
plurality of names is as easily used to-day as it ever was.   It
may be done in either one of two ways : A gentleman intro-
duces five different persons to as many different trainers with
a request that they will in each case take a horse or two to
train and to be run in the trainer's name.   I think the request
would be acceded to, and then it would not be possible to tell
either when the particular horses did run, or anything about
their real ownership.   In the second case, a man registers for
five different persons five different names, or they do it indi-
vidually at his request, and yet the horses running under these
names may all belong to the one man, with little or no fear of
detection.

Now that which should be done by people unwilling to run
a horse in their own name, is to find a friend in whose name
they can do so without the fact gaining publicity.   Or, if they
have no such friend, they should, rather than register an
assumed name, which so many of necessity are cognizant of,
let him run in the name of his trainer, who has an interest at
stake to keep his secret.   I do not say that this is done, but
it seems to me the best, if not the only way, for those to race
who do not wish others to know they do so ; whilst it is prudent
in addition to train in a quiet spot unmolested by touts.

There is but one thing more that occurs to me as necessary
to advert to concerning the responsibilities of owners in
regard to the race itself.   It is a subject I would willingly
leave untouched, were it not an evil, to my knowledge, of unsuspected gravity.   I refer to the anonymous letter-writer, the
cowardly assassin who stabs in the dark, fearing to face an
open foe.

It is true these men only work mischief when they play

upon the credulous or timid; but unfortunately there are those amongst honourable gentlemen who are imposed upon by false-hoods, concocted for the benefit of the writer, under the guise of friendship for the receiver. Personally, I have known, as the result of an anonymous letter, a whole stud of horses re-moved from Whitewall to Danebury in the time of the late Mr. Scott; and it is impossible to say how many others have been thus removed, or jockeys injured,[1] by the same cowardly and shameless means.

If no contempt is too great, as no punishment would be too severe for these cowards, yet blame for the subsequent action cannot be entirely removed from the shoulders of the one who heeds these communications. For if the receiver be of a credulous or suspicious nature, he communicates his doubts and fears to a friend, who in like manner tells his particular friends, and so amongst them it reaches the ears of those who have originated the scandal (for these men seldom work with-out accomplices), whose object is thus accomplished, for the rumour is easily and irresponsibly set afloat. In the case I have mentioned at foot, there is no doubt that the writer and his lordship's confidential servant were confederates; and that

---

[1] The incident in point was the following:—An anonymous writer informed a certain noble marquess, "that if his jockey rode a certain horse for him at Ascot, he would not win; of which fact he had indubitable proofs." It is needless to say that had he been called upon to produce them, they, as well as the writer, would have been *non est*. What did the nobleman do on receiving this startling piece of information? Did he, as he ought to have done, in justice to his jockey, and in vindication of his own action, see his jockey, and telling him of it, ask for an explanation, and then consult his trainer as to the expediency of changing or retaining his jockey? He did nothing of the sort; but he consulted his con-fidential friend in racing matters, his house-steward, who recommended a change. It was done, and the horse won; and shortly after, and from the same cause, the horses were all removed to Danebury. And all this was done at the instance of two intriguing and unscrupulous cowards, taking advantage of the credulity of old age.

the result of their connivance was the removal of the horses, the cause of which was probably unknown to Mr. Scott to the day of his death. It was not until some time after, that I learned from undoubted authority what had taken place, and the object sought in bringing about the change.

But the subject is a distasteful one, and enough has already been said to show that there is but one proper method in which to treat such communications, and that is, to put them, unread, behind the fire.

CHAPTER XX.

WEIGHTS AND DISTANCES.

Evils of the light-weight scale—Weight-carrying hunters and their performances ; instances—Successes of racehorses with heavy weights: *Rataplan, Fisherman, Chandos, Vespasian*—Admiral Rous's opinion and its contrariety—The trainer's view of it—Table of light- and heavy-weight handicaps and the lesson it teaches—The late Lord Derby on Lord Redesdale's bill : his objections examined ; their fallacy shown ; Mr. John Scott's advocacy of it—Advantages of a higher standard—Opinions of the press—Children as jockeys: rarity of their success ; evils of the system—Reforms instituted by the Jockey Club —Long and short courses : advantages of the former, and evils of the latter —Handicaps at Goodwood and Newmarket tabulated to show the preponderance of boyish riders ; injustice of the system to experienced jockeys— Examination of boys suggested—Reason for general predilection for welter races—Petition to Jockey Club recommended—The Duke of Portland and short races—Good example set by the Prince of Wales—Official table of weights for Queen's Plates, and suggested table for shorter races.

I PROPOSE in this chapter to discuss the subject of weights and distances, under the impression that I shall be able to show that the racehorse of to-day is as equally able to carry a man and go a distance as was his predecessor ; and that a higher standard of weight than that now current, would be better for owner and jockey, and more humane for the horse.

In the first place, as I have previously demonstrated by examples, children cannot manage the horses they ride, and they are driven all over the course, and often out of it, and galloped twice the necessary distance before the race.

O

Indeed, I fearlessly assert that if there is one mistake greater
than another, it is the adherence to the present ridiculous
system of assigning such low weights to horses of all ages in
handicaps.   Nothing craves a more speedy remedy, and that
remedy, to be effectual, should be the addition, not of a few,
but of many pounds. To this I have before cursorily alluded ;
but now it will be my endeavour to deal with it fully
and fairly.

It must be apparent to every observer, that if a horse can
carry 11 st. and 12 st., and run heats two or three miles ;
or if he can hunt through a long day, with over 20 st.
on his back without hurting himself, of which we have so
many instances : it is sheer nonsense to say he is over-
burdened with 7 st., and cannot carry it without endangering the safety of his legs over a two-mile course. We are
told Mr. Edges of Nottingham, an excellent sportsman,
is 19 st., and that he rides nothing but thoroughbred horses
and that no one rides harder. Now I daresay some of the
animals scarcely look strong enough to carry their master's
saddle to the end of a long day ; yet they have not only carried it, but 19 st. in addition, and I have never heard that
Mr. Edges had an exceptionally large proportion of lame
horses in his stud. Mr. T. Assheton Smith, again, used to ride
thoroughbreds ; as also did Mr. J. J. Farquharson (better
known as the Dorsetshire Squire), and he, like Mr. Smith,
could not be called a light man, riding, I should think, 15 st.
Yet no one ever went better than these two masters on their
thoroughbreds, nor were oftener found with the hounds at
the end of a long day.

A notable example of racehorses carrying heavy weights
for a long course was seen in Mr. Osbaldestone's match against
time, in 1831, when he undertook to ride 200 miles in ten

hours. "The squire" rode 11 st. and his saddle may be put down as another 14 lbs. Thus we see twenty-eight horses carrying twelve stone four miles; and of the number, six were only three-year-olds, one of which did the distance in eight minutes fifty seconds, whilst some of the older horses took ten minutes fifteen seconds—though the fastest time—eight minutes—was that of the five-year-old *Tranby*. We could scarcely require a stronger proof than this is, of the capability of thoroughbred horses to do long distances under heavy weights. But again, take a case in training, and we find it the same. "Druid," in his "Scott and Seabright," tells us that "*Voltigeur* could sweat week after week with 12 st. laid across his back, and quite deserves his (the trainer's) most glowing eulogy, '*his* legs and feet, my lord, are like *hiron.*'"

But let us examine the running of some of our old horses, commencing with their two-year-old-races, and see what weight they carried then and after, and with what sort of success. *Rataplan, Fisherman, Chandos* and *Vespasian* all carried, as two-year-olds, 8 st. 7 lbs., and neither then nor after did the weight hurt them : for we find *Chandos* ran no less than thirty times, carrying 11 st. and up to 14 st. 5 lbs., and winning with the latter weight, besides many other races at a little less. *Rataplan,* over long and severe courses carrying different weights up to 10 st. 4 lb., ran no less than seventy-one races, winning thirty of them. To this list hundreds may be added, but I shall merely say that *Vespasian* (with legs anything but likely to stand a preparation) carried 10 st. 4 lb., and won the Chesterfield Cup, besides many other races. *Fisherman's* subsequent performances were astonishing, showing that heavy weights did him no harm. He ran 136 races and won ninety-six, over

long distances, most of the races being run at heavy weights,
up to and over 10 st. : and he suffered no more than the
others from doing so much work and carrying weights so
heavy.   After this I think no one will say 7 st. is too much
for a horse to carry.   In my opinion no horse should be
permitted to carry less.   To raise the standard 21 lbs.
would, I think, be a judicious movement, and make it far
preferable to the present low scale.

Admiral Rous's dictum on the subject may now be appropriately quoted ; it is perhaps specially remarkable for its
advocacy of a higher standard, and its paradoxical reasoning
against the change.

"A high-weight standard," he says, "is never popular.
Owners of horses object to 9 st., although they have no
objection to run in a Queen's Plate, carrying 10 st.   I have
always," he continues, "been an advocate of a high scale ;
in 1852 I recommended that the spring handicap should
commence at 10 st. 7 lbs.   Experience teaches me that,
owing to the prejudice of trainers, a high standard is a
certain failure with the best calculation of weight ; and the
clerks of the course well know that a light-weight handicap,
like a fat horse, covers its own defects."

Here the Admiral frankly avers, in unmistakable language,
that he is in favour of a high standard, and that the weights
should be raised to 10 st. 7 lbs.   He even advocates it.   But
the light-weight handicap, he says, pleases the clerks of the
course and covers its own defects ; as if the clerks of the
course are the only people whose interest is to be studied.
With due respect to the memory of the gallant and lamented
gentleman, I submit that two weaker reasons were never put
forth as a pretext for the pertinacious adherence to a system
admittedly wrong.

The Admiral, it will be seen, alleges that the trainers were against the improvement. But if this were so, how came it about that twenty-five of their number petitioned Lord Redesdale to have the standard raised? a petition in which I am confident more would have joined had they not been, like myself, uninformed concerning its intended presentation. But I will ask a question in support of my assertion. "What races are more popular than heavy-weight handicaps?" The answer is, "None." To demonstrate this a comparison between the light and heavy-weight handicaps is appended in a tabulated form.[1]

[1] Handicaps for all ages, run for at Newmarket in the Houghton Meeting :—

LIGHT WEIGHTS.				HEAVY WEIGHTS.			
Number of Runners in each race.	Year.	Total.	Average.	Number of Runners in each race.	Year.	Total.	Average.
... ... 11 9 9	1873	29	.9	... ... 9 7 9	1873	25	8
... ... 11 11 8	1877	30	10	... ... 10 9 8	1877	27	9
15 10 10 7 7 3	1878	52	8	... ... 14 6 9 13	1878	42	10

Nursery Handicaps run for at Newmarket in the Houghton Meeting :—

Number of Runners in each Race in 1877.	Top Weight in 1877.	Bottom Weight in 1877.	Total.	Total.	Average.
	st. lbs.	st. lb.			
17	8 2	6 7			
15	8 12	6 10			
12	8 12	6 10			
15	8 12	7 2	85		
17	8 6	6 8			
9	8 12	7 8			
Idem in 1878.	1878.	1878.		180	15
23	8 12	6 5			
17	8 12	6 0			
17	8 13	5 12			
9	8 12	6 9	95		
20	8 11	6 3			
9	9 2	8 6			

By this table, taken promiscuously from the Newmarket Houghton Meetings, it will be seen that the welter-weight handicaps are liked and patronised, and are still increasing in popularity. For in 1873 the average number of runners of all ages (fractions not included) eight in the welter-weight against nine in the light-weight handicaps, similar in value and distance. And though in 1877 the latter were still one in advance of the heavy weights, last year (1878)[1] we find the runners in the welter races have surpassed those in the light-weight handicaps by two : numerically standing at ten and eight respectively.

To this table I have added the handicaps for two-year-olds run at the same place and meetings, to show that owners do not object to run their horses even at that age with between 9 and 10 st. on them; for we see the top and bottom weight of one of these, set at 9 st. 2 lbs. and 8 st. 6 lbs. Out of the twelve races the top weight carried 8 st. 11 lbs., or above it, no less than ten times ; whilst in the other two the weights were 8 st. 2 lbs. and 8 st. 6 lbs., respectively. The lowest weight among these 180 horses running in eight races out of the twelve was 6 st. 7 lbs ; whilst, in the others, only one went below 6 st., carrying 5 st. 12 lbs. Can any races be so popular as these ? for we see the twelve stakes bringing 180 horses to the post, averaging fifteen runners for each race. Truly what can this be called but the heavy-weight system ? and not, be it remembered, for three-year-olds and upwards, but for two-year-olds. It is also remarkable that not one of the above twelve races was won by a lighter weight than 7 st. ; although forty horses that ran carried less. But this is a result attributable, to my mind, as might be inferred from what I have previously said on the

---

[1] This was written in 1879.

subject, more to the incapacity of the boys put up to ride than to the demerit of the horses.

In a book entitled "Horse Racing," published in 1863, I find it is said,

"In 1860 Lord Redesdale introduced the light-weight racing bill into the House of Lords: by which it was proposed that after January 1st, 1861, no horses should start for any racing prize, carrying less that 7 st. weight, under a penalty of forfeiture of the horse so running and £200."

The bill, though it gave unqualified satisfaction to many, was disliked by some ; the then Lord Derby amongst others not approving it.   He said,

"If the minimum were placed at 7 st. the consequence would be in all handicaps the superior old horses would have to carry 11 and 12 st.   There was a reason, however," said his lordship, "why it was rather desirable that the weights should be slightly raised ; viz., the great difficulty of procuring jockeys to ride old horses in the present competition with the light-weight system."

This does not seem to me to be a slender reason ; for if we raise the standard, we get what his lordship desired—men in the saddle in place of boys. · It cannot be said, after what has been shown, that a weight of eleven or twelve stone is likely to hurt the horses.   Mr. Osbaldestone's match must have escaped Lord Derby's memory when he implied that horses could not carry this weight; although it must be allowed that the opinion on his part can only be inferred—he did not actually say so.   He goes on to say that it was the intention of the Jockey Club to raise the weights for the Derby, and some other races, from 8 st. 7 lbs. to 8 st 10 lbs., thus leaving untouched the whole gist of the matter, which is the raising of the lowest standard from 5 st. 7 lbs. to 7 st.

The late Mr. John Scott, the celebrated trainer of White-wall, Malton (his lordship's trainer), strongly advocated that the weights should be raised ; and no one was likely to know better than a person with his vast experience, or to give a more candid opinion. If the recognised standard for two-year-olds is 8 st. 10 lbs., and if early in the spring they can and do carry this weight (which in handicaps is sometimes increased to 9 st. 12 lbs.), why cannot all of them carry it in the following year ? A 7 st. minimum would put the good three-year-olds over two miles and a quarter in the autumn at 9 st. 10 lbs., and the old horses at 11 st.—a difference of 2 st. 10 lb., between the best and worst of the three-year-olds, and of four stone between the highest and lowest of all ages —a difference much the same as that now existing. I think that few will disagree with me in the conclusion that a horse that cannot win with such weights, is not good enough to keep in training. Indeed, it has become an absolute necessity, and notoriously so, that in fairness to owners, and in the best interests of the turf, the scale of weights should be raised and the courses lengthened.

This fact is not only an almost universal topic, it is markedly noticed by the sporting writers of the day. In the "Morning Post" of April 10, 1876, "Pavo" in an excellent article discussing the subject, says:—

"The success of welter-handicaps of late years shows the popularity of those races ; whilst the difficulty of finding competent boys to ride the present range of light-handicap weights is becoming more apparent every year."

The chance of winning any race over a short course with a child up, is so remote, that the best horse may not win one of ten or even twenty races he may run for ; though by com-petent judges each of them may have been looked upon as little less than an absolute certainty for him.   We find one horse running no less than thirty-six times (one year), winning but four races with a boy up, and over short courses (not one exceeding six furlongs) ; whilst *Fisherman* ran with a man on him, over long courses, 133 races, winning ninety-six—within a fraction of three out of four, against, in the other case, one in nine.

This one contrast should suffice, even if other conclusive arguments had not already been adduced, to show the necessity of having a man and not a boy to ride.   As it is, in the fields of to-day, amongst the ten or a dozen boy-riders, or often double as many, not a man is to be seen ; and the lads, left to themselves, ride harum-scarum, with the result, if disaster be escaped, of a bad start, a cannon, and a complaint against one or more of the jockeys for foul riding : the owner blaming the starter, the starter the boys, and the public every one concerned in it ; and whilst no one is pleased, the owner often suffers severely, being misled by what has occurred in respect to future and more important events.

The Jockey Club, it must be said, have applied a partial remedy ; and could their all-powerful aid be invoked, the important task would be finished.   They have wisely proscribed yearling races, and the running of any but two-year-olds half a mile, and they have at head-quarters also taken the initiative, and added to other improvements the introduction of welter-weights ; so that it only requires a little alteration— more long races with heavy weights, and fewer short courses with light weights—to complete the reform, so happily begun and so much needed.   This change would create a demand for staying horses, which breeders would soon supply.   It would, too, enable us to find the best of our non-stayers ; and be the means of showing many a supposed coward in a very different light over a distance of ground, who otherwise might die unknown to fame. It was by the accidental running in this way that the latent merits of two supposed veritable cowards were discovered.

It may be argued by lovers of short courses that the shorter the course the oftener the horses can run; and the lighter the weight, the less danger of breaking them down. But those that have seen a fractious horse with a boy in the saddle, will form a different opinion; and will think that the chances of injury in such hands, more than outweigh the advantages previously rated so highly. I have already named that *Noisy* was beaten in the Chester Cup through the incompetence of a lad of 5 st. 4 lbs. on his back, and may add that, for the same reason, he lost the City and Suburban. There was in this race a false start, when he, in company with another horse, ran the whole distance as if for the actual race. He was taken again to the post, and the real start took place immediately on his reaching it; and not having had time to recover from the effects of his former race —for race it was virtually—he only ran third, when he should have won.

I have no doubt if the races for three-quarters of a mile were proscribed for all but two-year-olds, and mile races substituted, we should find as many entries and as many runners at the post as now run the shorter course. Admiral Rous himself, admitted that short races spoiled jockeys and ruined the starter; both evils most assuredly requiring a remedy: the one for the sake of the jockey, who otherwise can only remain so in name; and the other on the broad principle, that every man has a right to the fair start which these urchins now prevent. But let us have the admiral's own words on this important question.

He says, "Short races are destructive to young riders; the custom encourages them to fight for the start, and to ride like chimney-sweeps on donkeys. I have never seen worse riding than amongst the young crack jockeys this autumn." Again : "The *bête noir* of racing is the unsatisfactory system of starting, and the helplessness of the official starter to control the audacity of the young jockeys, who frequently set him at defiance."

The existence, then, of these two evils—the helplessness of the official and the insolence of the light-weight jockeys—is admitted, whilst the authorities have the power to remove them by the simple process of raising the scale of weights. Indeed the dearth of *bonâ fide* riders, or men, and the superabundance of so-called jockeys, or boys, are so markedly contrasted that I have been led to compile a little table from the three great handicaps run last year (1878) at Goodwood, and from the three run at head-quarters. From this, which I append, it will be seen that at the former place, out of forty-six runners only six carried 8 st. 7 lb. or above, whilst forty carried lesser weights, down to 5 st. 7 lbs.[1]

But disheartening as such a discovery is, it is positively

[1] A Table of the three great handicaps run for at Goodwood; also of the three big handicaps run for at Newmarket in the October and Houghton Meetings, 1878; showing the number of horses that ran in each, and how many respectively carried 8 st. 7 lbs. and above it, and a lesser weight down to 5 st. 7 lbs. inclusive :—

Horses carrying 8 st. 7 lbs., or above it.	Horses carrying less than 8 st. 7 lbs.
The Steward's Cup 3	17
The Goodwood Stakes 2	14
Chesterfield Cup 1	9
6	40
Newmarket, Great Eastern Handicap.. 0	16
Cæsarewitch Stakes 0	20
Cambridgeshire Stakes......... 1	38
1	74

pleasurable, when contrasted with results found in examination of the doings at Newmarket. There, as will be seen, in the three handicaps, out of 75 runners only one solitary horse carried above 8 st. 7 lbs., whilst the 74 carried a less weight down to the minimum ; or a proportion of 1 man to 74 boys, of whom it may be said that three-fourths at least were better out of the saddle than in it. In two of the great handicaps at head-quarters, the result is entirely in the hands of these pigmies ; for, as we see, no jockey can take a part in them, and amongst 38 riders in the other, only 1 jockey is to be found.

It must be remembered that this result springs simply from the adherence to a scale of weights that precludes skilled horsemen from riding, and not from any scarcity of such able riders ; for it will be found that no fewer than 166 jockeys advertise their weight in " Ruff's Guide," besides the scores that do not. And of the former, 110 can ride 7 stone and above it ; whilst the services of the others, or at all events of most of them, could be well dispensed with. That this is so may be readily deduced from a few facts. It is a rare thing nowadays to see more than thirty horses running in one race, or more than one race meeting of any note in the same week. Allowing that of the 110 adult jockeys, 20 should be absent at little race meetings or from sickness, there would be 90 available at all our best race meetings, or about three riders for each horse in the largest races. As it is, under the present system, horses are frequently sent from the course unable to fulfil their engagements for lack of a light-weight boy to ride.

There is another point. How, under existing circumstances, as shown in these statistics, are the old jockeys to have the requisite practice ? or how, indeed, are they to gain a livelihood ? or, it may be added, how are we to obtain jockeys at all ? For it is not to be forgotten that the featherweights can only ride for two or three years, when they have to give place to others as incompetent as themselves.

But if the continuance of this baneful system is inevitable, may not something be done to lessen its evils? As it is, little fellows are put in the saddle more fit to mount a rocking-horse, and if they can only ride a short gallop or two with the assistance of an old jockey, or a trial without falling off, are pronounced efficient. I should require something more. Let the lad, before he goes forth to ride, be made to pass a competitive examination, and show proof of his ability, and so prevent the endangering of his own life and the lives of others. The riding of a trial or two with old jockeys, and in the presence of other persons capable of judging appointed for the purpose, would be enough to decide the point ; and without a certificate of competency, signed by such authorities, I would not allow any one to ride. For, indeed, it may be asked why should a so-called jockey alone have full power to maim for life, or cause the death of any, by his reckless assumption in undertaking to do what he is unfitted to accomplish ; and in the public trial hurt either himself or others ? It would not be allowed in other trades or professions, and should not be in this. Under such restraints, we should have better jockeys, and a smaller number of them, both desirable objects of attainment ; whilst the men would be more fitting recipients of the lavish presents now bestowed on children, so frequently, as has been shown, to their detriment.

As it is, most sensible people would prefer, in place of our present races, to go back to longer courses, even though we had fewer of them. For it is not the number, it is the quality of the competitions that gives the sterling interest to our great national contests. I may fearlessly say that three good horses with men on them, running a long course at Ascot, Goodwood, or Doncaster, would attract a larger concourse, and create more interest, than the sight of twenty or thirty useless brutes running all over the course with children on their backs for a £100 scramble.

When the riders are men and accomplished jockeys, if the horses be beaten the owners are satisfied and the public are content ; for it is known that the best horse has won, and that the defeat is not due to the ignorance of the rider. And if this be so, is it not a reason why all true lovers of the race-horse should take some steps to see *jockeys* more often in the saddle ? Probably the best method of procedure would be to petition the Jockey Club to take the revision of the light-weight scale into consideration, with a view to bring about so desirable a revolution.

I have named in Chapter XVII. the incident of a trial at Welbeck Abbey ; and I may here mention that the Duke of Portland's idea of racing was much at variance with the practice in vogue now. He disliked a short race, and was never known to give orders to wait. But when he had a horse that was a jade, he used to say facetiously to my father, " John Day, I suppose you had better make play ' behind.' " In contrast to this, we see, in the present day, two noblemen making a match, the shortest of allowable courses for three-year-olds, with some 6 st. on them ; in fact, shortly after-wards, one of these tiny jockeys is seen riding 8 st. 10 lbs., absolutely being preferred before the old jockey who usually rode for the stable. It is impossible to tell what risk owners run in putting up liliputians on saddles insecurely fixed on mountains of saddle cloth, unsafe for the boy, and dangerous for the horse. Moreover, to prevent the heavy saddle from slipping round, or getting back on the horse's flank, or the saddle-cloths from falling off, the girths and surcingale must be drawn so uncomfortably tight as possibly to prevent many horses so treated from winning.

After such scenes, it was refreshing to witness the example set by the Prince of Wales and Lord Strathnairn in their match, both as to weight and distance. Here was no five furlong scramble, with boys up riding helter-skelter from one post to the other; but a four-mile race, with men as jockeys, which tested the merits of the horse, the skill of the rider, and the ability of the trainer. This worthy example set by England's future king, himself a member of the Jockey Club, should bear good fruit.

The Master of the Horse has given us the different weights each horse has to carry for a Queen's Plate in a tabulated form which I append as useful for reference.[1] And I

[1] The following is the official table referred to, the weights being fixed by the Master of the Horse, and sanctioned by the Jockey Club :—

QUEEN'S PLATE WEIGHTS.

Age.	March and April.	May.	June.	July.	August.	September	October.	November
	TWO MILES AND LESS THAN TWO MILES AND A QUARTER.							
	st. lb.	st. lb.	st. lb.	st. lb.	st. lb.	st. lb.	st. lb.	st. lb.
Three years..	7 9	7 11	8 0	8 3	8 5	8 7	8 8	8 9
Four years...	9 7	9 7	9 7	9 7	9 7	9 7	9 7	9 7
Five years ...	10 0	10 0	9 13	9 12	9 12	9 12	9 11	9 11
Six and aged	10 2	10 2	10 0	9 13	9 12	9 12	9 11	9 11
	TWO MILES AND A QUARTER AND LESS THAN THREE MILES.							
Three years..	7 8	7 9	7 10	7 13	8 1	8 3	8 5	8 5
Four years...	9 7	9 7	9 7	9 7	9 7	9 7	9 7	9 7
Five years ...	10 1	10 1	10 0	10 0	9 13	9 13	9 12	9 12
Six and aged	10 4	10 4	10 2	10 1	10 0	10 0	9 13	9 12
	THREE MILES AND LESS THAN THREE MILES AND A HALF.							
Three years..	7 7	7 8	7 11	8 0	8 2	8 4	8 6	8 6
Four years...	9 7	9 7	9 7	9 7	9 7	9 7	9 7	9 7
Five years ...	10 2	10 2	10 1	10 1	10 0	10 0	9 13	9 13
Six and aged	10 5	10 4	10 3	10 2	10 1	10 1	10 0	9 13
	THREE MILES AND A HALF AND UPWARDS.							
Three years..	7 3	7 4	7 6	7 9	7 11	7 13	8 1	8 2
Four years...	9 7	9 7	9 7	9 7	9 7	9 7	9 7	9 7
Five years ...	10 4	10 4	10 3	10 2	10 2	10 1	10 0	10 0
Six and aged	10 8	10 7	10 6	10 5	10 4	10 3	10 2	10 1

This table, though complete in itself, and for its special purpose, requires, as I have observed, enlargement for general use. It assigns no weights for distances

think if we had another for shorter races it would be a welcome and serviceable addition. But as such a thing is nowhere to be found (as far as I know) I shall try and supply the omission by giving it. Though these figures do not exactly correspond with the scale adopted at any particular race-meeting, I think they are about the same as are generally in use. I have not thought it necessary to go beyond a mile and a half, as it would be but a repetition of the weights adopted in the Queen's Plates for two miles and upwards.

less than two miles, or for horses under three years old ; as those under that age are proscribed from taking part in Her Majesty's Plates. As it is, two-year-old races are one of the great features of modern racing, and it is very necessary to have a just scale for them ; nor should one be omitted for the relative weights to be carried by three- and four-year-olds over a shorter course than any given in the above official list, as the most important races of the year are run at a mile-and-a-half. A scale of weights for all ages over all courses, if issued in a tabulated form by the Jockey Club, would be an acceptable boon to the racing community ; as under the present system, clerks of the course often fix widely different weights for races run on the same course, and on the same day.

. Until such be forthcoming, I venture to give the relative weights that should be carried by horses of different ages over the various courses I have named, which, if in an abridged form, may in some sort serve as a guide :—

TABLE OF RELATIVE WEIGHTS.

A two-year-old should give a yearling :—

Over half-a-mile, in October .... 2 st. 7 lb.

A three-year-old should give a two-year-old :—

Over five furlongs, in the Spring .... 2 st. 0 lb.

,, six ,, ,, June .... 2 st. 0 lb.

,, ,, ,, ,, Autumn....................... A few lbs. less.

A four-year-old should give a three-year old :

Over one mile, in the Spring .... 23 lbs.

Over a mile-and-a-half, in June.................... ...... 20 lbs.

Older horses, over both these courses should carry 5 lbs. to 7 lbs. more than the four-year-olds.

CHAPTER XXI.

PROFESSIONAL HARDSHIPS.

Assumed incapability of trainers : how originated ; public slanders ; officious interference of friends—The result, removal of horses ; instances from my own
experience—The advice of the friend and of the trainer contrasted—Eccentric
owners and their doings—Influence of servants instanced in the case of Lord
Palmerston's stud—Payment of training accounts : hardships of deferred payments shown in diverse instances ; the credit system and the bill discounter ;
examples of liberality, and in my own experience—Unexplained removal of
horses : its prejudice to the trainer ; instance of Lord George Bentinck at
Danebury ; other instances at Woodyates ; arguments in support of the
trainer's right to an explanation—Groundless complaints against trainers and
jockeys ; illustrated in two instances—Why trainers and jockeys are poor—
Mr. Chifney and Mr. Ridsdale—The discussion of the subject justified.

IN the account that has been given of the process of
training the racehorse, it will be seen that the life of
the trainer has its full share of responsibility, cares, and
difficulties. But there are other anxieties which, in truth,
may not unfairly be termed hardships, that deserve some
notice. I am naturally diffident in introducing the topic,
because it is of a somewhat personal nature. But as the
existence of evils harmful to every one connected with a
racing-stable (whether as owner, trainer, or jockey) is due
I cannot doubt in most instances to ignorance of the facts
or to thoughtlessness, a few words on the subject will be
received, I must hope, in the spirit in which they are
offered.

P

One of the greatest of these hardships is changeability on the part of owners, some of the effects of which have been glanced at in the course of our examination.

In some respects there is no more thankless office than that of a trainer. Few men get more roundly abused as a body, or censured as individuals, by public opinion. Why this should be I cannot undertake to say; but that it is so there is proof enough, and possibly it has its rise in the disappointed hopes of foolish men.

Nor does the evil end here. Public opinion reacts on the wavering minds of owners; and as a result of the ignorance of the one and the caprice of the other, the fidelity of the trainer is suspected, for no other cause than because he has been unable to realise expectations baseless as the fabric of a dream. The public are too impatient of defeat. The exalted notion of their knowledge of the horse they back, must make him win. If he do not, then the trainer, and the trainer only, is to blame for incompetency ; or worse, for aiming to secure his own base ends.

It is fortunately not so with all. There are many excellent men, owners of horses and others who back them, that are far above reproach. But others, and many, like rationalists, only believe what they see, whilst unhappily, their vision is distorted by self-interest. Most men enjoy immunity from slander; but the trainer only so long as success attends his often thankless efforts. Should a change come, his life is destroyed it may be said, for his means of livelihood is taken from him.

As to the origin of this changeability on the part of employers, there are other causes than the idle talk of the public ; for this, did it stand alone, might be treated with indifference. But when friends will seek to make owners dissatisfied with anything short of continuous successes, the difficulty is greatly increased; and unless impossibilities be performed, estrangement follows.

This is not in any sense a theoretic proposition. I can give instances innumerable, and not a few which have borne very hardly upon myself. In one case I lost one of my best employers through the interference of an officer of rank, who, once that he got the ball in his own hands, was careless even that his agency and aims should be concealed. I have lost the support of good employers in other cases, simply because they listened to unfounded charges made by pseudo-friends, which in some instances would not be too severely stigmatised as machinations. An instance or two must suffice to illustrate an ungrateful revelation.

Some few years ago a gentleman sent me two fine yearlings to train, which, like many good-looking yearlings do, turned out to be useless. The owner when told of this could scarcely believe it. He had them tried over and over again, but with one and the same result. After hazarding all kinds of conjectures as to the prospects of their future careers, he inquired, "What can be done?" to which I replied unhesitatingly, "Sell them." We tried to dispose of one, and succeeded beyond our expectations by the following stratagem. The black horse was sent to New-market and run in a Selling Race (for £300), my own boy riding him. My instructions to the lad were, that when beat, he was to sit steady on his horse and not abuse him wherever he might be in the race. He was beat a hundred yards, a result thought to be too bad to be true, and he was snapped up at the price by the owner of the second horse; and as the jockey had neither whip nor spurs, the wiseacres putting this fact to the other, had their suspicions aroused—indeed many of them would have given a good premium for the choice of the claim. The horse was heavily engaged in all the following spring handicaps, his impost being 5 st. 7 lbs.; but he never went to the post for one. I was never thanked for my share in the matter, nor the boy rewarded for his successful and artistic services; but, stranger than all, the other equally bad horse was kept on until three years old, and entered for the Chester Cup, for which he became a good favourite. I expressed to the owner a hope that he was not backing him, because the animal could beat nothing. But he would not be convinced, and took the horse away from me, and after running him on several occasions without the least chance of success, ultimately sold him as useless. This, it may be allowed, was ill-treatment of the trainer; but the sting of it was, that previously to removing the horse he said to me, "I know that you think him a good horse, and have backed him for the Chester Cup." I may often have been accused of backing good horses, or of laying against bad ones, in either of which acts there is some sense; but this was the first time I had ever been accused of backing a horse that I knew could not beat a hack.

Another instance, I think the most impudent of many audacious experiences, was when an Irish gentleman, some seven feet high, came to see his friend's horses.; having, I must allow, permission to do so. Nothing pleased this son of the Emerald Isle. He took back with him a pitiful tale; in which the matters that met his approval may be briefly summed as nothing, against a list yards in length of grievances. There was nothing, to his mind, as it should be in a racing-stable; at any rate he had never seen things done in the same fashion in Ireland. He had much to say, although he did not back his charges with argument, except in one instance, when as might be expected, his reasoning was weak. The oats were inferior he said; and when asked the cause of the inferiority declared that they were *new*. Now oats in the month of April I consider not only good but preferable to those kept, as he said his always were, until they have seen two Christmas days. Indeed, if they have not been eaten before that period, very few will be after; for they would most surely smell disagreeably and be refused by the horses. His presumption was considerable when he stated that he could tell old oats from new by seeing a few in the manger; but it did not equal his lack of veracity in his report of his visit, which was literally beneath contempt.

I have no wish to overstate the case, or to add a word incapable of proof, in demonstrating the harm done by the tattle (if it be not worse) of friendly busybodies. But that the evil exists the following will prove :—

So long as certain gentlemen ran their horses in my name and their own was a well-kept secret, matters went smoothly ; but so surely as they substituted their own names, things went wrong. If they won, they ought, it was said, to have won more. Absurd as it may appear, this was actually said to me by a nobleman after winning a large stake ; as though I were the keeper of his purse-strings ! If, on the other hand, they were beat, it was the most extraordinary thing in the world. Beat and beat again ! there was no end to it ! The trial must have been wrong ; the race must have been wrong : in fact, the whole business was wrong, and there must be an explanation of it. All that before was so correct and pleasant, is suddenly transformed to the very opposite. Yet there had been no change of management.

What then was the solution ? Simply this : The owner
unfortunately had listened to his friends, instead of, as
previously, hearing what his trainer has had to say. It
cannot be doubted for an instant, that the trainer studies
his own interest in studying the interest and pleasure of
his employer ; and that to think or to wish to do otherwise
would be madness. There is a greater desire to serve an
old client, and more pleasure in doing so than to serve half-
a-dozen new ones, whose good qualities are taken on sup-
position, for they may be impostors. But amongst old clients
many are known to the trainer as valuable patrons and good
men. This one may be peevish, but he is genuine ; the
other has his crotchets, but he is liberality itself.

Sometimes the origin of the change is amusing. The late
Mr. Hilton, an eccentric gentleman, told me that he removed
his horses from the late Mr. Harlock, because one of them
was choked with a carrot in the night, and found dead in
the morning ; adding " his trainer should have prevented it."
Mr. —— took his horses away from Danebury because he
backed *Lady Elizabeth* to win the Derby and she did not.
A very worthy old friend and most estimable man, a client
of mine, without the least wish to create unpleasantness or
be thought officious, thinks no horse's feet can be properly
attended to that he has not seen cut out and the shoes put
on : otherwise his heels are too high, his toes too long, soles
too bare, his feet want paring down ; or it is the reverse of
all this with his shoes—they are always too thick or too
thin, too long or too short, and have too few or too many
nails, and the largest number generally placed on the wrong
side, or drawn on too tight or insecurely fixed. And yet
I think I have had as few lame horses as any one elsewhere,
notwithstanding all this terrible catalogue of existing wrongs

We understood each other, and as the expression of his · opinion was always in private it did no harm, and we still remain the best of good friends.

The removal of horses from one trainer to another perhaps has the most ludicrous basis in the following instance. An Irish gentleman sent me a horse to train, a two-year-old with a tail dragging the ground. I cut it, as is usual with race-horses; and in due course the owner arrived, and seeing it squared, was so annoyed at my presumption in cutting a hair of his horse's tail without his express permission, that he never forgave me. However, as it was near the time the horse had to run, he allowed him to remain till after the race. He ran and won (as was expected). But the owner immediately removed him, and has never trained with, or indeed spoken to, me since.

Other dread enemies to trainers and to the peace of mind of their employers are old servants, for these add to ignorance, officiousness in telling their masters how horses should be trained, and refer them to the looks of their own carriage-horses as a test of their masterly ability in the treatment of their stud. The intention is probably good and the zeal undoubted. But as the experience of these worthies, often invaluable in their own sphere, is limited to that gained from the box-seat of a carriage, they are not exactly the authorities I should like to quote on the condition of a race-horse. Yet not unfrequently masters not only listen to, but implicitly believe in, their doctrines. The late Lord Palmerston, who all his lifetime had trained with my father and with my grandfather before him, removed his horses from their old quarters at Danebury at the instigation of an old and petted pad-groom. This self-confident person wanted his lordship's horses to be tried when they were unfit; and when told that they were so, would not believe it. When he found his commands were not obeyed, he left for Broadlands in high dudgeon, and quickly returned with a mandate for the delivery of the horses, and immediately bore them off in triumph to Littleton.

But after all, changes are not so often brought about by the neglect, seeming or real, of his duties on the part of the trainer, as by inability on the part of the owner to meet his engagements. The removal is, in these cases, made with the intention of getting fresh credit elsewhere. Lord —— left me because after his account was two years standing, I was presumptuous enough to ask for payment. He paid it, and ordered his horses to be given up to a trainer at Epsom, whom he left very shortly after, and probably from the same cause, being about Christmas time, and retired from the turf. Trainers, it is commonly thought, have opportunities to become rich men; but here we have one reason why so many of them die poor—the method in which training accounts are paid. Employers having the reputation of great wealth are often short of money, or at least make that excuse to the trainer. Theoretically, training accounts are paid every three months; practically, it is very different. Some pay yearly, some in a number of years, some not at all. To these must be added those who pay by bills of exchange—as a rule the worst kind of payment, and unfortunately only too customary. As the bills represent racing transactions, your banker declines to discount them; thus, in order to provide money for current expenses, you must apply to a West-end money-lender, who kindly obliges you at fifty per cent., and if not paid at maturity or punctually renewed with interest at the same rate paid in cash, a writ is issued and judgment with all its attendant expenses follows. You apply to the acceptor, for whose accommodation the bill has been taken, and implore him to take it up ; but he either cannot or will not, and it is renewed with about as much probability of being met as in the first instance.   In sum, when ultimately paid at the end of some two years, you find you have been training other people's horses for nothing.

I do not say that this unsatisfactory practice is general, but I do not hesitate to affirm that it is too frequent.   Nor is it only the impecunious who settle their long-standing accounts in this ruinous fashion, for with them it is in a measure inevitable and therefore excusable.

I have trained for a gentleman whose reported income is over £30,000 a year, who has paid me in this way, renewing from time to time, without paying or adding the interest.   I remember training for a nobleman (to whose acts of kindness I am much indebted) for several years, who once sent me a cheque for £100, saying, " half a loaf is better than no bread," though a large amount at the time was owing, and before another remittance was made the total had increased to £7,500, which was settled by bills at long and different dates, only ultimately paid after the delay and unpleasantness usual in these cases.   These deferred payments are manifestly one cause of the comparative poverty of the trainer.   I could better afford and would much prefer to train horses for 30s. per week ready money (monthly payment), than for 50s. on the credit system such as I have described.   I have been told, and on the very best authority, that the late Mr. John Scott had at one time over £20,000 on his books owing to him, over and above his yearly bills, which temporarily so inconvenienced him, that he had to request time for the settlement of his own affairs.   He recovered, however, and died comparatively a wealthy man, notwithstanding his enormous losses.   It must

be apparent enough, that with such heavy drawbacks, training is not the lucrative business many would or may imagine
it to be. Of course with a large string of horses, and good
employers it does very well ; but few of us have such
opportunities.

Yet it would ill become me, in dealing with this part of my
subject, to withhold the meed of praise from those munificent
and liberal patrons of the turf who so richly deserve it. I
understand it is the practice of many noblemen and rich
commoners to pay monthly, whilst others pay large sums in
advance, in order that funds may be forthcoming to meet
current expenses, as need requires. I believe the late Mr.
Graham paid everything monthly, and made exceedingly large
presents to his trainer on many occasions ; besides in other
ways showing acts of the greatest kindness and liberality. It
is said the elder Mr. Boyce (now deceased), father of the
present Mr. Boyce, was, at the death of his employer, not
only left his string of racehorses, but the house, stables, and
the whole of the household furniture, even to the linen, plate,
and pictures—together, a most valuable bequest. The late Mr.
Joseph Rogers, father of Sam (the once celebrated jockey),
was also left a similar present, on the death of the late Mr.
Christopher Wilson. As to the accuracy of these statements
I cannot say, as they pertain to years gone by ; but I should
think they are substantially correct. But I can vouch for
the truth of the following instances in the present day. A
wealthy and generous foreigner not only always paid his
trainer's account monthly, but sent him on account on one
occasion a cheque for £8,000, not at the time owing him a
single farthing, and in every respect was equally as liberal to
his jockey as to his trainer. A certain nobleman but lately
elevated to the peerage, once said to his trainer, in reply to a

request for a little cash, " I would not give a fig for a man that could not let his trainer have a couple of thousand when he wanted it," and immediately wrote him a cheque for that sum. These and other munificent acts, show that there are those who pay not only well, but at the proper time ; which is doubly serviceable, for deferred payment is often not worth acceptance, and is little short of ruin to the trainer.

That the subject is one warranting the space given to it, is patent from the fact that at the end of every racing season we hear of so many studs being removed from this trainer to the other, and without a reason for the change. It is fair to assume that no valid reasons exist because none are ever offered in justification ; yet the fact of the removal leaves the inference that the motive is either caprice, or the tyranny of the strong over the weak.

This, it must be admitted, is not as it should be. No man has a right to fix a stigma on the character of another which he cannot remove, if subsequently he may be desirous to do so. If a servant be discharged, he has a right to demand the cause of his dismissal, and if his employer refuses to give a character (which seldom occurs) the conclusion is that the man is quite worthless ; whilst for an unfair one, he is liable at law. But in racing no such respect is paid to the trainer. His summary discharge exposes him to all kinds of suspicion without redress of any kind. I will give a few cases to the point that have come under my own observation.

The late Lord George Bentinck removed his horses from Danebury to Goodwood because my father happened to differ with his lordship in the matter of changing the clothing of a mare (*Crucifix*) ; he thinking it a dangerous practice in a cold March wind, whilst his lordship was of the opposite opinion. The intention of the proposed change; it should be added, had been to deceive one of the most harmless of old men, Mr. Isaac Sadler, who was incapable, I am sure, of doing an ungentlemanly thing, although his lordship could not be persuaded to think so. In the result, all kinds of rumours got afloat, which though quite unsubstantiated were nevertheless detrimental to the reputations of honest men. I remember a Glasgow merchant who, in twelve or fourteen years, employed as many trainers and dismissed them all through caprice ; but it stands to reason that all of them could not be justly accused of neglect or excess of duty. And his treatment of jockeys was the same ; rarely one rode for him again after the first defeat, even though the Derby itself had been the latest victory. In no single case was a reason given for this unfair treatment.

It may be thought that the ruin of many persons which followed as a necessary consequence in this instance was exceptional ; yet if we were to search for them, analogous cases might, I suspect, be found, although sufficient has been quoted to show the changeability of owners. I may, however, mention a few of my own experiences during the last thirty years as a public trainer of racehorses.

As a matter of fact, I have never been told why many of my numerous employers removed their horses, except on one occasion ; and that was for recommending a gentleman to take a mare out of training—he having seen with his own eyes over and over again, both in public and private, that she was good for nothing as a racehorse. He would not be convinced and removed her with the rest of his horses. But he never won a race with her afterwards, although large sums of money were staked on her when lightly weighted and in bad company ; but even so she failed to obtain a place. He

raced for several years afterwards; but I do not remember
his being possessed of a single winner throughout the time.
This case was the more remarkable, because he did not find
a fault with the mare's condition, or with anything I had
done.   The only fault was a difference of opinion; too small
a one, it must be allowed, to separate old friends, for I had
trained for him for many years, and with great success.   Had
I exonerated her, saying she would probably improve with
age; or after every defeat had I excused it, throwing the
blame on the jockey, the starter, on anything, in fact, but
the horse, we should have remained friends.

If a gentleman has, or thinks he has, a grievance, it is his
prerogative to complain; and it is better to do so, so that if
it exist it may be redressed.   But frankness should be mutual.
If owners prefer their horses fat, there is no reason why they
should be made otherwise; just as they are entitled to give
what instructions they like to their jockeys, so long as they
are honest.   But there are duties even here.   No man has a
right, from a sinister motive, to instruct his trainer to run his
horse fat, or his jockey to make play over a long course with
a horse known to be unfit, in order to deceive the public, and
then to remove the horse.   For the result is to raise the value
of his horse at the expense of the trainer and the jockey, who
are thus ruined to secure his end another day.   It is fair and
legitimate enough to instruct your jockey to wait with a horse
that you know to be slow, or to make good running with one
that cannot stay; or indeed to run them in any state of fitness for an ulterior purpose that may benefit the employer,
so long as the services of both trainer and jockey are appreciated.   It is only the truth to say that jockeys are not
always to blame for staying at the post, or coming too late,
or even for going the wrong course; nor are trainers, for

running horses palpably unfit—for they but receive and do not give instructions; and whilst they alone are censured, others receive the benefit.

The above argument will find illustration and corroboration in the following incident.

A gentleman, who shall be nameless, asked me to buy him a yearling. · I did, and gave 300 guineas for one, the only one I bought for him. As a two-year-old he was tried in the presence of his owner and won very easily—in fact, was found to be a good horse. He ran a few days after with a stable boy in the saddle and was not placed. I was not present. Without saying one single word, or even hinting at such a thing, the owner did not allow the horse to return to my stable, but sent him to his own. Shortly afterwards the rest of his horses were taken away, his retirement from the turf, which I knew was a fabrication, being the colourable pretext for such action. The horse next year won the Derby, trained by a stable boy cajoled from my establishment at the time of the removal of the horses. What could this act imply but dishonesty on the part of the jockey or myself, or both? The horse, it should be said, when he ran as a two-year-old amongst "hacks," was not backed for a shilling and was well and undoubtedly ridden to the orders of the owner, who, after reaping the reward of such conduct in this one horse at the ruinous expense of the jockey and trainer, never won a race after that I remember, and retired in reality from the turf.

In another case, after *Dulcibella* had won the Cæsarewitch, I claimed her half brother, *Romulus*, for 300 guineas, and sold him at the same price to a very wealthy young gentleman, "who," it was said, "was desirous of training his horses with me." In due course, *Romulus* was tried and found to be a good horse over a distance of ground, and entered for the

Cæsarewitch and the Cambridgeshire, in both of which he was bound to be in at a light weight from his previous running in other hands. He never ran in public whilst with me. He was, however, unfortunately entered in the Leamington Stakes at Warwick, at 5 st. 7 lbs., and was ordered to be sent there. When he arrived, the owner informed me that some one had forestalled him in the market, to which I replied, "At your own request the horse has not been trained. Why, therefore, do you want to back him, or even run him? Why not keep him for his two races in the autumn at Newmarket, as previously arranged?" The horse, after being kept wavering in the market to the very last minute, was struck out, and then his owner said to me, "I have backed *Petra* for £2,000, or rather I stand it in the stable commission;" and forthwith, without a word of explanation, then or since, ordered me to give *Romulus* up to the trainer of *Petra*. I may, perhaps, add that *Petra* was the first animal beaten, or was so to all appearance, pulling up long before the winning-post was reached, and that *Romulus* died a maiden. He was a very sound horse, although I heard he afterwards broke down in his new trainer's hands; but be that as it may, he never won a race whilst in them, and his owner soon afterwards retired from the turf.

It is such conduct as here has been illustrated that brings obloquy upon trainers and jockeys. Yet there appears to be some fatality attending the fortunes of those who stray from the path of strict honour; for in no one case can I call to mind any one who derived permanent benefit from such graceless acts.

As to the effects upon innocent trainers and jockeys, two cases may be cited in illustration from bygone days. Mr. Chifney—certainly the most accomplished, and probably the wealthiest jockey of his day—after winning the Derby and making a large fortune, ended his days in abject poverty, dying of a broken heart, caused by the duplicity of friends and scorn of foes. Mr. Ridsdale, who enjoyed the reputation of being one of the best trainers of his time, died, we are told, in a hayloft for the want of a bed to lie upon, with only three halfpence in his pocket. These cases are not without parallels in our day. It may not be easy to determine the cause of great wealth and poverty thus existing almost simultaneously; but in part it may be thus accounted for. Few trainers or jockeys begin life with a fortune, but some often quickly make one. They are then noticed and praised, befooled and idolized, by those who live on them— so long as they are successful. The lucky jockey is, after a few successes, proclaimed "a living wonder;" but reverses come, and he is as roundly abused and deserted. The trainer shares a similar experience.

But the chief hardships that befall the trainer have been pointed out in this chapter : the actions which, on the part of owners, their pseudo-friends and the public at large, are the unworthy cause of much unpleasantness between employer and employed. If I have dwelt upon the topic, it is because I believe if the errors be shown they will be avoided in the future. If the owners of racehorses had but less confidence in their friends and more faith in their own judgment and in the honesty and ability of their trainers, they would not only have no cause to regret it, but would make life pleasanter to those they employ.

CHAPTER XXII.

THE RACEHORSE AS HE WAS AND IS.

Has the thoroughbred improved?—Reasons for affirmative answer; Admiral Rous's opinion—Flyers and stayers of our day enumerated—Horses past and present contrasted : *Bay Middleton* v. *Vespasian, Blue Gown, Prince Charlie,* and *Green Sleeves*—The work of the present day more continuous—Tables of number of horses and distances run—Increase in numbers and foreign competition—The press on *Alep's* defeat by *Avowal*—Satisfactory result of this examination—Increased size of the racehorse demonstrated—Fallacy of the time-test—Improvement in hunters and steeplechasers.

ONE vexed question often debated, and which it appears is as fiercely contested as ever on any and every favourable opportunity, relates to the condition of the English racehorse. Has he deteriorated in speed, size, or stamina? Is he no longer the superior animal he was in the last, or in the earlier part of the present, century? On this subject I shall add to my own ideas, the views of those, in my opinion, the most trustworthy authorities to follow ; a plan that may help to clear up doubts which must of necessity exist in connection. with things that happened so many years ago. For in the comparison of the merits of the horse in the last century, when but very brief and imperfect accounts were kept of their doings, with those of the horse in the present day, much must be conjectural ; yet these accounts if carefully studied afford a mass of interesting information, and properly collated, give us, if not a just estimate of the merits of both, yet an approximation to it, little short of the truth itself and sufficient for our purpose.

The result of such an examination on my own part has been a definite conclusion. I believe our horses are superior in speed and endurance to the horses of past times, and, if it be an additional advantage, are increased in size.

The late Admiral Rous, the first great authority that I shall quote, says :—

" There is an ignorant notion abroad that the thoroughbreds have degenerated because so many are broken down before they are four years old. It is no wonder if we reflect' that in these railroad times the young horses are destroyed by galloping and racing for ten months in the year—two-year-olds running three and four times in a week. It is the old story, killing the goose for the golden eggs—otherwise there is no deterioration ; on the contrary, the racehorse never was so good."

Every sentiment of the gallant admiral, as above expressed, I fully endorse. I think the reputation for speed will be safe in the keeping of such horses as the following :— *Trappist, Thunder, Galopin, Prince Charlie, Springfield, Ecossais,* and *Lollipop ;* and for endurance with such as : *New Holland, Hampton, Petrarch,* and *Pageant*—some of the latter, and many others I could mention, being equally good at any distance up to and under four miles, though some few may have been sent to the stud, where we shall find many more good horses of both sexes. The names of a few of the latter may be given as follows:—*Sterling, Rosicrucian, Speculum, The Earl, Hermit, Doncaster, Blue Gown, See-Saw, Julius,* and *Palmer* as sires, and *Apology, Brigantine, Europa, Hannah, Formosa, Green Sleeves, Marie Stuart,* and *Fräulein* as mares ; besides a host of others too numerous to mention.

It will be well now to contrast the performances of a few of these modern horses with those of one of the best of former years ; for which purpose I select the running of *Bay Middleton* in 1836, a performance that I think had never up

to that time been equalled. *Bay Middleton* never ran as a
two-year-old, and only seven times as a three-year old, and
was never beaten. His best race was the Derby, when behind
him were *Gladiator, Venison*, and several other very good
horses. He was seven or ten pounds better than *Elis*, the
winner of that year's St. Leger, and twenty-one pounds
better than *Venison* at a mile and a half; and he could give
others of the same year twenty-eight pounds and beat them.
It is, therefore, undoubted that *Bay Middleton* was three
stone and a half better than some horses of his own age.
Now let us take the running of one or two of later date:
Blue Gown, for instance (though Sir Joseph Hawley always
said *Rosicrucian* was the better horse). We find that in
running for the Cambridgeshire he gave one of his own age, a
three-year-old, 3 st. 7 lbs. and a beating, and probably would
have given him seven or ten pounds more, or a difference of
four stone. Next, we see *Vespasian*, a six-year-old, giving
Judge, a three-year-old, 4 st. 10 lbs., and eleven pounds beating,
making him five stone and a half better than the winner of
the Queen's Plate, for *Judge* won this afterwards the same
day. Many like instances could, if needed, be found; but I
think those furnished will be sufficient to show that horses
now are better than they were in 1836, in which year they
were better than in any preceding year. As a natural consequence, therefore, our horses must be better at the present
time than they ever were before. Moreover, in 1836 and the
preceding year, horses did not run so often, and could be
better prepared and made more of than nowadays, when
they are continually being raced, galloped, or tried. Old
Mr. Forth used to say, "Horses were like peach-trees that
blossomed but once a year;" and the late Mr. S. Chifney
said, "They cannot be made to keep their form from one
day to another." Yet we are obliged, as trainers, to have

the horses under our charge running not only once or twice but twenty or thirty times a year, and we are also expected to have them fit each and every time, and looking like satin. Again, formerly, there were in the year only about 400 horses to contend against, and very few, if any, foreign horses. Now, how vastly increased do we find the numbers. According to Messrs. Weatherby's " Racing Calendar " for races past (1878) we see no less than 2,097 horses running in 1,699 races, exclusive of horses that run only for hurdle races and hunter races on the flat. The whole is given in an interesting form in the two tables at foot.[1] It should be

[1] TABLE No. 1.

Table showing the number of horses of different ages that have run in the undermentioned years :—

Years.	Yearlings.	Two Year olds.	Three Year olds.	Four Year olds.	Five and upwards.	Total.
1797	—	48	161	122	262	593
1802	—	31	117	108	280	536
1807	—	33	230	148	280	691
1812	—	55	324	188	254	821
1814	—	78	309	174	239	800
1822	—	112	285	194	387	988
1827	—	142	361	210	453	1,166
1832	—	200	395	237	407	1,239
1837	—	215	326	210	462	1,213
1843	—	213	384	236	456	1,289
1849	—	264	419	254	378	1,315
1859	9	576	496	240	324	1,642
1860	—	608	521	302	286	1,717
1861	—	661	550	214	342	1,767
1862	—	626	528	291	381	1,826
1863	—	643	510	291	393	1,837
1864	—	664	548	298	438	1,948
1865	—	659	572	364	447	2,042
1866	—	727	572	359	449	2,109
1867	—	752	661	408	637	2,458
1868	—	844	631	418	617	2,510
1869	—	842	673	402	617	2,534
1870	—	807	709	442	611	2,569
1871	—	732	740	450	561	2,483
1872	—	699	617	382	390	2,098
1873	—	694	602	356	427	2,079
1874	—	710	572	320	363	1,965
1875	—	784	550	354	396	2,084
1876	—	769	592	303	390	2,054
1877	—	805	624	318	330	2,057
1878	—	873	612	321	291	2,097

The Irish horses are not included prior to 1849. In 1843, 113 horses ran in the Irish races reported in the English Racing Calendar. Since the autumn of 1867,

remembered that we have to contend against the best horses of other nations, of which there were running in that year (1878), according to the same authority, no less than 600 —more than one quarter of the number we possess at the present time, and actually more than the aggregate of horses we had running in 1802.

In 1836, in the United Kingdom we had 1,489 brood mares, and in 1876 we had 2,858 accounted for according to Messrs. Weatherby's pages ; but there are many others not included in this stud-book—probably scores, *Jester's* dam being one, whose pedigree is unknown. Of the above mares thirty-seven were sent abroad before foaling.

Foreigners, who previously bought our yearlings but sparingly if at all, have of late years purchased great numbers at high prices; against which, as well as the produce of our best mares, which also they have freely bought, we have now to contend. In the same way our very best stallions go from us regardless of price. *Buccaneer*, one of the very best stallions we ever possessed, went, I think, to Austria. By his aid, Mr. Baltazzi, an Austrian gentleman, won the Derby with a colt

hurdle races have not been included in the foregoing Tables, and since the end of July, 1871, Hunters' Races on the flat have not been included.

TABLE No. 2.

Table showing the number of races of different distances in Great Britain in the undermentioned years, including the principal races in Ireland as reported in the English Racing Calendar :—

Distances.	1873.	1874.	1875.	1876.	1877.	1878.
Half a mile and under	246	233	261	269	251	256
Over half a mile and under one mile...	1,049	1,044	1,035	1,053	837	900
One mile	268	234	256	258	245	244
Over a mile and under two	307	268	261	239	220	223
Two miles and under three	91	78	79	77	73	64
Three miles and under four..............	18	14	11	9	11	10
Four miles	2	2	6	2	2	2
Total	1,951	1,873	1,909	1,907	1,639	1,699

(named *Kisber* after the place he was foaled at) out of an
English-bred mare.   The Austrians thus possess the sire and
dam of a winner of the Derby, besides many other mares and
stallions, once our own, equally well and fashionably bred.
Some idea of the number may be had from the fact that
from the year 1873 to 1876 inclusive, foreign purchasers were
found, from eighteen different countries, for 490 horses, chiefly
brood mares and stallions, yearlings and unnamed young
horses being reckoned in a different list, which would probably sum to as many more, or, together, something like
250 a year; and of the former no less than 146 went to
France and forty-seven to Austria.

I think, from the facts related, that nothing more is wanted
to show that our horses are better now than at any other
period in our history; but I cannot refrain from adding an
incident in support of my argument, because of its special
interest.   I have already adverted to the match made between
the Prince of Wales and Lord Strathnairn; and I may now
add that the race itself created considerable excitement on
account of the breed of *Alep* and his unbeaten career, and
is the more worthy of record because this one of the competitors was the first racehorse kept by royalty for many
years.   Its chief professional interest lay, of course, in the
fact that, in the result, it determined the superiority of a
moderately half-bred Arab crossed with English blood over a
pure Arab, and one of the very best of his race; and this will
be readily admitted, I should hope, as another proof of the
superiority of our thoroughbred horses over all others, however bred.   I am corroborated in this opinion by a leading
article in the *Standard* of July 7th, 1877, which runs thus :—

" Again we find that when it comes to a match between a
pure-bred Arab and a horse with English blood in his veins,

the latter carries the day. *Alep*, the Prince of Wales's horse, has gained a tremendous reputation in Egypt, never having been beaten in any of the eighteen races he ran in that country ; and Lord Strathnairn's *Avowal*, a half-bred animal with some Arab blood, is not a particularly brilliant specimen of a racehorse, but was nevertheless easily able to account for the hitherto unconquered *Alep*."

After giving the time in which Arabs had run two miles, the writer says in conclusion :—

" The four-mile race of yesterday was calculated to display the speed and endurance of the Árab, but even against so moderate an animal as *Avowal*, *Alep's* efforts were useless, and the value of English thoroughbred blood is again conclusively demonstrated."

When we come to consider the size of the thoroughbred we see the same (it may be, questionable) superiority. In the Book Calendar of 1749-50 is a list of stallions and their prices for serving mares, together with laudatory remarks, a few only of which I will notice. One advertisement (abridged) runs thus : " The fine Arabian horse brought over by Mr. Moscow from Constantinople, at three guineas, and half-a-crown the groom. He is near fifteen hands high." Again, *Disman*, at the same price, is strongly recommended on account of his great strength and size, being 15 hands high, which appears to have been the extreme height of nine out of ten, whilst the others are described as being very little taller. Now if we contrast with these our horses, many of which are 16 hands and a half and 17 hands high, we shall easily perceive how superior is their size to that of those I have been describing ; whilst the low fee for serving the mares formerly charged, contrasts strongly with that for stallions at the present date, viz. 100 and even 200 guineas, each mare.

I should perhaps remark, in conclusion, upon the fallibility of the time-test to gauge the merits of different horses even with all the accuracy with which it is now kept. The objections to it are obvious. One race may be run fast a part of the way only, whilst another is run the whole distance at the best speed of the animals contending. Thus in a slow run race over a long course, a fast horse may win and beat one that, if the pace were good all the way, would be able to distance his conqueror; and in the two instances the time occupied by the same animals in doing the same distance would vary considerably. The state of the ground, too, would tell materially for or against the making of good time. As no mention is made of all these differently operating circumstances, nor any calculation of the probable effect on either of two animals thus tested by time, I prefer to see horses tried side by side ; or if that cannot be attained, then I would rather they were tried collaterally horse by horse, than rely on information derived from the uncertainty of the time test.

If more were required to be said on the subject, I think it would be allowed that the superior stamina of the racehorse is even more conspicuous if we observe him under heavy weight, over deep ground—across country a long distance—as a steeplechaser, where he now takes a foremost place. Some twenty or thirty years ago, the half-bred hunters could beat our thoroughbred horses over such courses ; and to start one of the latter would have been deemed an act of insane cruelty on the part of the owner. Though some may argue that the transposition is more owing to the degeneracy of the one than the improvement of the other, yet I think this will not appear to be the case if we consider the high standard of prices given for hunters and steeplechase horses, which must tend to improve their breed and consequently their qualities in the same ratio as a similarly enhanced value has improved our thoroughbred horses. I may therefore fairly assume that our horses have made progressive improvement, and are now better than at any other period of their history ; and that we may congratulate ourselves on the happy and complete success that has followed the indomitable pluck, skill, and energy of breeders of the thoroughbred racehorse.

CHAPTER XXIII.

RACING, PAST AND PRESENT.

Rarity of races in old days; extracts from records—Racing in 1750—Value of
stakes in present day; table—Ancient estimation of the horse; King Athelstan's running horses—The earliest race on record—Racing as it was; dis-
tances travelled and hardships; the Duke of Queensberry and "Hellfire
Dick;" a six-mile race; heats; cruel feats of endurance—Racing as it is:
horses run oftener now; *Fisherman's* performances, and others; *Isoline,
Crucifix, Galopin*—Racing for pleasure, and modern increase of betting—
Cosmopolitan state of the turf—Evils of usury—Career of the Marquess of
Hastings; its assumed disastrous result refuted—Career of the late Earl of
Derby—The two contrasted, and satisfactory deductions therefrom—Betting
a chief cause of loss, greatly increased by usury—Example of the latter;
£2,000 for a box of cigars.

IF we come to compare racing as it is and as it used to
be, we shall find how vastly it has improved as a science
and increased as a national pastime.

In 1750, or thirty years before the first Derby was run, we
find the races so numerically small that in order to make a
volume recording the races of a respectable size, it was found
necessary to add "Cooking" and a list of battles fought.
The account of the first race given in this curious and interesting little volume I give *verbatim*. " Upon the 15th day of
March (1749) the annual Sixteen Guineas Prize was run for

at Kippling Coats (Yorkshire), as usual, for any weight 10
stone one heat, which prize was won by

> Mr. Holles's black g., *Chimney Sweeper* beating
> Mr. Osbaldestone's bay h.,
> Mr. Watson's bay h., and
> Mr. Read's bay h."

It was then the usual custom, it appears, to race from
March till October and, as in the present day, there was a
close time; at all events, there was no racing in the other
months, possibly because such a proceeding would have been
against the prevailing taste or fashion. One race a day must
surely have been scarcely worth the trouble of witnessing;
yet they seldom had more. Beverley had four days racing
made up of one race each day; and Bury (Suffolk) held a
three days' meeting with the like number, viz., one race daily,
and Newmarket was content with about the same meagre
sport—these races being mostly run in heats from one to
four miles.

This sort of sport, if it can be dignified by the name, must
have been of a very dull and unappreciable character; for
though the distance may have had to be traversed four or
more times, and each heat been well contested before the race
was finally won, it may sometimes have been decided by the
first, followed by a walk over the course for the second. In
the year 1750 I find it recorded, in the same work, that 450
horses ran, having 240 owners, a little less than two each;
Lord Poltimore having the largest stud, consisting of 12,
which secured him eight victories of the collective value of
£588 10s., none of his horses having run more than twice, and
only two so often. The 150 races run in that year ranged in
value from 10 to 135 guineas, or an average of about £80

each, bringing the sum total to about £12,000 for the whole
racing season—about half the value of one stake run for
nowadays. The whole amount run for in one recent year
(1878) reached the enormous sum of £391,049 4s. 0d. exclusive of matches, as given below in a tabulated form taken
from the " Racing Circular." [1] In this respect racing seems
to have made greater strides than in almost anything else; for
on comparing this sum with the £12,000 that was run for in
1750, we shall find it to be more than thirty times as much
as was run for in that year.

It is perhaps needless to say that the rapid and gigantic
strides which the national sport has made in recent years,
would teach us falsely should they lead us to suppose that

[1] Table showing the amount of money added to races of different distances
in Great Britain and Ireland, in 1878, and the amount won in stakes, including
added money :—

	£	s.	d.	Added Money. £	s.	d.
Half a mile and under	19,799	0	0			
Ditto, selling races	12,540	0	0			
				32,339	0	0
Five furlongs, and under six	42,613	0	0			
Ditto, selling races	25,877	0	0			
				68,490	0	0
Six furlongs, and under a mile	26,766	0	0			
Ditto, selling races	8,483	0	0			
				35,249	0	0
A mile, and under a mile and a half	47,735	10	0			
Ditto, selling races	5,355	0	0			
				53,090	10	0
A mile and a half, and under two	20,125	0	0			
Ditto, selling races	150	0	0			
				20,275	0	0
Two miles and upwards	15,950	0	0			
Ditto, selling races	100	0	0			
				16,050	0	0
Total				£225,493	10	0

Of this sum £63,246 was given to two-year-old races, £14,371 of which was
for selling races, and £115,879 10s. was given to handicaps.

Ireland contributed £9,015 of the total amount, and Scotland £7,192.

The total value of stakes won, calculated according to Rule XI. (iii.) exclusive
of matches, was £391,049 4s.

man's interest in his noble servant and friend, the horse, is any new thing. The horse has from time immemorial been thought much of, and, it may be, has been in ages long past more truly appreciated than he is in our day. We read that as far back as A.D. 930, the German Emperor, Hugh the Great, sent a present to King Athelstan of " running horses ; " from which we may conclude that they were highly prized and probably scarce and costly. At a little later date, we find the Saxon King giving orders that no horses should be sent abroad for sale or other purposes, except as royal presents. So the date of the Germans keeping horses may be coeval with that of the Saxons, if not earlier. In D'Israeli's " Curiosities of Literature," I find racing alluded to when Mr. Fitz Stephen, in his account of London, describes Smithfield as a " field where every Friday there is a celebrated rendezvous of fine horses brought hither to be sold." The writer continues by giving an account of a horse race there, remarkable as being one of the earliest on record in this country ; from which it would appear that racing was engaged in by the inhabitants of London before, as far as it is known, it existed at Newmarket.

But however interesting these ancient records may be, the comparison of the turf as it is and as it was, is most to the purpose when made between the practice of a generation or two since and that of our own.

In the days of yore, the Royal Plates were, after the Derby, Oaks and St. Leger, the most attractive and coveted prizes ; and so great was the rejoicing on winning one of them that the whole amount was often spent in commemorating the event in true Bacchanalian style. The start for a Race Meeting some 100 miles distant was commenced eight or ten days before, and the business usually took about three weeks in

performance, including the return journey. To-day, double
the distance may be done in as many days, thus economizing
money and time.   The late Mr. Scott used to send his horses
to Leatherhead where they were located for several weeks for
Epsom races.   Probably after travelling so far on foot, this
halt could scarcely have been well dispensed with. His horses,
too, were usually sent from Whitewall to Pigburn before
the Doncaster Meeting. This change probably was dictated
from the superior nature of the one ground to the other.   At
both Leatherhead and Pigburn they used to take one sweat, as
well as several gallops, before running their respective races
at Epsom and Doncaster: now, through the instrumentality
of the railroad, they are brought within a couple of days
of one, and the other may easily be reached the same day;
and yet for aught I see, horses were as well trained in those
days as now, and the worst horses made as much of.

Mr. John Lawrence, in his work from which I have already
had occasion to quote, gives some particulars of racing as it
was in his time.

"The Duke of Queensberry," he says, " raced for over half
a century and with unparalleled success in his matchmaking
and betting accounts. His carriage match at Newmarket,
the fame of which spread all over Europe, and his successful half and quarter mile matches with the *Rocket* gelding,
gave him the reputation of an original in the projects of the
turf.   The success of his short races was supposed to
depend materially on the presence of mind, keenness of
eye and activity of Hell-fire Dick."

This I have heard my father say was the sobriquet of Mr.
R. Goodson, the celebrated jockey of that day.   Mr. Lawrence
next sets out to describe extremely short races not exceeding a
quarter of a mile, and then gives an account of one, in 1772, just

the opposite ; *Flying Childers* beating *Chanter*, 10 stone each, 6 miles. I have seen matches run at Newmarket over the yearling course, 2 furlongs and 52 yards. Now we seldom run over two miles, or less than five furlongs, with horses older than two years old ; anything under that distance being proscribed by the rules of the Jockey Club.

Races in those days were run for in heats, a custom long since abandoned ; and nowadays, as has been said, shorter courses are substituted for those of four miles, except in a very few instances. Fortunately a morbid desire no longer exists to witness such cruel feats of endurance as the one which took place over the old course at Stockbridge between *Camerton*, *Shoe String*, *Office Dyke*, and *Scorpion*, when the last named died on the course, *Shoe String* ran herself blind, and the other two were never afterwards good for anything.

There is a great contrast, too, in the number of times that a horse will run in the present day, as compared with the past. To-day a horse will be raced ten times as often as in the old times ; for we find that in 1750, only one horse in ten was raced a second time. What would Lord Portman and his contemporaries of that year, who were content to run each horse but once, or at the utmost twice a year, think of the performances of *Fisherman* and other horses of recent times ! *Fisherman* ran in one year, thirty-five times, and secured twenty-one victories, amongst them the Ascot Cup, two miles and a half, and immediately afterwards on the same day, the Queen's Plate about three miles ; and it does not appear that these or his other numerous races did him the slightest harm. This feat, it should be remembered, was much more trying than to run heats in which the same horses only are met again and again. *Isoline* accomplished a similar task at Goodwood. These were good horses, if not like

Eclipse or *Highflyer*, who were never beaten. Yet we must
bear in mind that our system has shown us *Crucifix* and *Bay
Middleton* who in their day knew no superior: and in our own
times, *Galopin* and many others, who after years of racing
retired from the turf without equals—names as much entitled
to be enrolled in the "blazing scroll of fame" as those of the
never-to-be forgotten worthies of old.

Formerly gentlemen raced mostly for the pleasure of the
sport, and not so much for gain; as the total value in
stakes to the most fortunate could barely be enough to repay
their expenses. There are now thousands of men who con-
stitute themselves racing authorities, that probably never
owned a horse except a hack. Yet these men will bet their
hundreds and hundreds on other people's horses: and if not
right in their Utopian idea, soundly abuse every one connected
with such animals, to the great detriment of the turf. They
forget that if two bet, one must lose : and no one can expect
to hold all trump cards in every honest hand. If a betting
man, from over speculation, bad luck, or dishonesty, fails to
meet his engagements, he is, as he deserves to be, tabooed as
a poltroon, and no more heard of. But let a gentleman
do the same and the turf is blamed for his accounts, and
the matter is never forgotten nor forgiven by the enemies
of racing.

The turf is at present composed of all grades, from royalty
to the humblest subject. There are rich commoners and poor
noblemen; the first racing for position, the others for wealth,
which either or both may miss or attain, and be eulogised or
condemned for the manner in which they do it. The safe
keeping of the best interests of the turf is wisely entrusted
to the rich and noble; for the poor, though equally
honest in all their dealings with it, are often the cause of

much scandal from the misapprehension of facts connected with the deeds of others.

Racing requires capital, and if this be supplied by usurers it is not difficult to foretell the destiny of those who engage in it. Yet it is not racing which, though it has to bear the blame, deserves it ; rather should the obloquy cast by the ruin of needy clients fall on the extortioner.

One case amongst a few in which the patrons of the turf have escaped this destructive snare may be cited. I allude to that of the Marquess of Hastings. His difficulties commenced, it can hardly be doubted, at that period so fatal to many of our aristocracy—whilst at college. With youth and inexperience as their only guides, young men are at that time, often fleeced by more insatiable sharks than they will ever meet on the turf ; and from the clutches of these foes some never escape, subsisting on borrowed money, and as a last resource taking to racing. I do not wish to be understood to say that the nobleman in question was driven to these extremities ; but that he had suffered in this way to some extent, there can be no doubt, for he was never considered rich.

His lordship commenced racing early in life, his horses being originally trained and run in the name of a friend. Subsequently he removed them to Danebury, and raced in his own name, quickly becoming the "lion" of the turf. At this period no one hesitated to pronounce him a lost man. "He was in the hands of usurers and beset with harpies of every description," it was said ; either the one or the other being enough to effect his speedy ruin, it will be allowed. But the most that could fairly be said against him was, that he may have borrowed money at extravagant rates of interest, and as truthfully it should be added, that he repaid it. His

R

horses were always run on strictly honest principles, and those
in his name were all his own, until his health gave way and
put an end to his short and extraordinary career. It may fearlessly be averred that during this brief time, he revelled in his
favourite amusement, spending enormous sums yearly, only to
have them repaid with a good amount over, by way of interest. His gigantic expenses were all met and discharged,
with most praiseworthy and business-like promptitude; and
his liberality was unbounded. And yet all this was done
without the aid of a princely fortune; for as I have before
said, his means were limited and he started with a borrowed
purse. And I am told by one of his lordship's most intimate
friends (in whose arms he died) that he was richer when
retiring from the turf than when he commenced racing.

I shall now, by way of comparison, say a few words on the
racing career of the late Earl of Derby; a fearless and upright
sportsman, as well as a justly celebrated statesman and orator.
Two noblemen so thoroughly dissimilar as were these two
in all that concerns racing, except in their unflinching in-
tegrity, can scarcely be found. The Marquess hardly ever
bred a horse, but bought his yearlings and old horses, of which
he had not a few. The Earl bred, and never bought any
young or old, keeping only a small stud. Moreover, he seldom
ran them except at Goodwood, Doncaster, Epsom, and a few
other places, and backed only his own, and then only for
small sums. The Marquess did just the opposite. He backed
his own often, and other people's, for very large stakes; and
no place was too distant, nor race too small, for him to run
a horse in it. Again, whilst the Earl was a millionaire, and
the Marquess comparatively speaking poor, both raced with
success. I can vouch for the fact, on the authority of a nobleman well known to the late Earl, that his stud never cost him

a guinea, but each and every year paid its own expenses, leaving a balance in his lordship's favour. And I suspect if other people kept as strict an account, we should hear of more winners and fewer losers on the turf, and discover that, after all, racing, like other amusements, may be indulged in in a less expensive form than is generally supposed—possibly at half the cost of hunting. Large and small studs I have shown can be made self-subsisting; and what has before been done, may be done again. But it is not so with any other amusements. They are all more or less costly, and do not offer the remotest chance of returning to those who participate in them a guinea either of capital or expenditure. But racing, if regulated and kept within prescribed limits, has the advantage over all other field sports, that besides the pleasure derived from it, it is possible with a limited income to gain a fortune by it, if not in the first, then in subsequent years.

The gist of the matter is, that betting rather than racing ruins the majority of gentlemen on the turf. This is the real cause of all great disasters ; and yet without it, it must be admitted racing could not be carried on. You wage an unequal war with the bookmakers who subsist by betting. They back all, you back but one ; and, besides other advantages, they never lay too long odds, whilst you never obtain fair odds. Yet on occasion a good bet may, and should be made, when you have a good horse of your own. On the other hand, it should be a rigid principle never to back other people's horses ; for of their merits you can know but little, and of their condition less.

But, bad as is the result of indiscriminate betting, that of borrowing money from usurers is worse. Against such a revelation as that given at foot, who can stand ? Or what practices on the turf can compare with such extortion and

R 2

robbery?[1]   But the subject of betting generally will occupy our attention in the next chapter.

[1] The following appeared in the *Evening Standard*, of Friday, March the 30th, 1877 :—" In the list of bankrupts figured a nobleman, heir to large estates, who had given bills for large amounts ; amongst other items stood conspicuously one of £2,000, given to Mr. S—— D——, who of course owed his friend, a Mr. K——, money, and handed him the acceptance. The valuable consideration that was to be given for the bill was to consist of cigars ; but on examination it turned out that only a box of the value of £5 was supplied to his lordship."

CHAPTER XXIV.

BETTING AS IT IS.

Hints on betting—Value of the genuine bookmaker—His counterfeit and the amateur backer—Worthlessness of "tips"—The only safe grounds for backing a horse—Proneness to wagering; the De Goncourt fraud—Making a backing-book.—A race-course incident: fidelity of Inspector R———; changed career of two boon companions—The commissioner: evils of employing him; how commissions are worked; his dishonesty, plausibility, and easy gains; authentic personal experiences in illustration; *Pharsalus* and the Metropolitan, *Promised Land* and the Two Thousand, disappointment in the Goodwood Stakes; the result examined.

I HAVE shown, I think conclusively, that racing properly carried out, is very far from the ruinous business it is popularly supposed to be. I have also pointed out that to bet in reason, and on the proper occasions, is a legitimate and, as a rule, advantageous course on the part of the owner of racehorses. In this chapter I propose to give a few hints on betting to amateur backers generally, which may prove of service; if not to teach them how to find the best horses to back, at least to know with whom they may safely bet.

Bookmakers pursue a legitimate and lucrative trade by laying against all horses as they appear in the market at a certain price, and are indeed an important part of the turf, second only to owners of horses, and could as ill be spared. And of these, there are many men of standing and good

position with whom the amateur may bet and be sure of
receiving his money if he is fortunate enough to back
the winner. But with the men who take the money before
the race, and with others outside the recognised ring, he
should have no dealings under any ·pretence. These men
only receive the money with the intention of decamping
with it, should they lose.

Another great point is never to rely for information on
a tipster or a tout. These gentry know more of men than
horses, and are always in search of flats and generally find
them. They never make the fortune for themselves that they
are always professing to have made and to be still making for
others. As Butler has it in *Hudibras*, they,

> " Make fools believe in their far-seeing,
> Of things before they are in being ;
> To swallow gudgeon ere they're catch'd,
> And count their chickens ere they're hatch'd."

Rather rely on your own knowledge and judge from what
you see than from what others may say, unless you take the
advice of a friend that may happen to know or be the owner
of any horse about to run. By this means you may win,
though you will have to take a shorter price than the owner,
after the commission is executed ; but you have the satisfaction of knowing that you have backed a horse that may
have a fair chance of winning and will be content whatever
be the result ; for you will have the assurance you have been
honestly dealt by and have had in turf phraseology " a run
for your money." Says Lord Byron—

> " Most men, till by losing rendered sager,
> . Will back their own opinion by a wager."

This is so, it may be concluded ; for it is the dictum of a
great student of mankind, and will probably be found true

of all ages : therefore although betting, as I have before said, has ruined ten times the number of men that ever the keeping of racehorses has done, it is perhaps useless to advise people not to bet as a rule, but rather to recommend them to keep a few horses and back them, and them only, on fitting occasions. Gentlemen would thus combine pleasure with genuine sport, in witnessing the running of their own horses, and would be in the end richer men.

No better example could be given of the methods in which the tipster and his unscrupulous colleagues gull their friends (?) the public than that of the notorious case of Madame de Goncourt,[1] and it may be added that thousands of similar scandalous robberies, most of them on a smaller scale no doubt, take place. This instance is one lesson salutary enough to cause on the part of all sensible men, avoidance of the tipsters; for it is very clear that men who for years had done their duty as officers of the police, fell when brought into contact with their contaminating influence.

I should not omit to mention certain bettors who, as a

---

[1] In this case William Kurr, F. Kurr, and Benson, contrived to defraud a French lady (then living in France) of £10,000 in an incredibly short space of time. The extent to which they may have robbed other people does not appear, but £100,000 is possibly not too high an estimate of the total. Madame de Goncourt was fortunate enough to have the greater portion of her money restored, as it was traced to the men and given up to the authorities. In this case the swindlers' avariciousness defeated their own ends. The £10,000 might have been secured, had they not endeavoured to obtain a further sum of no less than £30,000, which it was shown the confiding lady was willing to send them, but, fortunately for herself, she had to apply to her bankers or solicitors before doing so, and thus inquiry was made and suspicion aroused. The trial exposed the wide ramifications of the evil ; for Mr. Froggatt, a solicitor, and others high in authority in the police force were found to be implicated as accessories, and were subsequently, on the evidence of the thieves themselves fully corroborated in the chief points, convicted, and sent to hard labour.

class, are more harmful in their operations to owners of horses than all the rest of the forestallers put together—those who make backing-books. They back, with few exceptions, all the horses at the first appearance of the weights or shortly afterwards. In most cases they commence by backing ten or twelve horses, from 1,000 to 10, 20, or 30 as the case may be, and then wait the result of the acceptance. The horses are then quoted as backed. The public see and follow, believing that the money is put on for the owners. The horse becomes a favourite and the backing-book-maker hedges and stands to win a certain sum, the best he can make of it, to nothing ; whilst some time later the owner, obliged to look on with intense disgust, strikes his horse out. Of course the backer has in this case to run the chance of acceptance; for should the owner not accept, he can have no chance to hedge. After the acceptance he again backs a few of those that appear to have the best chance and then waits till the day of running and again backs the most dangerous-looking ones. In this way the winnings of such men are seldom much, and at times their losses are heavy. The same thing is done for the weight for age races. Long odds are taken about well-bred horses, and those recommended directly or indirectly by the tipster and tout. Indeed but for these men, few would be bold enough to attempt to make a backing-book ; a process which almost surely ends in ruin.

I may fitly, here, mention a circumstance rather amusing in its result if alarming in the outset, which befell me as a boy, as showing an extraordinary combination of fidelity and hard living in one and the same person, Mr. R—— an inspector of police.

I went to Abingdon Races to ride for Mr. Sadler, and whilst doing so, asked Mr. Montgomery Dilly to take care of my pocket-book and purse ; which he kindly did. On my return he informed me that he had been robbed, and with mine had also lost his own purse, containing £150 besides vouchers and other things still more valuable. Mr. R——, a great friend of Mr. William Sadler's, was applied to in hopes of recovering the lost property, and he promised to do all he could to get it restored ; but said he was afraid that everything except the notes would be destroyed before coming into his hands. He appointed the same evening at ten o'clock to meet us at the Lamb Hotel to give the result of his inquiries. At the time named he appeared and told us " that it was not in the possession of any of his men." We then suggested that he might know others who might have it, and expressed a hope that he would use his influence for its recovery. He promised to do so, and carried out his promise ; for on the next night he came again bringing the missing books with the treasure absolutely intact. When asked how much we were indebted to him for its restoration he replied, " Nothing ; " and only when pressed would accept two sovereigns to give to the men to drink our healths. But neither for himself nor his associates through whose instrumentality the money had been obtained, would he accept a farthing. R——'s end was unfortunately one his many friends in the sporting world had to deplore.[1]

---

[1] Many people living will doubtless remember Mr. R——, or, as he was commonly called, " Jack," as one of the genial spirits " wont to keep the table in a roar." He and his boon companion, the eccentric Mr. F—— C—— (the owner of *Deception* and other horses) who would never admit of a prefix to his name, used nightly to meet and indulge in singing comic and otherwise. But " a change came o'er the scene." I only once met poor R—— afterwards. He had then left the force, and had turned teetotaller and Methodist preacher. Strangely, about the same time, Mr. F—— C—— left the turf and took to a strictly religious life. A strange coincidence in the career of two roysterers, possibly illustrating the adage, " our indiscretion sometimes serves us well."

The commission agent, or commissioner, is an important factor in the present system of betting, and now deserves a word, for with him most racing men have unfortunately too much to do for their own benefit.

As a rule, few owners of racehorses keep them purely for the pleasure of seeing them run. Some are content to rest their hopes of profit on winning the stakes alone, but the majority prefer to back their horses. It is to the latter, and to the latter only, that the following remarks chiefly apply. Gentlemen of princely fortune can afford to keep studs, and large ones too, without the uncertain aid of success. These require no agents. They consult only their own pleasure when and where and how often they shall run their own horses. But it is a very different matter with those whose means are limited and who race for gain as well as for love of the sport. Such gentlemen hope, and very properly so, to turn to profitable account the knowledge they possess of the merits of their own horses; and a well-digested plan often brings the coveted success without the aid of the commissioner.

But the purchase and keep of racehorses and the attendant expenses are so very heavy, that racing for stakes alone is not a sufficient inducement to attract the many; it is only a very few that can indulge in a sport so costly. Hence it is that betting is so popular with owners, and that the commissioner is unfortunately so often called in to do what the owner could do so much better for himself. The very first thing a gentleman does after finding a good horse, is indirectly to impart the fact to his commission agent, with a request that he will back the animal for him for £1,000 or £2,000 as the case may be. This is generally done badly, and the trainer or jockey (who may have ridden in the trial) blamed for insincerity, whilst the commissioner or his satellites alone are culpable for the mismanagement or imposition.

A commission given in this way often defeats its own ends. Long before it is half executed, the horse is injudiciously rushed in the market and becomes first favourite, and the shortest possible price has afterwards to be taken, or much of the commission left undone.   Thus the average price becomes a bad one, a result which many have too much reason to regret from bitter experience.   It is only natural that fault is found all round, the commissioner, who is in fact the delinquent, alone escaping.   The trainer, the jockey, nay, even the poor stable-boy, are mercilessly condemned.   The commissioner expatiates on his own merits and those of his colleagues.

" Had it not been for strategic movements," he cries, " and for well-timed diplomacy on my part, the result would have been a total failure, instead of obtaining, as I have done, a very fair average price for nearly the whole of the money.   I saw, as who did not ? that the field was a weak one.   The book-makers would not bet, for our horse's excellent chance was patent to every one.   If I had not smartly taken the price, others would have snapped it up and things would have been very much worse."

This charming language, this unbounded candour and persuasive argument, carry the day.   The owner concurs in censure of the one, and eulogy of the other, section of those he employs.   And so the farce is repeated again and again, unfortunately with the same disastrous result.   I willingly admit that there are commissioners who do not serve their employers thus dishonestly, enriching themselves at their patron's expense ; but I have no hesitation in saying that there are too many who thus " arrive at fortune on their first lord's neck."

It is my last wish to make sweeping assertions without advancing facts in their support. I will therefore give a few instances to show the *modus operandi* of those who thus modestly feather their nests.

In 1855, when the Metropolitan was a race on which there was much betting, long odds being as a rule freely obtainable, I asked a very noted commissioner of the day to back *Pharsalus* for the race for £500 in my behalf immediately after the weights came out, the horse figuring in the betting at all sorts of prices from 50 to 1 to 7 to 1. He returned me 8 to 1—£4,000 to £500. Now without his aid, I could have obtained this £4,000 to £100, or at the utmost £150, showing a clear loss of £350, simply through putting the commission in his hands. In this case there was no hedging for any one but the takers of long odds, in which category the owner and his friends did not figure; although it is perhaps needless to say the trusty commissioner did, having them in fact pretty well to himself. It is in this fashion that owners are made "to stand to be shot at." The faithful commissioner has all the long odds, and lays his patron the short ones; and thus, as he proceeds, hedges all his own money, and on all occasions stands, without a chance of loss, to win a large stake on the success of the horse he has backed for the owner *and himself*.

In another instance in 1859, some time before the Two Thousand, I asked my commissioner to back *Promised Land* for me. But he declared this could not be done. "No one will lay," he averred, "except at a very short and unfair price." "Very well," I replied, "I shall not run him." It is almost absurd to add that this had the desired effect. "How much do you want to back him for, and what price will you take?" came the rejoinder in the shape of a question. I

named the amount and my price, and in the course of the
same day was informed by my worthy commissioner, " Rather
than you shall not be on, Mr. Day, I will lay you the money
myself." A similar thing occurred with the same horse and
the same person for the Goodwood Cup. The horse was first
favourite before a shilling of my commission was executed.
But I changed the face of things by informing this worthy on
the night before the race: " I shall not run the horse here in
this case ; I shall keep him for the St. Leger." And again it
was found my money could be speedily put on for me at my
own price.

Now, in both these cases, it cannot be for a moment doubted
that the money had been actually put on the horse, but the
particulars had not been handed in to the principal; and so
long as the horse kept well it was never intended that they
should be. On the other hand, had the animal been taken ill and
died, the account, circumstantially stating how every shilling
had been laid out, would as assuredly have been sent in to
me. In sum, had it not been for my firmness, I should have
seen the horse win both races without a guinea on him in
either of them. Nor would the pecuniary loss have been all ;
my friends would have blamed me for selfishly keeping all the
money to myself, and no statement to the contrary, though
true in every particular, would have been accepted. As it
turned out, people thought that in both cases I had received
double the odds I had given them.

One other more recent instance in respect to the Goodwood
Stakes must suffice. Our commissioner at the time was requested to back a horse for that race for £1,000 immediately
after the publication of the weights. Between this period
and the declaration of minor forfeits there was a great deal
of betting, our horse standing at 50 to 1. On the latter

declaration, he rose to 33 to 1, at which price he stood some
time, and then advanced to 20 to 1, when the commissioner
said that most of the money was on. But when asked for
his account, he replied that the returns from the country had
not yet been received, and that he would send it in so soon as
these came to hand. But the so-called returns were, as might
have been expected, delayed, and before their arrival the
horse had reached the short price of 7 to 1. Then he enclosed the account, saying: "With great regret I have to
inform you that my country agent has spoiled the whole
thing. He has missed the long shots and has been compelled
to take the shortest price, which only has since been obtainable ; and the unfortunate result is a considerable reduction
of the average which now stands at 12 to 1." This is not
an unfair example of how commissions are worked ; and it
might be added that the excuses are often less plausible
than the one given in this instance.

But let us sift this matter a little and see who won and
who lost money by this transaction. Basing my opinion on
the amount of betting on this race, I have little doubt that
30 to 1 would have been nearer a fair price than the one
returned ; indeed, I may say that 25 to 1 was the very least
that the account should have averaged. The horse won,
and what was the result ? Instead of receiving the £25,000
which we were fairly entitled to, we received only £12,000,
or a little less than half.

Startling as is this statement, it is approximately correct
if it be not true to the letter. An act of suspicion could
not pass unchallenged ; but the agent had his reply cut
and dried. "The commission as worked," he said, "was a
failure deeply to be deplored. I have myself been deceived ;
but it has been an error of judgment on the part of the

country agent I trusted.   In fact, it has been an unfortunate combination of untoward events over which I have had no control."   He finished up the whole with the following peroration :—" I hope the explanation given will be accepted, and that things will work better in the future."

It may, at this point, be urged that whilst it is easy to declaim against the evil, is it not possible to point out some safeguard for the future?   Such a comment would be very appropriate ; and as we have now reached that stage in our examination of turf matters, at which I have proposed to offer a few suggestions on practicable reforms, it will be convenient in the next chapter to venture to point out remedies, that, with a fair prospect of success, might be adopted in regard to current evils in betting.

CHAPTER XXV.

BETTING AS IT MIGHT BE.

Suggested remedies : to legalize betting—Restrictions on commissioners—Gentlemen recommended three courses : to do their own commissions; to employ
their equals ; or to name and adhere to a price—Suggested alteration in
system of nomination and entry : a different time of entry ; a new mode of
acceptance ; the proposed method sketched, and the result, betting on the
nomination—Benefits of the proposal illustrated from the Waterloo Cup ; the
tipster and tout done away with—Bookmakers and their procedure ; a rever-
sion to the old tactics recommended—Betting on the Waterloo "draw"
examined ; the one disappointment, *Coomassie* forestalled, and its warning—
The criticism of able writers commended and desired.

ONE of the most effective remedies applied to betting would
be to legalize it.   This would not only influence commissions, but would extend to cases calling for the law's restraint
—to welshers, and to those who, often winning thousands,
decamp on the first reverse of fortune.   If transactions on
the Stock Exchange are legal, why should it be otherwise
with those on the turf?   Honest men of every grade desire
they should be ; only dishonest men require provision of such
a nature as to permit non-fulfilment of their engagements
to the great injury of those that complete them.

Now, just as the solicitor who wilfully neglects a case that
he undertakes to conduct, or from incapacity destroys rather
than assists it, is amenable for such shortcomings ; so it should
be with a commission agent, who, from any cause save a just

one, takes less than the fair market odds, or refuses to give his employer what he, or others for him, may have taken, he should, in like manner, be held responsible for such acts. Moreover, he should be held accountable for bets taken, if those he has had reason to suspect might not meet their engagements, should fail to pay up. Again, it should be made a *sine quâ non* that all bets be given in daily as they are made until the commission is executed. Were betting legalised, we should strike a deadly blow at the root of this evil. But till this is done, the commission agent, who acts in a suspicious way, should be called before the committee at Tattersall's, when the charge preferred should be rigorously investigated ; and if substantial proof of dishonesty be adduced, let restitution be made to the last farthing, or proclaim such a one a defaulter, and no longer allow him to associate with his honest *confrères*.

The fortunes that these men make without a guinea in the world, or the *nous* to make one except as racing commissioners, may well make one wonder. But I think an explanation will be found in what has been said. This gentry, starting with a book and pencil as their whole stock-in-trade, suddenly emerge from obscurity as the possessors of thousands—and how ? Simply by betraying the confidence reposed in them by their patrons, whom they soon outvie in everything, save manners, honesty, and honour.

There is an easy remedy. Gentlemen should make their own bets, or find some one of their own class to do so for them. But if they do neither of these, then let them, as a saving clause, declare at the outset the price they will take, and be satisfied with nothing less. By this simple method, the owner of a horse may get what he is entitled to and may reasonably expect. It is but the application of

S

an old and simple rule—show that you know what is right and that you intend to accept nothing short of it, and you have gone a long way towards its accomplishment. Were this the custom, commissioners would perforce have to act honestly. They would see that such conduct is a necessity in a matter of trust, and that by serving their employers well they would be best serving themselves. They should not be permitted to make a bet for themselves until the commission entrusted to them was fully executed ; not an unreasonable condition, for they can, and as a matter of fact always do, stand in for any reasonable sum in it. Some such plan must necessarily be adopted by owners who wish to remain long on the turf, and who do not choose to work their own commissions and totally ignore the agent ; for then they would, if nothing else, have the satisfaction of knowing they have taken the market-price from a responsible man.

Another effective blow might be dealt to the evils of the current practice of betting, by an alteration in the system of nominations and entries for the big handicaps, which, if tried and found successful, might easily be applied to other races.

In cases when the stakes close some time before the day of the race, I should suggest that instead of the entries being made as now, the following plan should be adopted—taking the Cæsarewitch Stakes as an example. I would have it run pretty much as follows :—

> " *The Cæsarewitch Stakes, a free handicap of* 25 *sovs. each,* 10 *forfeit,* 3 *sovs. entrance. The names of the owners and horses to be put down at Messrs. Weatherby's on the* 1st *of August, the weights to be declared on the* 1st *of September, and acceptance to be signified three weeks before the day of the race.*"

The names of the owners and the names and ages of the horses would be arranged as follows :—

Name of Owner.	Name of Horse.
Duke of Redhill	*John Barleycorn*, 4 yrs.
Lord Southdown	*Bay Windham*, 3 yrs.
Mr. Jones	*Iron Master*, aged.

In due course the weights would be allotted thus :—

	st.	lbs.
John Barleycorn, 4 yrs. old	10	7
Iron Master, aged	10	0
Bay Windham, 3 yrs. old	7	0

Three weeks before the race the acceptance would be signified and the nomination be made, thus, let us say :—

	yrs.	st.	lbs.
Lord Southdown nominates *John Barleycorn* .	4	10	7
Mr. Jones nominates *Bay Windham* . . .	3	7	0

The Duke of Redhill did not accept, and Iron Master *is struck out.*

In all races for horses of the same age, the entries could be made by subscribers' names only, and a week or two before the race the names of their horses (and their ages if a weight-for-age race) should be sent in by the nominators. The betting in all cases would be on the nominations and not on the individual horses. Of course every nominator would be at liberty to name and run his own horse, or any other that was duly qualified, provided the owner or nominator were not a defaulter, or otherwise incapacitated from doing so by the rules of racing.

I must guard myself from being understood to propose that nominators should run their horses in each other's names as a rule ; what I propose is that it should be thoroughly known that they have the power to do so should they choose. The plan if adopted would give owners a fair chance of being able to back their nominations, because it would check forestallers who would probably wait until the day of nomination rather than invest their cash in the dark. It would admirably meet the spirit of one pertinent remark of the late Admiral Rous, who said, " He would be insane to sacrifice the interest of the horse-owner for the benefit of men with a monomania for gambling." And it would do away with the heartburning and the grumbling of the fraternity who insinuate favouritism in the adjustment of the weights ; for the handicapper would not know which horse would represent Lord Southdown's nomination or indeed any other ; and knowledge of owner-ship would be profitless to him.

By this method, too, every one that made an entry would be sure to get his horse fairly weighted, as no possible motive could be assigned for his being otherwise treated : and this may help the entries and increase the number of starters. I do not mean to imply for a moment that the weights now are improperly or unfairly adjusted ; in most cases handicaps are most admirably done, although, as is inevitable, discrepancies will now and then appear. But the plan will deprive the grumblers who find fault where none exists of the last peg on which to hang a complaint.

I shall be told, I daresay, that the system if adopted will restrict betting and so spoil sport. In answer, I can point to the large sums betted months and months before the " draw " for the Waterloo Cup takes place, and ask, If the principle is found to answer so well with greyhounds, what is to prevent its being carried out on a more extensive scale in racing ? A glance at the list given below taken from the sporting intelligence of the "Evening Standard" of February 11th, 1879,[1] will suffice to dispel any apprehension of a dearth of speculation on the introduction of such a system of wagering, seeing how the betting on the Altcar-blue riband has superseded that on the Derby itself, as well as on all the spring handicaps—one only of the latter being mentioned, and that one patronised very mildly.

This list is, I think, conclusive of one thing. There is more betting in the month of February on a few grey-

[1] THIS DAY'S SPORTING.

LONDON BETTING.—THREE P.M.

WATERLOO CUP.

100 to 9 agst. Lord Fermoy's nomination (taken and offered).
16 to 1 — Mr. Salter's nomination (taken).
20 to 1 — Mr. Douglas's nomination (taken and offered).
25 to 1 — Mr. Harrie's nomination (taken and offered).
33 to 1 — Mr. Stone's nomination (taken freely).
33 to 1 — Duke of Hamilton's nomination (offered ; 40 to 1 wanted).
33 to 1 — Mr. Deighton's nomination (offered ; 40 to 1 wanted).
33 to 1 — Mr. Codling's nomination (offered ; 40 to 1 taken and wanted).
40 to 1 — Mr. Evans's nomination (taken and wanted).
40 to 1 — Mr. Jardine's nomination (taken and wanted).
40 to 1 — Mr. Allison's nomination (taken).
40 to 1 — Mr. Trevor's nomination (offered).
50 to 1 — Mr. Nicholson's nomination (taken).
50 to 1 — Mr. Haywood's nomination (taken and offered).
50 to 1 — Lord St. Vincent's nomination (offered ; 66 to 1 wanted).
50 to 1 — Earl of Stair's nomination (offered ; 66 to 1 wanted).
100 to 1 — Mr. Abbot's nomination (taken and offered).
1000 to 8 — Mr. Briscoe's nomination (taken and wanted).
300 to 250 agst. Mr. Salter's nomination v. Mr. Douglas's nomination (taken and wanted).

LINCOLN HANDICAP.

33 to 1 agst. Morier (taken).
33 to 1 — Ridotto (taken and wanted).

hounds through this system of nominations when no one
knows the individual animal he may be backing, than there
is on all the horses put together that may be engaged in
hundreds of races at the same time. There must be a
cause for this, and I think without much seeking a reasonable one may be assigned. It is this : there is no sufficient
inducement to tempt the public to precede owners in the
market to any extent, and the latter are thus enabled to
back their nominations at a fair price, and the public follow.
It will be noticed that more than half the quotations in
this list are at or above forty to one, whilst in two instances
the odds are 100 and 125 to 1 respectively. But were the
greyhounds backed by name, and the tipster and tout on
the *qui vive* to send their patrons the results of trials that
never took place, and reports of greyhounds that are well
as being ill, and of others that are as fit as fiddles as being
broken down (as is the current practice of those who do
this kind office for the patrons of the turf [1]), it may safely
be affirmed that not a moiety of these odds would be
obtainable.

The system as pursued with coursing puts the public on
a fair footing ; for it (the public) has discrimination enough
to see that no one besides those immediately connected with
the greyhounds can know which or what dog would represent
a certain nomination ; and will not be cajoled and induced
to act on the doubtful reports of paid agents : who must
say something or they will fail to impress a sense of their
importance on their employers. After the draw, any and
all may legitimately bet to their heart's content ; whilst

---

[1] We see in print horses represented as being well and worth backing that
actually have been dead some time. This may be sheer ignorance in most cases,
but the result is the same : to enrich the bookmakers at the expense of the public.

throughout, no secret need be kept as to the merits of the greyhounds. You may have the best in the world, and all the world may know it, and also that he is well: but it availeth the public nothing; they can't back him. They may back the owner's nomination, and he, from prudential motives, may run his dog in another and a worse, or in his own nomination. And if in racing, in the same way the betting should be on the nomination instead of on the horse, then and there would be an end to the career of the tipster and the tout, and the horses at Newmarket, Epsom, and elsewhere, might gallop, walk, or be kept in the stable without reports of trials that never took place, or of horses doing wonderfully well that are perhaps dead, or if not *de facto* defunct, are so to all intents and purposes so far as their chances of winning are concerned.

As for owners, they would scarcely be able to realise at first the immense advantages accruing to them from the change. They would be able to see their horses without any one knowing that they even took an interest in such an animal as a thoroughbred. And there would be one other great change. Stable-boys would no longer have inducements to betray their employer's secrets, or in other ways be tempted from their allegiance; for no information would be needed, and promises would no longer be made before the race of rich rewards afterwards, that were never meant to be or never are kept.

But I should observe that of recent years betting has undergone a complete revolution. At present, the bookmakers may in a restricted sense be styled backers; for few now-adays make a genuine book, but rather keep some particular horses to represent their interest as well as "the field." The limited state of the money-market, and the precedence taken of owners by the public, together leave little for the stable commission, which generally has to go unexecuted, and the horse be struck out : to the injury of the owner, who thus loses the chance of winning the stake (which may be a large one) ; to the detriment of the backer, who loses his money; and to that of those of the bookmakers that have not laid against him. I think if bookmakers would fall back on the old system and make a genuine book and bet to it, and it alone, they would oftener get "round" than they do now; and though perhaps their profits might not at times be so large, they would be less problematical, and the result better for themselves and for backers of their own horses. But whilst they continue as now to employ questionable characters in every direction to tell them what this, that, or the other horse is doing, so long will they act on erroneous information. They will refuse to bet against many bad horses that are thought to be good ; and they will back others which are said to be good that are hopeless as though they were already struck out: whilst they will refrain from betting against other horses because they learn from the same doubtful authorities that "they are sure to reach a short price "—which they never do. Thus what might have been a good book is now turned into a losing account, and it is no wonder that we hear complaints of the badness of the profession.

These suggestions however are only offered for what they may be worth. I do not profess to teach bookmakers their business, being myself but a novice at it. But the system seems feasible, and for the reasons given, it would be better for those that backed horses of their own and for the bookmak er themselves.

, Recurring to the proposed system of nominations. I append

a list[1] of quotations taken from the "Evening Standard" of February 19, 1879, to exhibit the state of the odds "after the draw," for the Waterloo Cup, for comparison with their state before it as given in the previous extract.

From this list it will be seen that on the substitution of names for nominations, no fewer than thirty-four dogs were *backed*, whilst the extreme odds of 200 to 1 were obtainable,

[1] 1000 to 4 agst. Banner Blue (t.)
1000 to 15 — Star of Oaken (o.)
1000 to 10 — Vivari (o.)
45 to 1 — Blackbeard (o.)
1000 to 6 — Ariosto (t.)
1000 to 15 — Plunger (t.)
1000 to 10 — Shepherdess (t.)
1000 to 70 — Doon (t.)
1000 to 40 — Market Day (t.)
1000 to 9 — Skipworth (t.)
1000 to 8 — Silver Hill (t.)
1000 to 20 — Iphigenia (t.)
1000 to 5 — Nellie Miller (o.)
1000 to 20 — Waterwitch (o.)
No betting agst. Marquis of Lorne.
1000 to 80 agst. Dear Erin (t. f.)
No betting agst. Hark Forward.
11 to 1 agst. Lady Lizzie (t. & w.)
1000 to 8 — Barabbas (t. & o.)
1000 to 6 — Misterton (t. & o.)
No betting agst. Witzenia.
33 to 1 agst. Sutler (o.)
1000 to 8 — Blackheath (o.)
1000 to 7 — Boy o' Boys (t. & o.)
1000 to 30 — Whoa Emma.
1000 to 15 — Spinet (t. & w.)
1000 to 9 — Musical Box (t.)
1000 to 15 — Wood Nymph (o).
1000 to 40 — Whistling Dick (t.)
1000 to 8 — Pretty Polly (o.)
1000 to 12 — Civility (t. & o.)
1000 to 18 — Shasta (t.)

1000 to 25 — Hilda (t. & w.)
40 to 1 — High Seal (o.)
1000 to 10 — Hamlet (o.)
No betting against The Runner.
1000 to 14 agst. Commerce (t.)
1000 to 20 — Sir James (o.)
1000 to 15 — Patella (t. & o.)
1000 to 10 — Hake (t.)
1000 to 8 — Comus (t.)
1000 to 7 — Boyne (o.)
No betting agst. Rinald.
1000 to 4 agst. Fancy Dress (t. & o.)
1000 to 20 — Honey Bee (o.)
1000 to 8 — Alice Conroy (o.)
1000 to 12 — Dolly Mayflower (t.)
1000 to 10 — Queen Sybil (t. f.)
1000 to 10 — Standard (o.)
1000 to 10 — Athlete (t. & o.)
1000 to 15 — Lady Stanley (t.)
1000 to 5 — Debdon Belle (o.)
No betting agst. Master Owen.
1000 to 3 agst. Ben Cruachan (o.)
1000 to 10 — Barquest (o.)
1000 to 10 — Potentilla (o.)
1000 to 15 — Wood Reeve (t.)
1000 to 20 — Self Taught (o.)
No betting agst. Hark Back.
1000 to 5 agst. Regal Court (t.)
1000 to 8 — Barefoot (t.)
1000 to 20 — Hagar (o.)
900 to 100 — Zazel (t. f.)
40 to 1 — Don't be Headstrong (t.)

and in the case of the winner as much as 166 to 1 was taken
and offered.   Where is any such list of quotations to be seen in
which half the number of the horses entered in any large handicap are backed at one time ?   Here are sixty-four dogs, against
sixty of which liberal odds are offered ; the bookmakers only
refusing to lay against four out of the whole (this I take
to be the meaning of the term " no betting," placed against
certain names) whilst in most of the other instances the offers
are very liberal, and many of the animals heavily backed.
I have ventured to give the list *in extenso* to confirm my
theory that as much speculation as, if not more than, now
exists might be expected if the system were adopted in
racing.

The extraordinarily long odds laid against so many nominations for months before " the draw," must be a boon to all
owners ; the prices laid subsequently cannot be otherwise
than agreeable to the public ; and in both cases the result
must be satisfactory to the bookmakers, or they would not
be so unusually liberal in their offers.   Owners of racehorses
do not, as a body, object to other people backing their horses.
What they do dislike and resent, is being forestalled in the
market, which is, and always has been, a never-failing source
of unpleasantness and worse.

Though a lover of the " leash," I am but a novice at the
sport, scarcely initiated in what appears to me a difficult
science ; but from information derived through the medium
of the press, all the betting is on the nomination up to and
before the " draw : " this being the case with the Waterloo
Cup also, so far as I can see, with but one exception.   This
one exception was *Coomassie*, the winner in the previous year,
and one is almost tempted to add " of course she was an
absentee."   I know nothing of those concerned with the

animal and offer no opinion on the matter.   But it is an admirable instance to bring forward to show how coursing
would degenerate, if the wagering on it were brought down to
the practice in racing: and inversely, as evidence how
racing might be improved, were its custom of betting assimi-
lated to that of the other.   Look what insinuations the absence of such a dog gives rise to?   If the public will throw
their hundreds and their thousands before owners, they must
expect that some will condescendingly stoop to pick them up.
It is the system of betting on races introduced into coursing and with immediate fearful consequences.   Owners are
subjected to severe animadversion, and all concerned must
hear remarks couched in no flattering terms from the unbiased
chroniclers of sport.   *Coomassie*, it was stated in some
papers, was lame before; in others, behind; and again, had
broken a leg; whilst others averred she had received an
injury in her stifle.   Now these contradictions cannot be
spread abroad without fruit, and that fruit is often suspicion.
For myself, I think with Falstaff that though " reasons were
as plentiful as blackberries none should be given ; no, not
even on compulsion ; " but if a reason were volunteered, it
should at least have been the right one.   I have referred at
length to this case-for the point it gives to my argument.   A
man's conduct concerning his own, demands no vindication ;
he does with it, as he has a right to do, just what he wills.
But we see that when, in coursing, the system of nominations
is abandoned, the old "bone of contention" in the racing
world immediately crops up.   *Coomassie*, when backed by
name, was, like the racehorse is, thought to have become
public property, and was by the public backed.   She did not
run, and the vials of the public wrath were opened upon
those who had the management of her.

In all that I have said in this long chapter on the subject of racing tipsters, I must strictly guard myself from the imputation of desiring to restrict fair criticism in any shape or way. Many of our sporting writers are known to be gentlemen, unbiased and far above suspicion of any kind. No class would more heartily rejoice than they would to see the sport shorn of its abuses; whilst their influence for good upon the turf can hardly be overrated. They not only graphically describe turf doings to a daily increasing circle of readers amongst the race-loving public, but they point out and help to rectify abuses; and certainly supply the information that may most confidently be followed by those of their admirers who will back horses, but have not the special sources of information which, as I have shown, are peculiar to the owner and trainer.

CHAPTER XXVI.

PRACTICABLE REFORMS.

The stable-boy and his tempter, the tout—A method to frustrate espionage ; its working and advantages explained—The light-weight jockeys and their riding ; numerous accidents through incapacity of boys ; necessity and advantage of having men in the saddle—A protest by able jockeys suggested —Doubtful result of Education Act—A growing evil, "galloping for a start," and its remedy—Sales with engagements considered in reference to reform of present hardships—Four days a week racing commended and advantages shown—Judicious enactments of the Jockey Club.

OF all remedies in turf matters, not any would be more desirable than one that should defeat the wretched system of espionage ; and I therefore venture to suggest a simple method by which the tout may be in a great measure rendered harmless, if he be not totally checkmated.

Contrary to the generally received notion, it is not on the downs, but in the stable, that the tout works so much harm. On the former he is seldom in the right place at the proper time ; but from boys in the stable he derives information as to all that is going on inside—for as matters are now conducted, nothing escapes detection. The boys, be they big or little, good or bad, know every horse, and whether he be ill or well, lame or sound ; and more—whether the lameness be of a trivial or fatal character, or the illness likely to be of long or short duration. Once in possession of these facts, they communicate them nightly, as far as they know to the touts; these immediately transmit the information to their employers, who, more inexcusable than themselves, use this dishonest means for their own emoluments.

This is a practice that all who care for the turf must wish should be stopped. For, I emphatically repeat that it is in the stables that the mischief is done. The boys, who can hardly be said to know right from wrong, become the tools of designing knaves. By these men they are entrapped to act dishonestly towards their employers by the bait of a trifling money reward, or luxuries and pleasure—the latter frequently of an immoral kind. The result is, ruin to the lads, and to yourself (unless you can counteract the machinations of their tempters) the subversion of all your plans. To put an end to such a state of things is obviously no easy matter; but yet I think something may be done towards inserting the thin end of the wedge, which time may be trusted to drive home, to the benefit of the boys and the extinction of the tout.

My plan is: in the first place, to have all stalls and boxes numbered, and to call their inmates by the number of the stall or box each occupies. As a matter of fact, it is easier to say "No. 1," or "No. 10," than "colt out of Camera Obscura," or "Old Gipsy Boy." This simple plan properly worked is thoroughly effective. For if the boys are ignorant of the age and pedigree of the horses, they cannot know for what races they are entered, or whether this or the other horse is doing well or ill; and of course they cannot transmit to others information they do not themselves possess.

When your employers with their friends pay a visit to see the horses, you hand to each of the party a card with the following printed on it:— *You are requested to ask no questions as to the age, name, or pedigree of the horses, as this information will be found in detail set forth on this card against the number corresponding with the number of the stall or box in which the animal referred to stands.*

Questions, of course, may be inadvertently asked, but may safely and simply be answered by referring the inquirer to the number on the card, where he will find all he wants to know. Before the company separates, the cards are given up, and kept in a place of safety until again needed. Of course, from time to time the cards require to be replaced by fresh ones, or alterations made in them by omissions or additions.

By this method your visitors can with as equal facility comment upon or ask questions concerning the horses by number, as they could by name. "I like No. 1;" "No. 10 is too big:" or "No. 20 is too light," are remarks as easily made as "I like *Tom Thumb;*" "*The Giant* is too big;" or "*The Dwarf* is too little." And whilst conversation would be just as pleasant as it is under the present system, the boys would learn nothing, or at least nothing worth transmission. They might tell the touts that No. 1 was in physic, No. 10 was lame, or No. 20 was well; but as neither they nor their tempters would have the slightest idea as to whether No. 1 was *The Giant, The Dwarf,* or *Tom Thumb,* their lips might as well be sealed; there would be no cash forthcoming for information so useless, and the tout's occupation would be gone.

Of course I admit that this plan would not be practicable with old horses (though it would be an undoubted success with yearlings and two-year-olds, or indeed with horses of any age that had not run) for they of course would be known, and secrecy would not be possible. But look at the immense advantage of having the first run of the market yourself, if only for a single race—the Middle Park Plate, Derby, or St. Leger, it may be—until the eve of running. For by means of a closely kept arcanum you may win one of these and secure a well deserved fortune.

I have myself used the cards and found them to answer the end intended admirably. This, and this only to my mind, is the way secrets can be kept. In large stables, where thirty or forty yearlings are annually added to the "string"— what an inestimable boon it would be to owners and trainers to have the knowledge of the merits of their horses to themselves; defying the touts at exercise, and the boys in the stable!

So much then for stable secrets. It may now be well to turn our attention to the other mere boys whose employment as jockeys has been shown to be so hurtful, and to examine the reforms that may be beneficially introduced in their case.

It requires no philosopher to tell us that a boy of 7 stone must be preferable in the saddle to one of half the weight; for he possesses as much knowledge and infinitely more strength than the little urchin who, after ruining his employers and all connected with him, retires from the scene, to be replaced by others as useless and audacious as himself, if they do not succeed in surpassing their predecessor in these qualities.

These self-styled jockeys, who are physically debarred from riding properly (I will not say, with skill, for the term is absurd when applied to children) start as masters of the art without a rudimentary knowledge of it. Often they are unable to sit on their horses, whilst they are seldom able to guide, and never to assist, them. Many frightful accidents prove this; the fearful one in the Metropolitan Stakes at Epsom when a boy not only lost his own life, but endangered the lives of many others, being only one example out of numbers. This danger is in itself a proof of the necessity of doing away with these pigmies as jockeys. If clerks of courses and handicappers will continue to adhere to the present ridiculously low scale, and the Jockey Club do not take the matter into its own all-powerful hands; then, it may be expected that the legislature will interfere, and by fixing a minimum weight of seven-stone, confer a benefit on the racing community, and put a stop to a reckless and useless waste of life and limb. Action was taken, not very long ago, with respect to performances on the trapeze and other things, in which the sacrifice of life had been trivial compared to that which is caused on the race-course. In fact, it is almost a common occurrence to hear that this or the other jockey has been killed on the course or maimed for life; the result of the sensational exhibition of tiny lads, who would be in the proper place out of harm's way in a dame's school, instead of endangering not only their own but the lives of all jockeys unfortunate enough to be riding with them, besides risking injury to spectators who are frequently knocked down and ridden over.

It is a wonder to me that the old jockeys do not in a body respectfully solicit their employers not to ask them to ride in such company, or indeed with any one under seven stone. Should a deputation selected from our able riders ask permission to wait on the Jockey Club, or one of the stewards, to represent the real state of the case, I think that very likely the request would be granted, and the grievance complained of, be redressed. The evil unfortunately is on the increase; and nothing will in my opinion, as I have said before, stop it, but the raising of the weights to a seven-stone minimum.

T

I know the theory set forth is, that unless boys learn to and do ride at three stone or thereabouts, they will never be able to do so at heavier weights. A more fallacious idea I think I never heard uttered, or one more likely wholly to stop the progress the theory professedly seeks to advance. Admit for argument's sake that it is necessary for boys to commence their tuition at an age so very early ; then, let them ride at two stone, or any other weight, until practice has given them something beyond the rudiments of a business they are supposed to be thoroughly well acquainted with, if not perfect in. It is not the learning at an early age that I complain of in these boys, but the assumption of duties they are utterly incapable of performing, and the coming forward to ride in public, much as John Gilpin did, as regards the amusement afforded to onlookers ; although unfortunately it is the reverse of diversion to the luckless owner and backers of the horse.

Everything I see connected with the light weights, convinces me more and more of the absolute necessity of employing men instead of boys ; and whilst on this important subject I cannot refrain from expressing my views copiously, even at the risk of being thought tedious. Can any one seriously believe that, of two boys weighing three stone apiece and in other respects equal, the one after a year's tuition as a jockey, shall, in after life, be better than the other who has received four or five years extra tuition in his art before appearing in public ? Yet this is what some people would have. By the same parity of reasoning they might assert of two students equally gifted, that the one leaving college after a year's tuition, will be equal in learning to the other who has continued his course of study with unremitting labour for four or five years longer. If this be the logic brought forward in support of retaining the services of mere

boys, I think no more need be said to prove on my part that
the sooner the scale of weights is raised the better.

I must confess that I am not a great admirer of the
Education Act in its application to the youths intended for
the racing business. It prevents them being taught anything
but their school lessons until they are too old to be taught
riding as children ; and the probability is, that when they
come forward to ride in public, they will year by year know
less and less of the rudiments of the art. This, in itself, is
an additional reason, were one needed, for having boys of a
certain weight, or men, as jockeys. I fear, too, that the influence of the Act in the stable will be still further to elevate
the ideas of both men and boys already too prone to think
themselves above their work.

Before finally leaving the subject, it may be well to point
out a most pernicious practice that has lately sprung up in
connection with the light-weight system. I refer to the
galloping from the saddling paddock, harum-scarum, like so
many wild Indians, up hill and down dale, over uneven ground
wet or dry, to obtain a supposed preference in the choice of
the side from which to start. As a consequence, older
jockeys, who, properly consulting their employer's interests,
go steadily to the post, are, at the instance of these boys,
made on their arrival to take what place they can find—a
practice unfair, and which cannot be too strongly deprecated.
Owners, unable to restrain these impetuous youths, suffer by
having their horses broken down. But the stewards, if informed of the practice, which is a nuisance both intolerable
and dangerous, might put an effective stop to it by fining
every jockey who should be first at the post more than once
on the same day, and by suspending him for a repetition of
the offence.

T 2

The sale of racehorses with their engagements is another matter on which some observations may be offered.

When sold as yearlings, the rule is clearly defined and well understood, both by vendors and purchasers. A list of the engagements is given in the printed catalogue of the day ; and these are taken over by the purchaser. If no engagements are specified, it would be taken for granted the animals had none ; and if it should turn out otherwise, the seller would not be able to compel the purchaser to take them over afterwards, if he refused to do so. But older horses are often sold with or without their engagements, and sometimes under what are termed Lord Exeter's conditions, which are not always well understood, though really so simple as to need little explanation ; the fact being that horses, bought under such conditions, are virtually bought without their engagements—for the purchaser need neither run them, nor pay their forfeits. On the other hand, should the buyer prefer running, no one can prevent him doing so, so long as the nominator is alive, and the new owner pays one half the stake and gives the original vendor one third of the results if the horse wins. These very excellent conditions were made by the late Lord Exeter, and no purchaser can wish to buy under better. But in selling horses in the ordinary way, with their engagements, one objectionable result is that the seller passes the right to scratch from his own to other hands. It may then happen that the minor forfeits, a mere bagatelle when duly declared, are neglected and swell to a serious item, which it is compulsory on the vendor to pay in default of the purchaser doing so ; the remedy of the former being to place the latter's name on the forfeit list until he refunds the amount.

Now there is evidently some need of redress here in justice

to the seller. A man of straw may buy a horse heavily engaged, and from neglect or design refuse to declare the minor or any other forfeits, and put the vendor to an extra, unjust, and vexatious expense.

A case came under my own observation which I will briefly relate, to show how unfairly the practice operates against the seller : a person who bought a yearling with his engagements died, and his executors sold the horse again, on the same conditions, by public auction. The animal was bought by a man who neither struck him out nor run him ; and as no one else had the power to do so, the forfeits were augmented to a serious sum. The executors refusing to pay this, the vendor (the nominator) was bound to do so by the rules of racing. Thus the vendor was deprived of every sort of remedy for the recovery of this unlooked-for outlay. It was equally useless to place on the forfeit list the name of a defunct person, or the names of others who refused to pay or had not the means to do so. Now to enable the vendor at the sale to have what he expects and what he is most justly entitled to, it would be well, I venture to think, if the aggregate amount of the smaller forfeits were stated in the conditions of sale, and the sum deposited by the buyer in the hands of Messrs. Weatherby before the horse was given up. And in default of payment of these minor forfeits, the horse should be at once put up and resold, the defaulter paying the expenses of the resale and any loss accruing to the original vendor. Such a rule as this would, I think, meet the exigencies of the case. Or it might be made that before the larger forfeit became due—if it were not duly paid, the vendor should have the power of striking the horse out, notwithstanding any conditions to the contrary in the catalogue of sale.

There is another ground for very general discontent in the

rule that disqualifies a horse on the death of the nominator ;
and I think a judicious revision of the rule might be made.
The purchaser of any horse with his engagements, should, if
so notified to Messrs. Weatherby within a given time, be
able to have him transferred from the nominator to himself,
and should alone be answerable for the horse's stakes and
forfeits, and should be looked upon in every respect as the
original nominator.   Of course if any one, to evade his responsibilities, sold a heavily engaged horse that was good for
nothing, and gave as the purchaser a man of straw, or even
one not known, or who could not satisfy the Jockey Club of
his power to pay the forfeits or stakes as they became due,
the horse should then still remain the property of the vendor
as far as his stakes and forfeits were concerned, unless the
amount were paid into Messrs. Weatherby's hands to cover
them.   This would simplify matters and operate justly to all.

The comfort of all true lovers of the turf, would, I feel sure,
be increased, and the condition of those connected with it
improved, by restricting racing to a certain number of days
in each week.   Lord George Manners exercised his influence
with the Jockey Club beneficially, by restricting all meetings
at Newmarket, the Houghton meeting excepted, to five days ;
an example that might be worthily followed by the officials
elsewhere.   But the restriction might be carried further with
increased advantage.   I would have the racing at all meetings
confined to four days in the week ; leaving the Monday for the
settling at Tattersall's, and the Saturday for yearling sales—
for men can only be in one place at a time.

If it should happen that all the races set down could not
be run off within the four days, some of the minor stakes
might be amalgamated to reduce the number and increase the
individual value of them with advantage ; or should such a

plan be thought inadvisable, then an extra day, or two days if needed, might be given in the following week—the latter, a provision that his lordship made, which it may be remarked, was the cause of the re-introduction of the Second Spring Meeting at Newmarket, after its discontinuance for so many years. Even at head-quarters, four days a week should satisfy the most ardent sportsman. If the time did not permit all the races to be run off, it would be better to have eight annual meetings instead of seven, concluding the racing season at head-quarters as now with the Houghton meeting.

Apart from the increased comfort to racing men, there is an incentive for the change in the benefit accruing to those professionally engaged in training. Five days racing means an augmentation of the Sunday labour which, in almost every other direction, it is endeavoured to limit as much as possible. Racehorses must travel to and from the scene of action, and men must take them. Workmen must be employed in the construction of booths and temporary stands, and horses and men in the transport of the material. Sunday must be largely devoted, too, to the cooking of provisions, and the conveyance of drinkables from place to place. The present custom was commenced, and is continued, for the benefit of the few; it finds no sympathy with the bulk of the people, or with the generality of racing men.[1]

I should add that certain recent enactments of the Jockey Club have, with excellent judgment, in a certain measure helped in the diminution of Sunday labour. I refer to rule 54. By it, all entries previously made on a Sunday, are in the future to be made on the Monday, or for races falling on Monday on the Saturday previously.

---

[1] Since this was written Saturday racing has been (in April 1879) abolished at Newmarket.

CHAPTER XXVII.

MINOR EVILS OF THE RACE-COURSE.

Evils of suburban meetings; first-past-the-post betting—The suburban meeting and its frequenters; practicable restrictions on the behaviour of the masses—The extermination of the welsher possible through institution of outer ring for protection of small bettor—Restraint in use of language; example of the influence of order in Inspector Tanner; responsibility of the clerks of the course—Removal of the ballad-monger—Beneficial result of reforming the customs of the course—Dramatic restrictions, a lesson in point—Necessity to restrict sale of drink and dancing—The race-course as it was (1817)—Admiral Rous on the powers of stewards and others—Apology for introducing the topic.

THE suburban meetings, as they are called, are those which cast the greatest blot on the reputation of the turf. It is only a natural result that in the neighbourhood of large towns, more especially of the metropolis, races should attract a concourse of people amongst whom manners and morality are only conspicuous by their absence. The racing, too, is poor. Even for large stakes, good horses seldom compete at such places; and indeed few run at them, for the races are mostly plates.

The disgraceful exhibitions often seen at such meetings were recently made more objectionable by the introduction of " first-past-the-post" betting, which was simply this: the horse that is first past the post, and is so placed by the judge, wins the race so far as his backers are concerned, for they are paid. It does not matter what the horse may be, or his age, or the weight he carries, or the course he runs ; or that immediately afterwards he is disqualified, and the race given to the second horse : he has won to all intents and purposes. Fortunately the practice was stopped in its infancy through the vigilance of the Jockey Club ; and I only refer to it here as showing the lengths to which the promoters of these meetings would go if they were permitted.

Such meetings have no attraction for gentlemen; and in the absence of the restraining example and influence of the upper classes, the crowd, wild with excitement, is prone to excess in every conceivable form. I well remember the Hippodrome races at Bayswater, and those at Harrow, now most happily done to death by their own inherent viciousness. The scenes witnessed at Harrow would beggar description. The few policemen, utterly powerless to preserve order, consulted their own safety in flight. Life itself was endangered ; whilst any one having property was ruthlessly despoiled of it, with little risk on the part of the thieves, of detection, and none of punishment when detected. One visit was my first and last appearance on the scene. The Hippodrome was no better, the difficulty of preserving order, there, being admittedly increased by the number of footpaths across the inclosure. The company was chiefly composed of welshers, prize fighters, and the disreputable beings that always follow in their wake, and the downfall of a meeting reliant on such elements was as certain as it was speedy ; the press of the time [1] pointing out that a mob "displaying such brutal coarseness and immorality" must drive away "the stay and props of all race-meetings—the respectable portion of the community."

I am not so optimist as to suppose that the objectionable frequenters of the race-course can be as summarily removed

---

[1] *Sunday Times.*

from it, as an intruder is ejected from your own house. "In every crowd there is a thief" is an old proverb that holds good with the athletic sports or the cricket match ; the ball or the rout, or with an assemblage of any kind. The frequenter of the race-course cannot, therefore, look for a special immunity from this plague. And I am far from wishing to deprive any class, even the great unwashed, of its right to witness the national sport, although its numbers be often so great as to hinder rather than help the diversion. But there is a duty imposed upon the crowd, as there is on the individual. It must behave itself, and assert a right to its own freedom of action by respecting that of others. But when, with horse-play and coarse brutality, it rides rough-shod over every one, the panic-stricken public fly, and the result is the place is left to the mob and the meeting discredited for all future time. It must be admitted that the turf would benefit largely were means taken to prevent the recurrence of such scenes ; or, failing this, to obliterate all such meetings from the calendar.

I think something might be done to get rid of the wretched "welsher," or to minimise the evil he does, by apportioning a piece of ground on each race-course close to the grand stand, or on the nearest eligible site, for the so-called ready-money bettors. It should be inclosed with iron railings, with gates for ingress and egress ; and into it all these men should be forced to go, and no betting be allowed elsewhere except, of course, in the ring proper. This would effectually checkmate those who now take money before the race and decamp with it. A small fee should be charged for admittance, which the frequenters, whether professional or the public, wishing to bet, could well afford to pay. In this ring, no money should be allowed to be taken before the race, in open transgression and in defiance of the law ; nor should any betting-man be allowed to leave until he had paid after every race, nor any one else till all just claims on him had been settled. A small distinctive badge might be worn on the arm to denote that the wearer was a bookmaker, with his name legibly written on it ; and there should be persons appointed to hear any complaints, and the offender should be at once expelled and proclaimed a defaulter, and not allowed again to enter until he had satisfied all just demands upon him. The fantastic garments now often worn for the sake of attracting the attention of investors should be forbidden.

Such a provision would put an effectual stop to ready-money betting, which, although proscribed by the law, is still practised to an alarming extent, and winked at by the authorities. A few policemen at each gate, and a small reserve force at command to take into custody offenders against this salutary rule, would soon enforce it. The transgressors, like those of the other ring, should be taken at once before the magistrate and relegated to the police-station until the charge of taking money for bets before the race could conveniently be preferred. A few convictions would soon convince the delinquents that though they might not admire the law, they must, like other people, obey it. The same sharp measure would put an end to the other illegal practices, such as the exhibition of lists, of any structure, an umbrella, stool, or bag to mark a fixed spot ; and the result would be, one and all would be compelled to resort to the appointed spot prepared for their reception and for the protection of others. That pest of the turf, the welsher, would be done away with, and the poor man would be able, as he is entitled to be, to bet his shilling or two with the same amount of protection as the larger bettor who lays his thousands, and can appeal for redress, when injured, to the Committee of Tattersall's.

Of other objectionable features of the race-course not any is more vicious or repugnant to good sense than the unrestrained licence given to the tongue, which chiefly characterizes what I should term the outer ring, in close vicinity to the more refined and delicate portion of the company. It is but fair to say that the reputable bookmakers are decorous in their language, and detest the use of vile expressions on the part of other members of the ring as much as any one does, and would hail with as much delight its effectual suppression. But the evil exists ; and it only remains to inquire if there may not be found some practical remedy. It occurs to me that what is wanted might be brought about by the employment of a few extra policemen, including some detectives; whilst the extra expense incurred would be amply covered by the additional receipts from members, who, as matters now stand, are debarred from frequenting a place in which such language is allowed—or, if need be, by raising the charge.

It is certainly incumbent on clerks of the course and lessees to do all in their power to put down the evil, either by persuasion or by force. So long as ladies and gentlemen pay the sum demanded for admission to the stand and its inclosures, so long have they a right to demand to be protected from insult ; that decent order be kept ; and that all offenders, in this respect, should be immediately expelled. At a theatre, if the comfort of a visitor who has taken a ticket for the stalls, or any other part of the house, be interfered with by a maudlin fool or talkative person, the latter is immediately removed by the attendant without solicitation or charge. So it should be on the race-course with those whose language is

an annoyance to others.   In the days of the late Inspector
Tanner, his simple presence had an immediate salutary effect
on all indecorous people, although he was engaged to look
after the pockets and not the social behaviour of the visitors.
His wide influence extended beneficially over the fraternity of
welshers.   It is clear, therefore, if the power of one man high
in authority was so effective, that a system once set in motion
by men of equal position, would require little addition to the
ordinary staff to render it efficient in the future.   I submit,
therefore, that such a system is worthy of a trial, and if it
succeeded, clerks of the course and lessees would gain the
gratitude of their chief supporters, and undoubtedly make
their own position easier and stronger.

Their influence, aided by the strong arm of the law, could
make itself felt in the alleviation or removal of evils which
extend beyond the grand stand and its enclosures.   These
evils may be best pointed out in the fewest words.   Chief
amongst them are the ballad singers, not only the dirty, half-
clothed creatures who sing offensive doggerel, but the well-
dressed men, women and children who troll forth songs
hardly less coarse, and often more harmful in their significance.   It is hardly possible to imagine a worse evil.   No
visitor, whether in carriage or in drag, on horseback, or on
foot, can, as matters now are carried on, enjoy immunity from
the pest; and it is not possible to say that even the most
innocent escape contamination from the repetition of words
and sentiments of the grossest suggestiveness.   If one party
of these tormentors be bribed to go away, its place is quickly
filled by another ; in the result levying a continuous black-
mail on any one who is desirous to free his party, often
consisting of his own family, from such surroundings.

I suspect the law, if set in motion, would quickly put an

end to the career of these disreputable beings. Money obtained under such circumstances would probably be ruled to have been obtained under false pretences, and the impostors would be sent to prison as rogues and vagabonds.

But here, too, I think the simpler remedy of having a few extra policemen would be found effective, whilst the expense would be met by an additional charge of a shilling, or so, on carriages making use of the reserved inclosure. But I do not think such a charge would be found necessary ; my impression being that the course, once freed from obnoxious elements, would receive a sudden access of visitors who now avoid it. Clergymen of many denominations are deterred from attending races, not because they disapprove the sport in itself, but because of the Saturnalia into which, unchecked by any authority, the scene is turned.

There is no reason why a race-meeting should not be as charming and inoffensive as any concourse of the people. The English delight in outdoor recreation. Melody adds to such diversion a pleasure of its own; songs that would delight and not offend the senses, would be an acquisition to such a scene, whilst instrumental music would help to beguile that period which, in the intervals of racing, might become, by comparison, wearisome : and those who should contribute such accessories, deserve both encouragement and reward. The former pests of the race-course and its approaches—the thimble-riggers and card-sharpers, astrologers and sooth-sayers—have long since become a thing of the past. It would not, therefore, be impossible to sweep away the offensive ballad-mongers, and with them the wretched objects, who, to excite charity, exhibit monstrous deformities, often painfully shocking the sensibilities of the fair visitors. The latter is a sight that is needless ; for we know these objects of compassion are well provided for by public institutions, and would not be permitted thus to exhibit themselves in any town or country village.

Freed from these blemishes, the amusements offered by the race-course would be both enjoyable and innocent, affording to old and young that recreation which prepares them to encounter with fresh vigour the duties of to-morrow. The drive to and from the course, with all its pleasant surroundings, is a scene which has often been graphically depicted by our sporting writers, and is one, allowably, that can find no equal elsewhere, in which all is good fellowship and innocent merriment and fun.

When a building is licensed as a theatre, the Lord Chamberlain satisfies himself that it is so constructed and arranged as to insure the well-being, comfort, and safety of its frequenters. But he does not limit himself to these precautions. He proscribes any piece that has an immoral tendency, permitting only such to be put upon the stage as cannot offend the most innocent. It is a practice that might be worthily followed by clerks of the course, who should use the powers they possess in the same discreet way.

The sale of intoxicating drinks on the race-course is another matter to which some restraint should be applied. The legislature has wisely curtailed the hours in which liquor may be sold in public-houses, and some such prohibition should be extended to the sale of it in the booths on race-courses. The sale might, I think, be safely permitted for a certain period of the day, commencing an hour or two before the first race is run, and extending until two hours after the last race is over, on each day of the meeting. As things are at present, it is the custom for the lower classes to rush off at the conclusion of the day's sport, to the booths, often accompanied by their wives, daughters, or other female friends, who may be under their care. Drinking is then carried to excess, followed by dancing in semi-darkness; and it is needless to say how baneful such a form of dissipation must be to men and women who are, it may be said, in a measure entrapped into it. Sobriety and modesty often become things of the past only. The restrictions I have named would do much towards stopping this lamentable practice, and would turn into a real day's pleasure for the poor man, what is now too often an outing he can only look back upon with regret. If to do so much be beyond the authorities, then the magistrates should interfere; and if they, too, are powerless, then surely some true lover of racing holding a seat in Parliament would bring forward a bill for the purpose, if only the matter were agitated.

My observations on these matters are not intended for a moment to attach blame to clerks of the course and others for evils which in many cases were pre-existing. Indeed, these officials as a body deserve a large meed of praise for strenuous efforts, often successful, towards reform. Nor would I have it supposed that the race-course of to-day is worse than the race-course in times gone by. Indeed, if we examine the subject, we shall probably find that we have much less to complain of in this respect than our forefathers had.

In the beginning of the present century, Newmarket not only abounded in touts of all kinds, but in other degraded characters, who stood on no trifles in the commission of actual crime. These miscreants were tutored to villainy by men who because of their superior education and talent were worse than their tools. So widely spread was the mischief, that the turf showed signs of decline if not of absolute collapse. A sporting authority (the *Morning Herald*), writing in 1819, says, that the races at Epsom had fallen into such low repute, owing to the ill condition of the course and the scanty accommodation afforded, that it was thought they would be given up on the death of the then Lord Derby. "How changed," exclaims the writer, "from the days of O'Kelly and *Eclipse!*" Defaulters, too, seem to have been very plentiful at that time, collecting every guinea they could obtain from their honest associates, and levanting with the sum so received, whether big or little, £10,000 or £10, without paying a farthing of their losses. These and other discreditable acts, which are substantially the same as found in the newspaper referred to, had brought racing to a very low ebb. Here is what is said on some other points:—

"These were not the only unfortunate circumstances attending the races held at Epsom that year, for we are further informed that they were greatly attended by 'thieves,' and other bad characters. The Races this year had the honour of being particularly patronised by the 'borough gang,' who committed unheard-of depredations: one day Mr. Bolton was attacked by upwards of thirty men, near the course, and, as a matter of course, they relieved him of his watch;"

After describing how others were robbed, it is added, that a gentleman who was looking at the races had his pockets turned inside out, and a constable, who, seeing the act, seized the rogue, was surrounded by about 200 thieves, who knocked him down and kicked and beat him with sticks. The bare recital of these barbarisms is sufficient to show the improvement made in our day in the proceedings on the course, and that it is not without reason I affirm that the racing authorities deserve praise for successfully carrying out many difficult reforms.

U

It may be pertinent to our topic to inquire briefly what is the extent of the power vested in racing authorities. The general routine and management of the race-meeting devolve upon the clerks of the course and the lessees under the acknowledged, but seldom obtruded, guidance of the stewards of the respective meetings; and it will be appropriate if I submit a few extracts from the late Admiral Rous's book on horse-racing, in which he gives his opinion on the subject:

" It will be well," says the Admiral, " for a gentleman who undertakes the duties of a steward at a country race-meeting, to be informed of the liabilities he takes upon himself in accepting that office, and of the rights and privileges conferred upon him by virtue of it. In law a steward is liable in respect of all things done or ordered in his name, by his authority, either expressly or impliedly given."

A little further on we read :

" As a general rule it may be taken that during the day of racing, the race-course and enclosures are in the legal possession of the stewards, and that they have for all purposes connected with the races, the authority of the owner of the ground to order off every person whose removal they deem desirable."

The removal of the objectionable persons here alluded to is no doubt that of defaulters in respect of stakes or bets lost on horse-racing, and those who misconduct themselves in other ways; and others who having been proved guilty of any malpractices on the turf, had been warned not to attend under penalty of expulsion. But it is clear that authority, and authority brief in its action and potent in its consequences, is vested in racing officials, and it therefore seems feasible that similar excellent enactments might be put in force to repress what we have here discusssed as " the minor evils of the race-course."

That I, as a trainer writing on training, have ventured to devote a chapter to these matters may be thought to demand some apology. The fact will not, I trust, be viewed as an attempt to set myself up as a moralist. But writing on the racehorse, and incidentally and necessarily on certain turf matters, I hope it may not be deemed an excess of zeal to point out those blots, which to a certain extent exist only because their existence is not known, or its grave consequences are not fully appreciated. The removal of the anomalies I have here glanced at, is all that is wanted to complete that improvement in the customs of the race-course which I have shown has been progressive if slow; an improvement that it may be confidently hoped will be carried out by the competent authorities, if only the general desire for such a reform be pressed upon their notice.

CHAPTER XXVIII.

ATTACKS ON THE TURF; AND CONCLUSION.

Frequency of attacks on the turf—Contrasts in its favour with other occupations—
Professor Low's attack specially considered: errors of his statements and
their deductions shown ; the alleged cruelty to the horse refuted by contrast
with his actual treatment ; wasting not injurious ; his indiscriminate charges
against trainers and jockeys shown to be groundless ; instance of Chifney—
Absurdity of his allegations against owners laying against their horses dis-
played, and the real origin of public favourites shown—CONCLUSION.

IT is so common an expression that the practices on the
turf are corrupt, and its frequenters actuated by sinister
motives, that I feel I ought, in bringing my work to a
conclusion, to say something to exhibit the fallacy of this
notion.   To defend or excuse those of my own calling, and the
others more or less directly connected with it, is no part of my
intention ; for defence or excuse would imply an admission
that the attacks on the turf have some solid basis, which is
not the case.   My object is merely to show, by contrast with
other occupations, how utterly erroneous is the popular
estimate of my own in this respect.

Amongst trainers and jockeys there may be those who
are guilty of malpractices, as there are offenders in all
sections of the community ; but I think it is not too much
to say, that the worst practices on the turf are outdone
daily in other occupations.   We have dishonest bankers,

stockbrokers, solicitors, and tradesmen, whose culpability will outvie any charge ever whispered against the owner of a racehorse, or his trainer or jockey. Without giving cases in number, I may shortly refer to the Glasgow Bank as an example of what men of commercial position will descend to do for their own ends; and to the frequent cases of adulterations on the part of the retail trader: and ask, if the annals of the turf can show anything to equal these frauds in systematic dishonesty.[1]

The abuses of the turf, and the errors of the trainer and jockey may well be left, the one to the vigilance of the

---

[1] The *Evening Standard* of 22nd October, 1878, in speaking of the Glasgow Bank, says :—" The report relates a tissue of dishonesty, fraud, concealment, and malversation wholly without parallel. Advances of enormous extent have been made to prop up rotten houses : bad debts have been made to an amount many times exceeding the whole capital of the bank ; false balance sheets have been drawn up to deceive the shareholders and the public ; lying returns have been made of the amount of gold in the coffers of the bank ; and an immense over-issue of notes has been sent out ; large dividends have been declared when the bank was in a hopeless state of bankruptcy : and in fact it is difficult to mention a single description of monetary fraud that has not been perpetrated at the bank."

With respect to food adulteration, the same authority says :—"According to Dr. Harper, and other chemists and analysts, tea is adulterated with no less than seventeen different substances, milk with eight, sugar with four, the staff of life is tampered with to an enormous extent with four spurious ingredients, butter with three, curry powder with ten, pickles with five amongst which figure sulphuric acid and corrosive sublimate, besides other things." It further goes on to relate how spurious are the drinks we must consume, if we do not confine ourselves to water. " Beer," it says, " is adulterated in several different ways, and it may be startling to the reader to hear some of the effective ingredients, such as strychnine, and sulphate of iron, and wormwood. Soda water, commonly so called, in nine cases out of ten, contains no soda at all, but is simply water into which carbonic acid gas has been pumped. Brandy is mixed with nine different substances, and sherry, champagne, and port are more or less shamefully adulterated." The frauds of Sir John Dean Paul, of Redpath, and others, and recently of the solicitor Froggatt, show that no profession can claim immunity from scoundrelism, whilst one of the most harmful of all offenders, the purveyor of diseased meat, often escapes the just punishment of his gross misdeeds on payment of a nominal fine.

recognised authorities, the other to that of employers, to
the restraints imposed by law, and to the penalties which
invariably follow unfair or careless performance of duties ;
whilst reformers would find ample scope for the practice
of their designs, in the many abuses which affect the welfare
of the world at large.

But from this general view of the subject it will be well
to turn to consider special attacks on the turf.

Professor Low, in his work entitled "Domestic Animals of
Great Britain," is perhaps fortunately too partial and too
consistently pessimist in his views, to cause his authority on
racing matters to rank high with lovers of fair play.   After
telling us something of notable persons connected with the
sport from the time of James I. to that of Oliver Cromwell, he
speaks of the sport itself; of which he, at least, says, and in
so far we may agree with him, that it is not productive of more
gambling than other things, nor so harmful as cards or dice ;
nor is there, he allows, more gambling with us than in other
countries in which horse-racing is unknown.   But when he
comes to discuss the professional aspect of the topic, it will
be conceded, I think, that his conclusions have no trustworthy foundation, either of experience or logical argument.

" The humblest class," he says, " connected with the business
of the turf are the boys of the stable ; to each of whom is
assigned the care of one horse with the duties of riding it at
exercise."   (He here starts with a palpable mistake, as each
boy does two horses.)   He proceeds to state on the authority of
Holcraft, " that the boy rises at half-past two in the summer."
Speaking of wasting jockeys, the Professor says that, under
the system which he has been describing, " a man may reduce
his weight a pound or more in the day without injury to his
general   health   or   temporary   impairment   of   his   natural
vigour."   Of the young horse itself, he states, " he is cruelly

misused ; to fit him for his future task, he must be deprived
of liberty, and subjected to artificial feeding and training,
almost from the time he quits the side of his dam.   No time
is allowed him for that exercise in the field which his instinct
points out as the most suitable and natural, nor for partaking
of that food in the open air, which is best of all others to
preserve health, and answer the demand of the sanguiferous
system in the young animal.   He must be trained, bled,
physicked, sweated, and subjected to restraint in his natural
motion, at the time when the animal functions should have
their natural play."

These assertions are positive enough.   Yet I think it is
easy to prove that the Professor is wrong in every point.
The cruel treatment and restraint to which the foal is
subjected from the time it leaves the side of its dam, of
which he speaks, may be summed up in the following
brief description.

The colt is, when weaned, confined in a stable with a
companion or two, until he has forgotten his dam.   Then
he is with the others set at liberty, depasturing in well
sheltered paddocks and comfortably housed at night ; when
he has the best of corn and natural and artificial grasses of
all kinds, and has in every other way all that he desires for
his comfort.   It will be seen that he does not lose his liberty,
as the Professor would have us believe, at the time of his
quitting the side of his dam, or indeed until some twelve or
fourteen months after, when eighteen or twenty months old.
Up to this time he enjoys the most perfect freedom of action.
He daily exercises himself according to his natural propen-
sities, either galloping or idly taking his rest.   What is this
but natural exercise ? and where is the restraint so much
objected to ?   I am free to confess I cannot see it ; and more,
I am bold enough to say it does not exist.   But the time

has arrived, as it does to all horses, when the colt must be accustomed to restraint; and even then a proportionate allowance of exercise allotted to suit his tender age is given —and he is not overworked, whilst he is well cared for.

Again, as to his being trained, bled, physicked, and sweated, I can vouch for it that his training is little more than gentle exercise until he is old enough to bear work; and that in a state of health, he is not subjected to bleeding, and that a mild dose of physic is only administered occasionally as a preventive of disease, or in illness.

Having shown, I think, beyond all doubt, that the Professor is wrong in his remarks on the horse, I shall next essay to demonstrate that he is not more happy in his strictures on the manners and customs of those that have to do with him.

In his statements as to the early hour at which the boys rise, and as to one boy being kept for each horse, it must suffice to say that he is in error, as he is in a general sense in other ways. For as to wasting one pound a day, I have myself wasted for years, and often reduced myself six pounds in a day, and day after day several pounds. I reduced myself to ride *Belissama*, at Bath, from 10 stone to the required weight, 7 st. 13 lbs. which included the saddle. I have never injured myself by the process, and I do not doubt others have wasted even more with a similarly innocuous result.

But the Professor still further commits himself to untenable statements, and does so in a much more reprehensible fashion, when he categorically attacks trainers and jockeys and would brand them with infamy; as indeed he is inclined to attack all and any who happen to differ with him in opinion. But it is only fair to submit his own words, even though the quotation be somewhat lengthy; for by this method, points will not be brought forward that specially assist my theory, nor on the other hand, others suppressed to the injury of his arguments.

" The betting," he says, " of jockeys and trainers, to a vast amount, has now become a system extensive, open, and avowed. It is no longer the restricted and temperate betting which prevailed in former times, on horses in which the master and employer of these people had an interest, but they must have their books as regular as the boldest gambler of the course. Now, here is a system which strikes at the very root of all confidence in the affairs of the turf. What ! the horses of sportsmen to be entrusted to a set of avowed gamblers, who may have a direct interest in causing their defeat ! What confidence can be placed in a jockey on whose success in a match with another horse he or his confederates may have thousands depending ? Will he win in opposition to an interest so great ? Those who believe so, must have a higher confidence in the virtues of Newmarket than our knowledge of human nature elsewhere justifies. The first admission on record of a jockey betting on the horse opposed to that which he himself rode, is the elder Chifney. He lost the race, but he justifies himself by saying, that he knew the horse he rode was unfit to win. The argument of the jockey is not worth the tassel of his velvet cap ; and the principle contended for needs only a little extension to justify every kind of roguery. This very jockey lived to acquire a splendid stud, to build houses, to sport his equipage, and to experience the revolution of fortune's wheel, by dying a beggar. But the training grooms, more trusted still—what can be said of their concern with the gambling speculations, by which their interest and their duty have been placed at variance ? What need of their master-key to guard their troughs from the introduction of the arsenic or the sublimate ; or of the live fishes, to show that the water is as pure as their own thoughts ? A few orders of the head groom on the training-ground, a few doses out of time of Barbadoes aloes, a gentle opiate from the apothecary's shop, all for the health of the horse, will answer every end. Or should these disgraces not be perpetrated, how many are the means by which races may be lost or won ! A simple breach of confidence may answer the end, information may be conveyed sufficient to neutralize the hopes of the confiding employer, and the one book be made square, although the other may become a memorandum of ruin."

We may pause for a moment in our quotation to examine the relevancy of what he has said to this point. If such things were done, there would be some ground for such an argument. But he bases his thesis on an utter hypothesis. No jockey or trainer bets in the way he describes, and therefore does not fall under the temptation. And it is on hypothesis only that he ventures to condemn a class. He says, "The elder Chifney was the first to back a horse in a race other than the one he rode, and he lost owing to the horse's unfit condition." This was the rider's opinion, soundly based no doubt and justified by the result, though he might have been mistaken in his opinion, and might have had to pay dearly for it. I confess I cannot conceive the dishonesty that is attached to such conduct. It cannot be the mere fact of the jockey's betting, or of his being the first that did so, and nothing of an improper nature is proved against him. All he did was to ride one horse and back another in the same race. But why should he not have done so ? What reason can be given to show, that if a jockey rode a carthorse of his employer's, he should be required, if he betted at all, to back him against an *Eclipse ;* or if you will, against one of his own horses of which he thought well and had confidence in his brother professional in the saddle ? For racing has its glorious uncertainties. One horse may fall down, or go the wrong course, and from various reasons others may be disqualified and the carthorse may be the winner, and his jockey having backed another horse, may lose and would pay. But there would have been no dishonesty if the horse had been beaten. The fact is, horses are beaten from other causes than the roguery of owner, trainer, or jockey. It is possible to cite numerous instances in which the jockey, by consummate art has, at the critical moment, turned what would have been an easy defeat into a splendid victory, and not unoften at his own cost. At Goodwood on one occasion this was so palpably done at the cost of some thousands of pounds to the jockey, that the prefix of "honest" was ever after attached to the rider's name. The contest for the blue riband of the turf itself can contribute a case, a parallel to which it will not be easy for the Professor himself to find off the race-course. In this instance a jockey rode the winner for his employers when his own horse ran second. In one minute he could have made a splendid fortune and would never have been called to account. But the temptation, great it must be confessed, had no charm for him. He preferred honour to riches.

Fortunately these facts are known and appreciated by the chief supporters of racing, and therefore the jockeys as a body can afford to treat with contempt attacks upon their honesty. For myself, I find it difficult to believe that the writer really supposes the occult practices he condemns have existence. According to him, trainers and jockeys, by combining to deceive their employers, make their own fortunes, and the unhallowed process is kept an undivulged secret from all save the nefarious accomplices. According to the professor, the evil is by no means fleeting, it is chronic. Annually similar frauds occur, and fresh owners take the place of their ruined predecessors, to be dealt by with the same unrelenting dishonesty. But such a theory carries its own refutation: were it so, no owner, even a millionaire, would be able to withstand these terrible losses, coming as they would with each revolving year; whilst we should see trainers and jockeys the possessors of the ancestral estates of their victims. It is difficult to say which of the two results is the more improbable. As a matter of fact, there are on the turf, owners who make money and owners who lose it; and a similar experience awaits the adventurous jockey or the speculative trainer. It is a game of hazard to a certain extent, and has its lucky and unlucky followers.

If we turn once more to the book, we shall find that the professor has little good to say even of the unfortunate (as he would make him) owner.

"It is seen," he says, "that the owner of a horse may, by betting against his own horse, gain by his losing the race: and by having his own horse largely backed, and then running to lose, pocket enormous sums."

The merest tyro will be here inclined to remind our critic of the sound advice of Mrs. Glasse: "Before cooking, first catch your hare." First then, let it be shown who are the people who will back the horse, that the owner may win enormous sums by betting against him, and the matter may be worth discussion. As things are—and this is all that need trouble us, we do not wish to start from hypothesis: as things are, then, owners of other horses will not back our hypothetical owner's horse, nor will the bookmakers whose business it is to lay; whilst the little staked by the public, naturally limited if the owner do not essay to lead the way, when sifted by the commissioner, will leave but a meagre nucleus for the "enormous sums for the owner's pocket." The fallacy of the argument requires no demonstration.

But let us hear the writer further on betting.

"One of the practices pursued," he goes on to say, "is to get up favourites for the great stakes. This is done by means of lies, false trials, deceptive bets, high prices paid for horses, so as to enhance the public opinion of their value, and by devices of all sorts. Large sums are staked on the favourite horse by the public. But is it intended that he shall win? No, it is settled he shall lose. A little management of the jockey will save appearances, and thousands are to be duped that the owner and his confederates may pocket the spoil. Enormous sums, as 3,000 guineas or more, have been paid for a colt; we will suppose, to start for the Derby. What is the meaning of this? Is the owner to back this colt against a hundred horses he has never seen, twenty or thirty of which (many of them, for anything he knows, better than his own) are to start? No: the purpose is not to win the Derby. The owner and his confederates are to gain by the loss of the race, and the dupes are to back the favourite."

Now as only owners could do this wretched business, if such a thing were done, on them alone must fall the blame. But a brief examination will show the crudeness of the notion. No one would put any faith in reported trials of living wonders, unless the stable backed the report with money. Then who is to get up false trials, circulate lies and make sham bets for nothing? or to give thousands for a horse not worth a copper with the vain hope of persons more shrewd than himself backing him? Who would thus part with a certainty for a doubtful expectancy, and give up the substance for the shadow? A shallow trick of the sort would be unworthy of the merest novice, and would certainly recoil on the head of its inventor. Owners are like other people, I am pretty certain; and as such, consult their own interests in preference to that of strangers, friends or enemies, and would scorn the idea of acting in a way at once mad and disreputable. The truth is, favourites are not made by those connected with them, "by lying and other devices." Their chief

supporters are the public, led on by touts and tipsters. Thos
who back and those who advise, continue to sing the praise
of the animals in hopes that a shorter price will enable ther
to hedge, and so stand to win a good stake but lose nothing
whilst the unfortunate owner, wishful to back his own hors:
at a fair price (knowing its real chances) has often to look or
and ultimately in self-defence to withdraw him from the race
—as I have before explained.

It is therefore clear that the owner has no motive for
dishonesty. But for argument's sake, we will assume that
owners, trainers, and jockeys conspire to defraud the public
of their money by the vilest deception. No one, not even the
Professor, can believe that the public will be hoodwinked by
the most ingeniously concocted scheme. At least, the success
of such a thing has not come within my experience, nor I
venture to say within the experience of any careful observer
of the turf and its patrons.

On paper, nothing looks easier than to lay thousands
against a horse and thus ruin credulous dupes and make your
own fortune. But in practice it is very different. Then,
experience shows that there is considerable difficulty in
hedging one's stake, though only for a small sum, and even
that this cannot always be done. But when anything beyond
it is attempted, the bookmakers and the public are on the
alert, and the facts (or what they surmise to be the facts) are
telegraphed to thousands of people in a few hours, and your
horse is driven from favouritism to an obscure place in the
betting ; perhaps reported lame, and certainly predicted to
be an absentee on the day of the race.

I think I have said enough to show that it is not possible
to win enormous sums by laying against horses in our day.
And I hope I have succeeded in making clear that Professor

Low in his attacks on the turf writes on the slenderest information, and that more often incorrect than not. But if one
more instance be required to show the emptiness of the
charge so gravely made, it may be found in the following
question, as simply put as it is profoundly answered.

" Is the owner to back this colt," he asks in reference to
an animal for which it is supposed a large sum has been
given, "against a hundred horses : twenty or thirty of which
(and of these many, for anything he knows, better than his
own) are to start ? "

" No. " The fact is, owners not only back their horses
against a hundred they have never seen before, but against
double that number or more, any one of which may be
better than their own. I may add in conclusion, that the
Professor is not singular in his aspersions of the doings of
owners, trainers, and jockeys.   Other writers glibly attribute
motives which have no existence ; amongst them Mr. Lawrence,
from whom I have on more than one occasion quoted. But
an answer to one, is an answer to all ; and it is only necessary
that that answer should be a direct and complete refutation,
in language unmistakable, fearless, and frank.

I HAVE now said all I have to say strictly bearing on the
subject which in the commencement of this work I proposed
to treat. I have resisted throughout the temptation to introduce anecdote, even when relevant, lest in so doing the essential purport of the treatise, which is to be directly serviceable
to the individual rather than amusing to the multitude, should
be frustrated by the introduction of extraneous matter. The
nature of this temptation may be illustrated here by a few
examples, not uninstructive in themselves.

It would have been easy to relate how on one occasion a

match was made to be run at Newmarket, when the one hors died and the other was unfit to run, and stratagem was use on either side. When in the end the match was declared off, little pleasantry was indulged in, the one sportsman declarin; his horse was scarcely able to walk out of the stable, whils the other retorted that his was dead and buried in it. Or another occasion, a jockey was bribed not to win, and telling his employer, was recommended to take the bribe, which he did ; and the owner himself rode the horse and won. Again, a gentleman who shall be nameless, matched his horse —— for £200 a side against that of a baronet, now deceased. The baronet had, as it afterwards appeared, no intention of running, and merely sent his horse, in order to frighten his oppo- nent. But the latter, whose horse in reality was too ill to leave the stable, substituted another for it, and sent the impostor to the spot (Newmarket), with strict injunctions to his trainer to give all inquirers an evasive answer. The baronet, by the aid of his trusty touts, learned of the arrival of the false horse, and believing it, on the same trustworthy evidence, to be the real Simon Pure, paid forfeit. This was no doubt sailing rather near the wind ; yet the baronet had tried to frighten his opponent with "false fire," and clever tactician though he was, was perhaps deservedly outwitted by one more wily than himself.

There is a savour of "Munchausen" in these stories, it may be thought; yet they have a substratum of truth which few of the marvellous conceptions that appear in books on racing matters can boast. And they must suffice.

In my treatment of the various subjects it has been my desire to introduce only those things that are relevant to it ; although perforce some matters will appear of more interest and greater importance than others to racing men. The breaking of the colt and his following preparation, his subsequent performances in trials and in public, are subjects demanding the ample treatment which has been given to them ; and the method followed will hardly be charged with redundancy, which, at the worst, would be less censurable than incompleteness. The chapters on betting, on the scandals of the race-course, and the present one on attacks on the turf, are open possibly to the charge of being the least cognate to the subject. As such they are, I am free to confess, the least satisfactory to myself ; but, on the other hand, they are not absolutely foreign to our examination, and, indeed, it is hoped may in some fashion serve to round it off. I may add that the suggestions for reform which fill Chapter XXVI., as well as the earlier comments on the light-weight jockeys, have, I am fully convinced, every warrant for their amplification in any work on the racehorse. If any doubt that the conduct of the young jockeys is an evil loudly crying for redress, let him attend the room next the weighing-room after one of the large handicaps, and he will find that if their faults have not here been extenuated, at least nought has been set down in malice.

If nothing more is required to be said specially on other points, I may yet venture to submit that the whole, as an original work, has had to contend with many difficulties in the endeavour to eliminate golden truths from popular errors, and to avoid plagiarism.

It has been my studied object throughout not to weary the reader by giving a detailed account where it was unnecessary or punctiliously to define matters and things when the bare, name was sufficient. For instance, when physic is recommended, I merely mention it. I have not said what it should be composed of, or the quantity sufficient for the dose, or the

X

treatment of the animals whilst under its influence ; simply because I assume all people connected with racing stables would understand a part of their management which admits of little or no variation.

I trust I have succeeded in being, without tediousness, explicit in describing racing matters to the comprehension of the uninitiated as well as of the *cognoscenti.* I have endeavoured to the best of my ability to refute the baseless and virulent attacks on my profession, and to forward the cause of morality in it, by exposing its errors, condemning its faults, whilst giving to honour and honesty their meed of praise. The result of my experience is recorded impartially, and I trust intelligibly, and without the aid of rhetorical embellishment. That the work has its blemishes I cannot doubt ; but I trust the weight of information may be thought to outbalance them, and, if I have achieved little, that the reader will generously accept that little as the best I can give. The words of the great moralist may, in this sense, perhaps fittingly bring my labour to a conclusion, and serve at once as the best apology for the attempt I have made and a plea for its indulgent reception.

" He that in the latter part of his life," says Dr. Johnson, " too strictly inquires what he has done, can very seldom receive from his own heart such an account as will give him satisfaction. We do not indeed so often disappoint others as ourselves. But he has no reason to repine though his abilities are small and his opportunities few. He that has improved the virtue or advanced the happiness of one fellow-creature ; he that ascertained a single moral proposition, or added one useful experiment to natural knowledge, may be content with his own performance ; and with respect to mortals like himself may demand, like Augustus, to be dismissed at his departure with applause."

INDEX.

X 2

Lightning Source UK Ltd.
Milton Keynes UK
UKHW020727060120
356457UK00007B/625/P

9 780469 377837